CYCLIN
NORTH
FRANCE
CYCLE ROUTES NORTH OF THE LOIRE

RICHARD PEACE & ANDREW STEVENSON

EXCELLENT BOOKS
94 BRADFORD ROAD
WAKEFIELD
WEST YORKSHIRE WF1 2AE
TEL: (01924) 315147
www.excellentbooks.co.uk
Printed 2013

ISBN 978 1 901464 28 3

Whilst the authors have researched the routes for the purposes of this guide, no responsibility can be accepted for any unforeseen circumstances encountered whilst following them. The publisher would, however, welcome any information regarding any material changes and any problems encountered.

Front cover photo: Malestroit, on the Nantes-Brest canal, Brittany
© Emmanuel Berthier
Rear cover photo: View of Notre-Dame cathedral, Paris
Frontispiece: Île St-Louis, Paris

Richard Peace is founder of Excellent Books, specialising in cycle publishing, and has been writing about cycling for more than 15 years.
Andrew Stevenson has written for Cycle and The Ride magazines, and appeared on The Bike Show on Resonance FM. He has ridden extensively in France, The Netherlands and Spain, as well as in Malaysia, Sri Lanka and The Czech Republic - almost exclusively aboard a folding bike.

Contents

Introduction

Touring Routes

Greenways & Véloroutes

French Biking Glossary

Index

Introduction

THE ROUTES

If you have always fancied taking in the sights of Northern France on two wheels away from traffic but wondered where the best routes are this is the guide for you. Since 1997 a French organisation called AF3V has been promoting the development of a network of waymarked cycle routes and greenways.

This growing traffic-free network, with many routes based on old railways and canal towpaths and known as *voies vertes*, gives you access to stunning French landscapes, be it the famed white sandy beaches of Brittany, Normandy's rural charms or the vineyards, canals and mountains of Burgundy and Alsace-Lorraine. There are also longer signed touring routes known as *véloroutes* linking the most interesting sights in an area using a mixture of minor roads and traffic-free tracks and paths. For the majority of the routes in the book a touring or mountain bike would be more than adequate and the broad tarmac of many routes will also suit racing bikes. Indeed many *voies vertes* are used not only by family and leisure cyclists but by groups of racers making them of the widest possible appeal to all groups of cyclist. The signage you are likely to see on the ground is dealt with opposite, whilst long -distance and the trans-national EuroVelo route system is detailed on pages 8-9. However it's also worth knowing that since 2010 a route numbering system for a national network has been agreed; 'trunk' routes will be signed as EuroVelo routes eg EV1 whilst shorter connecting routes will be signed as V1 etc. It's likely to be a few years before this standard numbering and signing system starts to be widely reflected in actual signage on the ground.

CYCLING IN FRANCE

It is simply a pleasure. France is a cycling nation and accords cyclists status on the road and some great facilities, from wonderful off-road riding to city centre automated bike hire. If you're unfamiliar with cycling in France here are a few handy tips.

You will no doubt know to ride on the right hand side of the road, path or track you are on. However, you should also be aware of an old rule of the road called priority from the right which is still a consideration. In the absence of all other road signs this rule still applies - effectively it means traffic joining from the right has priority - even if on a seemingly minor road. If, though, your road has yellow diamond on white background signs you have priority, until you come to one with a black line through. Side roads in the main have stop or give way markings and roundabouts also usually have give way systems so this rule won't apply here. However, this is not always so and in any case it's wise to make a habit of treating traffic coming from the right with extra caution as some drivers may still adhere to the old law, even if road markings say otherwise!

In France traffic lights go directly from red to green but do go to amber between green and red. A red light accompanied by an amber flashing arrow pointing to the right means you can turn right as long as you give way to other vehicles. A green light replaced by a flashing yellow light means you may proceed but have to give way to crossing traffic and pedestrians.

Where a cycle path is indicated by a white bicycle on a circular blue background, it is obligatory to use it in preference to the road. Where it is on a rectangular background, it is optional.

ROUTES & SIGNAGE

France has very roughly the same population as the UK and roughly twice the space; so outside urban areas you'll find an often virtually deserted network of minor country roads. Some of these are used in the eight touring routes described in detail in this book.

Different routes and areas often have very different signing systems although official cycle routes are commonly signed in green and white (see opposite for the planned EV and V system).

There is a national system of Grandes Randonnées (GR), long distance routes for hikers (and sometimes cyclists), all of which are on the IGN map 903. Marked on the ground by red and white stripes, they may be OK for cycling, although a mountain bike may be needed, so these are largely outside the scope of this book. Petites randonnées, more local paths, are also often cycleable by mountain bike.

The white cyclist on a green background is extremely common in signage. It may be fairly obvious where you are supposed to go (above); this *voie verte* is typical of the wide and slightly sandy greenways in Normandy.

In towns and villages you may need to pay a little more attention as the sign to the left demonstrates; here the standard signage appears alongside signs for a bewildering variety of other routes, including one for EuroVelo 6 (see pgs 8-9).

The *Route Info* section at the start of each chapter has advice on local signage relating to that route.

Cycling in towns and cities is pretty common but cycling levels, like the conventions and rules that govern local cycling conditions, vary quite a lot. In some places it can be the norm to cycle freely in pedestrian precincts, but not in others, although there's usually signage to tell you what actually should be. As in the UK, cyclist behaviour at traffic lights can be unpredictable. It seems to be fairly normal for cyclists to treat one way streets as two way, even if there is no signage.

A city centre street scene in Paris (below), with cyclists and pedestrians easily mingling. The cycle lane here runs alongside the Bassin de la Villette. Cyclists are also often at home with motor traffic, for example on the left, near the Arc de Triomphe.

GETTING THERE & AWAY

Taking a bike along with your car, caravan or motorhome is obviously one popular option and is much the same experience as in the UK. However, it's definitely worth knowing a bit in advance about bikes and other forms of transport in France whether going with your own motor transport or not; combining bike and train even on day rides means you can often see and do so much more.

TRAINS

Getting your bike to France and taking it on trains when there is not normally a problem with a bit of preparation; indeed in 2011 Eurostar carried over 5,000 fully assembled bikes on its specialist bike carrying service. As this figure doesn't include folders or dismantled bikes taken as hand luggage it's safe to assume the figure for all bikes is quite a lot higher. Both Eurostar and the French railways (SNCF) will carry, free and as normal luggage, folding bicycles and bicycles dismantled and in a bike bag. Eurostar say this should be no bigger than a normal suitcase and SNCF say 120cm x 90cm maximum. If you're happy to travel with your bike only from Folkestone to Calais, Eurotunnel is a lot cheaper and will carry your bike on the same train as you (you load the bike onto a bespoke trailer then hop in the vehicle that tows the trailer which drives onto the train!). If you're taking bikes by motor on Eurotunnel, see their website for further information.

If you want to take a fully assembled bike, this will go on Eurostar on the same train as you, if booked in advance and space is available, or via the registered baggage service when it will arrive within 24 hours of registration (often sooner). Many French trains will carry fully assembled bikes:

TGV – many services between Paris and the east of France accept bikes but there is a charge and reservation is needed. The new Duplex (two deck) TGV services do not accept bikes. To get between stations, crossing Paris by bike is not that bad, especially with the aid of a map showing cycle routes – find Carte des itinéraires cyclables on **www.paris.fr** to download one.

Other services – consult the timetables. Trains which will carry bikes are identified with a bicycle logo on both paper and on-line timetables (although the absence of a logo doesn't always mean that they won't - check locally for specific services). On local trains there is no charge but on long distance journeys there is and reservation is required (these longer distance inter-regional trains are known as Corail).

French rail tickets can be booked online from the UK - Rail Europe can give you details of the current system of doing this and can also sell you your train tickets direct. When buying tickets at a French railway station, do allow plenty of time – you can often be faced with a queue and a long wait.

www.sncf.com is the website for French trains. **www.sncf.co.uk** and **www.raileurope.co.uk** offer similar online booking services. Rail Europe can be contacted on 08708 371 371 or in person Monday to Saturday at 178, Piccadilly, London. Eurostar is on www.eurostar.com or telephone 08705 186 186 (£5.00 fee for telephone bookings). Eurotunnel is on **www.eurotunnel.com** or telephone 01303 282201.

On the train:

TGV (High speed services) Bicycles travel in a separate compartment to which you may not have access during the journey.

Corail Téoz (luxurious inter-city services) wall racks (hook type) in a spacious cycle compartment. Your seat is normally in a carriage next to the one where your bike is.

Corail Lunéa (overnight inter-city services). Most Lunéa trains have a separate cycle compartment with wall racks (hook type).

Corail Intercité No specific cycle facilities.

TER (local trains) Some trains have racks, others don't. There's normally a bicycle logo by the doors where you should load your bicycle.

Car If on a timetable a service is by car, or autocar, this is a road journey by bus and is not supposed to carry bicycles. You may find a friendly driver with a quiet bus who will accept your bike but if you do want to get where you're going, don't rely on this happening.

There are excellent mapping products of the French railway system at **www.iterritoires.com**

Some French local trains go to great lengths to accommodate bikes. This TER service in Alsace is typical of many in the region. Elsewhere in northern France bikes are usually allowed on most services, though space may be more limited.

FERRY

Taking bikes on the ferry is usually a lot simpler than by train. If you're going as a foot passenger, you usually have to board with the motor vehicles and lash your bike to the deck side or elsewhere as directed by crew. When booking you should include your bike (which needs booking on even if there's no charge for it). For route options, times and frequency see overleaf.

If you're taking bikes by motor vehicle it's worth checking the rules and charges, particularly for total dimensions and particularly if you want them on the roof.

EUROPEAN BIKE EXPRESS

Easy and efficient travel designed specifically for cyclists. Stops in Northern France for 2013 include Calais, Paris, Thionville, Nancy, Nemours and Auxerre. Their air conditioned coaches have reclining seats and pull a purpose-built trailer capable of carrying all manner of bikes and bike trailers. Runs throughout the summer serving western France on an Atlantic route and central, Alpine and Mediterranean France (and even into Spain) on other routes. Single or return journeys. Great for touring - you can go out on one route and return on another. UK pick-up points down the eastern side of England between North Yorkshire and Kent, with M62 / M6 feeder service on certain dates.
www.bike-express.co.uk 3, Newfield Lane, South Cave. HU15 2JW Tel: 01430 422111

AIR

A wide range of departure points and destinations can make this worth considering. Bikes need to have the handlebars flush with the frame and the pedals flush or removed. They should also be boxed or bagged, which gives you the problem of what to do with a box particularly at the other end. One solution is leaving your box/bag at the luggage facility of Blue Marble Travel at 2, rue Dussoubs, Paris (centrally located near the Bourse / Les Halles about 1km north of the river). 01.42.36.02.34 www.bluemarble.org

NB When travelling as a group by any form of public transport always contact the carrier in advance to see that they can accommodate you.

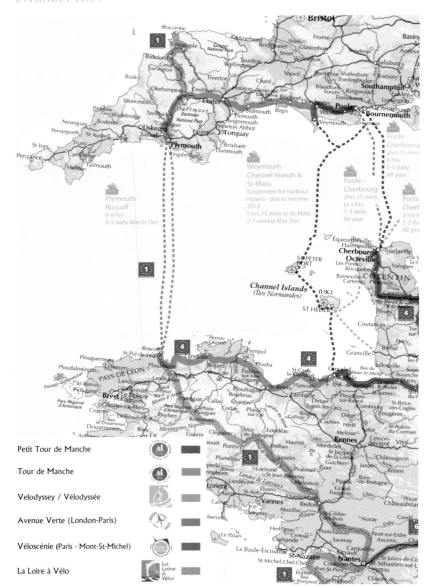

Petit Tour de Manche

Tour de Manche

Velodyssey / Vélodyssée

Avenue Verte (London-Paris)

Véloscénie (Paris - Mont-St-Michel)

La Loire à Vélo

LONG-DISTANCE & TRANS-NATIONAL ROUTES

2012 and 2013 heralded a slew of routes linking the UK and France

Petit Tour de Manche Launched 2012. 440km. Linking Dorset's Jurassic coast between Poole and Weymouth with a ferry crossing via the Channel Islands. In France head via Mont-St-Michel to the Cotentin peninsula. Much of this route (and lots more) is covered in the touring routes *Around the Cotentin* and *St-Malo - Mont-St-Michel Circular*. **www.cycle-west.com**

Tour de Manche Launching 2013. 700km+. An extended version of the Petit Tour taking in a long, wild stretch of Brittany's coastline. www.cycle-west.com

Velodyssey / Vélodyssée Launched 2012. 1200km. Including the UK's Devon Coast to Coast and a route the entire length of France's Atlantic coast. **www.velodyssey.com**

Avenue Verte Launched 2012. 406km. Using a high proportion of traffic-free trails to link London and Paris. **www.avenuevertelondonparis.com**

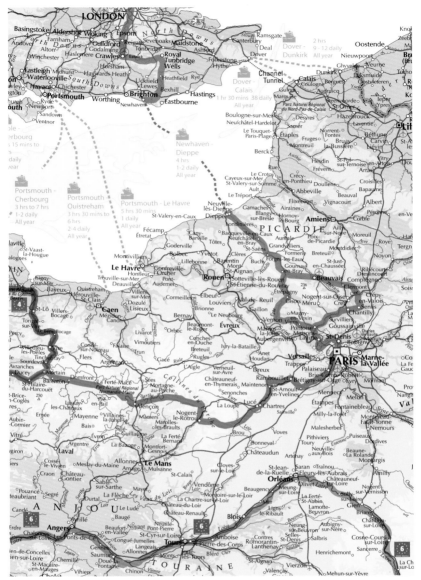

Véloscénie (Paris to Mont-St-Michel) To launched in 2012 with several sections to interim standard only. **www.veloscenie.com** See pg 188.

La Loire á Vélo Launched 2008. 800km following the river's banks. The area falls just outside the scope of this guide, but is covered in our *Cycling Southern France* guide.

EuroVelo Routes (**www.eurovelo.org**) link several European countries. Most are incomplete, but substantially complete sections in Northern France are:

EuroVelo 1, Atlantic Coast, North Cape to Sagres 8186km

EuroVelo 4, Central Europe, Roscoff to Kiev 4000km

EuroVelo 6, Atlantic to Black Sea, Nantes to Constanta 4448km

EuroVelo 15, the Rhine Route (Andermatt to Rotterdam 1230km) is also complete in Alsace. See **www.rhinecycleroute.eu**

ACCOMMODATION

More plentiful and cheaper than in the UK. Hotels, guest houses and hostels are usually very welcoming to cyclists and even if they don't have dedicated cycle storage will generally have somewhere secure for bikes. Tourist offices are plentiful and tremendously helpful in sourcing accommodation. Chambres d'hôte are often billed as the equivalent of bed and breakfast and often are, but sometimes they are more like small hotels. Logis de France is a hotel chain with many Logis Vélo hotels where you are offered such help as luggage transfer, weather forecast, cycle washing facilities, local route information and of course secure storage. Youth hostel information can be found on **www.fuaj.org** and indicates which hostels have cycle storage. Gîtes d'étape can be similar to a hostel or more like bunkhouses where you'll get basic dormitory facilities but need a sleeping bag - see **www.gites-de-france.com** or **www.gites-refuge.com** for more info. If you're wanting to hire a gîte rural, (a holiday home - usually self-catering) see **www.gites-de-france.com** again or local tourist authority sites. Clévacances are flats, chalets and houses for holiday hire - **www.clevacances.com** is a good starting point. Camping sites are generally very good whether you've got a small tent on a bike or several bikes on a motorhome - websites and publications on this abound - **www.campingfrance.com** is good.

VÉLORAILS

Vélorails are lengths of disused railway with the track intact and used now to carry pedal-powered railcarts. The usual arrangement is two people pedalling with a bench behind for two or three passengers. For a list and location map, see **www.velorail24. com**. They are at: Fédération des Vélos-Rail de France, Gare de Labaurie 24800 Eyzerac

WITHOUT YOUR BIKE

French cycle holiday companies abound - sometimes they're aiming to explore a particular area or theme, sometimes guided, sometimes self-guided with back-up available, sometimes touring, sometimes fixed base. They can offer baggage transfer and deliver you into the lap of luxury each evening or they can be fairly minimalist affairs relying more on camping or basic accommodation. A good start point for investigating is **http://www.freewheelingfrance.com/bike-hire-in-france/** If avoiding holiday companies and needing a bike, bike hire is reasonably common and you should enquire locally. Grand cities such as Paris and Strasbourg have city-wide automated cycle hire suitable for short hops across town and the idea has even percolated down to the relatively tiny city of Rennes.

MAPS

The majority of maps in this guide are based on Michelin 1:200,000 maps - usually sufficient outside urban areas. In larger towns and in cities you should pick up a street map (a cycle map if possible) from the tourist office. Specific cycle maps and guides for a particular route or area are listed under the *Route Info* section of a chapter under *Maps, guides and websites*.
Should you want even more detailed information on an area IGN 1:100,000 maps are excellent, showing the majority of minor roads and many tracks in an area as well as having cycle tracks traced in red. See **www.ign.fr** for more details.
Free online digital mapping can be useful but those sites outside the specific cycling ones listed opposite should be treated with caution when claiming to show cycle routes. Perhaps the most useful is www.openstreetmap.org though this sometimes misses out existing routes or shows routes that are not fully complete.

WEATHER

Northern France's climate is often on a par with that of the UK and with the majority of the coast being west or north facing it is wetter and stormier more often. The good news however is that the summers in Brittany and Normandy tend to be more reliable and a little longer than in the UK. The south coast of Brittany in particular has the luxury of warm summers *and* warm sea temperatures, ideal for cyclists who like to take the plunge at the end of day's pedalling. Brittany and Normandy can feel mild enough for comfortable cycling well into October though rainfall may be double the driest summer months. Away from the coast winter months at places like Rouen can be almost as dry as summer months, despite the drop in temperature and later winter-early spring may actually hold the driest months hereabouts.

Inland things are usually even drier and calmer and rainfall drops as you move east from Paris to Strasbourg. The big exception to the UK pattern of weather is the far east; by the time you reach Lorraine, Burgundy and Alsace summers can be very hot and sunny and stretch well into what we would consider autumn, when heavy rain storms presage the onset of an often subzero winter (cross-country skiing is popular in the Vosges).

A good generalisation is that late spring to mid-autumn often holds the best cycling weather, though be aware of the mid-July to August holiday crowds and the associated high prices (it's also wise to avoid Easter holidays for similar reasons).

For a forecast one of the most useful sites is **www.meteofrance.com**

FURTHER CONTACTS

The AF3V **national office can be found at:**
AF3V Association Française de Développement des Véloroutes et Voies Vertes.
30 avenue Eugène Gazeau 60300 Senlis
09 63 29 52 52   info@af3v.org www.af3v.org
The website for AF3V gives much information and has a route search facility for well over 200 véloroutes and voies vertes and an expanding English language version. There is a biennally published guide book, the "Guide Touristique des Véloroutes et Voies Vertes de France" listing 150 or more routes and available from AF3V or **www.cartovelo.com** or join AF3V as a member to receive one free.

A very comprehensive English language website for cycle touring in France can be found at **www.freewheelingfrance.com** and centres around detailed contributor articles on just about every topic.

France Vélo Tourisme is a new organisation promoting cycle tourism in France with details on all major long distance routes. Whilst there is an English language option to click work on translating all pages into French appears to be ongoing. **www.francevelotourisme.com**

The Vélib' public bike hire in Paris is truly impressive; over 20,000 bikes at 1,800 docking stations mean there should be a bike available for hire every 300 metres or so. For more details see the *Route Advice - Riding in Paris* panel on the *Tourings Routes Map*.

Brittany Coast to Coast

Route Info

Brittany Coast to Coast

Replaced by 'sea area Fitzroy' in the BBC shipping forecast in 2002 Finistère is a good region for a four day trip, with day ends chosen to provide quiet camping spots. 'Finis terre' (from the Latin for end of the earth) is home to a mixture of quiet, well-surfaced and signposted greenways, country lanes, gentle slopes and out of the way campsites, which keep you away from the crowds.

The route begins at the ferry port of Roscoff in the north and ends either on the beaches of Erdeven or at the end of the Quiberon peninsula.

The first three days of the ride for the most part follow signposted greenways with oodles of road and trackside guidance. Day 4 meanwhile follows quiet roads down to the coast and is based on knowledge gleaned from the local cycling community.

A new signed route for 2012, Vélodyssée, will use much of the Roscoff-Pontivy section, so you may also see signs for this (for more details see pages 8-9).

Grade EASY

Start / Finish Roscoff / Erdeven
or Quiberon

Route Length 251km / 156 miles

Length of Suggested Days
4 day linear route 36-81km / 22.5-50 miles
Day lengths are relatively long on this route but it could easily be stretched into a more easygoing 5 or 6 day tour.

Route Surface & Signing
52% off-road
Partly good quality off-road track, partly quiet road. Suitable for tourer, hybrid or mountain bike. Brittany's official long distance cycle routes are designated 'V' plus the appropriate route number (see map on page 173).

Access to Roscoff

Overnight ferries from Plymouth and Cork **www.brittany-ferries.co.uk**

i Offices
Roscoff Office de Tourisme, 46, rue Gambetta, 02.98.61.12.13
www.roscoff-tourisme.com
Morlaix Office de Tourisme, beneath the viaduct, plages des Otages, 02.98.62.14.94, www.morlaixtourisme.fr
Huelgoat Office de Tourisme, 19 place Aristide Briand, 02.98.99.72.32
www.tourismehuelgoat.fr
Carhaix-Plouguer Office de Tourisme, rue Brizeux, 02.98.93.04.42
www.poher.com
Pontivy Office de Tourisme,
Péniche Duchesse Anne, 2 quai Niémen
02.97.25.04.10
tourisme@pontivycommunaute.com
Erdeven Office de Tourisme
7 rue Abbé Le Barh
02.97.55.64.60   ot.erdeven@wanadoo.fr
Quiberon Office de Tourisme
14 rue de Verdun
02.97.50.07.84   www.quiberon.com

Guide
Les Voies Vertes de Bretagne fold-out map (in French but quite easy to follow, with signed routes detailed and information about campsites, hotels and bike shops), available from tourist offices and online at www.tourismebretagne.com

Brittany's greenways (*voies vertes* is French for greenways) are signed according to which of several long distance routes they are on. Pictured left is a signed section of V7 approaching Scrignac. The logo here appears on much of the network signage along with a 'V' number relating to a particular route (see pg 173 for more detail).

Don't Miss

Morlaix Viaduct

You'd have to be riding blindfold to miss this. Trains take the high route across this towering granite structure which spans the valley in which Morlaix, with its cobbled streets and improbable architectural angles, sits. The viaduct here is an imposing, impressive two storey whopper, 180ft high and 900ft long. There's a walkway on the lower tier; you can look down the valley and listen to the Paris-Brest express train rumble above your head.

The Breton Railway - disused, but used

Between 1891 and 1967 the rail route between Morlaix and Carhaix shunted Bretons about their business. Sadly, the cheap narrow gauge which was used for the tracks left the network out of step with the demand for speedy travel in the 1960s. Though no longer used by trains, the V7 greenway section is favoured by cyclists and horse drawn Breton Romany caravans, whose colourful horse-drawn vehicles make a welcome interruption. Unlike rail commuters, most cyclists don't mind their journeys being interrupted.

Breton Bikes

Situated on, but predating, the campsite, Breton Bikes sits by the Nantes-Brest Canal cycle route near Gouarec at Camping Tost Aven (see pg 18). This small, informally run set-up is an excellent base for those who might prefer an 'all in' cycle-camping holiday experience. Bikes of all shapes and sizes, tents, technical support and imaginative routes are all provided, backed up by a rescue service and a deep knowledge of the area. Even for independent cyclists, Breton Bikes can be a helpful source of informal route advice and minor technical adjustments.

Tour de France Connections

On the road from Mûr-de-Bretagne to Pontivy you'll be riding in the wake of an illustrious peloton. Stage 2 of the 2008 tour de France came this way en route from Auray (down south) to St. Brieuc (up north). Norwegian 'rouleur' Thor Hushovd emerged victorious from the wind and rain that July day. But the region's links to the tour stretch back to the 20th century. The celebrated rider and 1947 tour winner Jean Robic is a local hero in the Pontivy region, coming from the village of Radenac, south east of Pontivy. If you want to see exactly where he lived, pedal 18km south-east of Pontivy, where you'll find Rue Jean Robic in the village centre.

Chapel of St. Gildas

6km along the River Blavet from St. Nicolas there's an apparitional sight across the water. The chapel of St. Gildas marks the spot where a pair of 6th century monks (Gildas and Bieuzy) preached Christianity to their pagan flock whilst living in a nearby cave. The chapel itself appears to labour under a considerable weight. An outsized granite outcrop sits ominously over the chapel, seemingly about to heave the whole place of worship into the river. The chapel is open every afternoon except Monday during high season, though the most stunning point of vantage is probably from across the river.

The Alignments

Many people who visit Carnac are attracted by the three alignments of megaliths which lie 1km north of the town. Due to the crowds these days the stones themselves are protected by fences. They are thought to be relics from 3300 BC and are certainly a unique spectacle, even viewed through a mesh.

© Rhian VK Creative Commons

The Chapel of St Gildas on the River Blavet (day 4)

Day 1 Roscoff → Carhaix-Plouger / Huelgoat

TOTAL DISTANCE / ELEVATION: **81 km / 884 m ascent** 50 mi / 2900 ft ascent

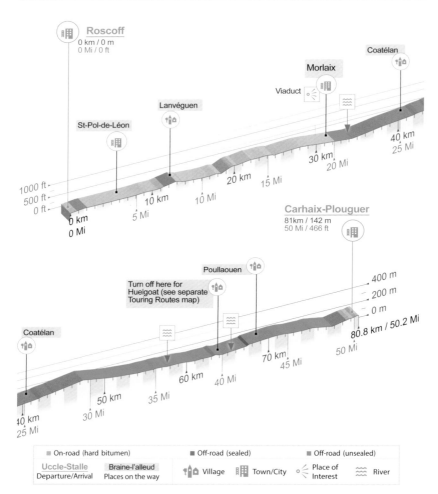

On-road (hard bitumen)	Off-road (sealed)	Off-road (unsealed)

Uccle-Stalle Departure/Arrival Braine-l'alleud Places on the way Village Town/City Place of Interest River

Day 1 Ride Notes

This is, marginally, the longest day of the trip, designed to make the most of an early morning landing in Roscoff. The first section to Morlaix is a popular ride on a gently undulating, mainly road section, with roadside signs indicating the cycle route (though the signs stop at Milinou and thereafter there are some busier road sections). Onward to Carhaix you'll take the V7 greenway, which is flat, being a disused railway line.

If 80km is a little far for the first day's ride you could head off along the

6.5km detour to Huelgoat, cutting off around 10km (6 miles) from your first day's ride and adding it on the second day's ride to Gouarec. This option also allows you to explore the unusual forest and boulder landscape around the area. For this option see * at the end of the Day 1 Ride Notes for this option. Leaving Roscoff ferry port, turn left (right takes you into town), following Port du Bloscon to a T-junction. Head left here and immediately across the railway line on your left you'll see the first sign for the V7 greenway, signposted to St-Pol-de-Léon.

Strangely, the first 80 metres is rocky, but don't be deterred. Thereafter the route wiggles gloriously through back gardens and quiet roads, with bonus glimpses of the Bay of Morlaix to your left. Follow the clear V7 roadside signs, meandering through the onion fields for 7km, into St-Pol-de-Léon. The main square in front of the cathedral makes a good stop, perhaps for breakfast if you're straight off the overnight ferry. Once nourished, the signed V7 to Morlaix continues on the D769. After 1.5k, follow the cycle sign to Milinou to your left. The next 7km is a helter-skelter of quiet lanes, roadside tracks, switchbacks, road crossings and short, steep hills. This eventful section passes through a string of small hamlets including Kérézéant and Penquer before switching to virtually traffic-free roads at St Nep, just before the D58, and affords more explicit views across the bay. Finally a left turn onto a path through a cultivated field, ends in Lanvéguen. From Lanvéguen, stick with the D769 (and roadside signs to Milinou), though these do run out shortly after 2km (a roadside sign delivers this sad news). Roll downhill into Penze, staying on the D769 over the river. Just through the tiny centre the road forks and take the unsigned left up Rue du Croissant. After 1.5km cross the D769 and continue on a minor road. Continue ahead at all junctions. The route should be signed here by the time you ride it, but in any case it's simply a case of ignoring minor turnings for some 2km after the 769 to come to a small T-junction and right. Keep ignoring turnings off this lovely quiet road and head over a level-crossing to descend to a roundabout. Head left over the busy D58, onto the D19 signed Ar Brug. Keep following these signs at the next roundabout, now paralleling the D58 to your right. Take the first left to climb steeply to a T-junction and right signed to La Garenne. The route then heads left to come to a T-junction and right to pass straightaway under the thundering traffic of the N12. Now on the outskirts of Morlaix, head over a tiny roundabout and through quiet suburbs to a larger roundabout and left onto rue St-Germain. This long

fast road bends right under the railway and descends to the port. Turn right here and head for the towering railway viaduct in the distance with the river on your left.

This brings you to the town centre, well worth exploring.

Leaving Morlaix, find the V7 greenway by first of all following the town centre signs to the museum, which is 500 metres from the tourist office in place Jacobins. From the front of the museum, head steeply up rue Vignes, becoming rue de Brehat, for 1km until you see the first green V7 sign off-road, signed to Poullaouen and heading right. The surface of this ex-Breton railway is good and there's plenty of green V7 signage en-route. Look out too for the well-preserved railway stations - especially Scrignac, which has water and toilets, as well as maps and additional information about the route. The V7 runs all the way to Carhaix-Plouguer (though see *notes below for the alternative finish at Huelgoat), where it hits the D787 to turn right on a traffic-free path alongside it before diverting onto a private road away from the 787 to rejoin traffic at a roundabout. Go second right here up rue Salvador Allende a short, steep climb into town, past the train station on the left and right at the next junction, up avenue Général de Gaulle, towards the town centre.

* Huelgoat finish: Heading down the V7 greenway leave it some 32km after picking it up in Morlaix to head right onto the D769. Follow signs onto the D769a to Huelgoat. Note: A signed route via Lochmaria-Berrien may be available by the time you ride the route.

Accommodation

Plenty of hotels in Roscoff centre but if you find these full or too pricey try the following, just to the west of town:

🏨 *Hôtel Armen Le Triton*
rue du Docteur Bagot, Roscoff
02.98.61.24.44 www.hotel-letriton.com

🏨 *Hôtel du Lac*
9 rue Général de Gaulle, Huelgoat
02.98.99.71.14
www.hoteldulac-huelgoat.com

🏕 *Camping du Lac*
Huelgoat 02.98.99.72.50

🏨 *Hôtel Noz Vad*
12 boulevard de La République
Carhaix-Plouguer
02.98.99.12.12 www.nozvad.com
🏕 *Vallee de L'Hyeres Municipal Camping*
Carhaix-Plouguer 02.98.99.10.58
www.ville-carhaix.com

Bike Shops
🚲 *Mor'Les Cycles*
26 rue de Brest, Morlaix
09.51.38.15.06
Opposite the theatre
www.mor-lescycles.com
🚲 *Technic Bike*
boulevard Jean Moulin (on the D264),
Carhaix-Plouguer 02.98.93.07.50
www.technic-bike.com

Roscoff & St-Pol-de-Léon

You can bypass Roscoff town centre from the ferry and head straight onto the cycle route, although a 2km detour into town means you'll find a lively introduction to Brittany, with an attractive old harbour, ornate sixteenth-century church and plenty of restaurants and other commerce. Much of Brittany's coastline is clean, fresh and inviting, with a good beach west of town at Laber. Lovers of unusual museums may want a trip to La Maison des Johnnies et de l'Oignon Rosé de Roscoff - especially if you want to learn about the famous red onions of Roscoff and those who sold them. More interesting than it sounds!

St -Pol-de-Léon is a quiet country town, dominated by an elegant cathedral. Also look out for the Kreisker Chapel, with it's thin pointed spire, a design copied all over Brittany.

Morlaix

Highlighted in the 'Don't Miss' section, the viaduct is literally unmissable when visiting Morlaix, but the town has numerous other charms. Notable historic buildings include the Jacobin convent on place des Jacobins, which houses the town museum (Queen Mary of Scots stayed here in 1548). The beautifully restored Maison à Pondalez at 9 Grande Rue and the Maison de la Reine Anne are also worth seeking out. It's a nice town for just roaming though, with steep stairways leading from picturesque place des Otages and place de Cornic providing fine walks. The port area north of the viaduct is also an entertaining stroll.

© Bjaglin/Creative Commons

Morlaix's viaduct dominates the town centre from most angles

© Emmanuel Berthier

St-Pol-de-Léon's cathedral makes an impressive backdrop to its market

© la Maison du tourisme Baie de Morlaix Monts d'Arrée

If you want to try out electric bikes Morlaix tourist authorities provide the opportunity to do so (middle). From Morlaix you follow this wide earth track (left) almost all the way to Carhaix-Plouguer.

Day 2 | Carhaix-Plouger →Gouarec

TOTAL DISTANCE / ELEVATION: **36 km / 245 m ascent** | **22.5 mi / 804 ft ascent**

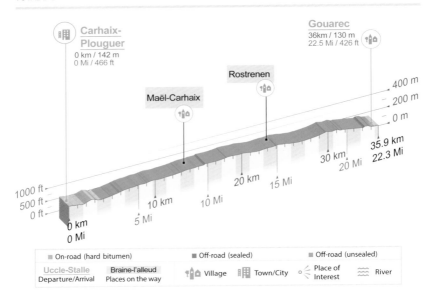

■ On-road (hard bitumen)   ■ Off-road (sealed)   ■ Off-road (unsealed)

Uccle-Stalle	Braine-l'alleud				
Departure/Arrival	Places on the way	↑♦☗ Village	🏢 Town/City	○ Place of Interest	≈ River

Day 2 Ride Notes

Today's is a much shorter, simpler ride than yesterday's, with a pot of gold (or maybe a free beer) waiting at its end. The only section requiring any thought is the escape from Carhaix; first, retrace your route into Carhaix to the roundabout at the bottom of rue Salvador Allende. Here, turn right onto rue Duguay Trouin, then left at the next roundabout, onto rue Tanguy Prigent. Atop this short climb go left onto route de Trebrivan and ride down for 500m until you reach another large roundabout, which the busy D787 intersects. Carefully cross the D787, go straight on and take the first turn on your left, signed to Kervoasdoué. Now take the next, rather unevenly surfaced (but only for 30 metres) turning on your right, which soon becomes signposted as the V6 greenway proper. Thereafter the surface improves and the route is signed along the path to Maël-Carhaix (16km), which is actually a 1.5km diversion to the right of the track, but makes a good coffee stop. The V6 surface deteriorates a little shortly after Maël-Carhaix, especially if wet, though it improves again towards Rostrenen. Some cyclists eschew this part of the greenway, perfectly acceptable though it is, instead choosing the road which runs parallel to

the signed greenway on the right. Whether by road or greenway, continue all the way to Gouarec and follow V6 signs into the village. At the bridge over the Nantes-Brest Canal, head right for Camping Tost Aven, which is signposted. You'll be hard pressed to find a more cycling friendly campsite than this quiet, spacious, low-key canal-side haven.

Accommodation

🏠 *Ty Aven B&B*
45 rue du Moulin, Gouarec
02.96.24.87.99 www.tyaven.com
⛺ *Camping Tost Aven* Gouarec,
02.96.24.85.42   baxter.david@orange.fr
Route advice, cycle hire, laundry facilities all on site, plus an informal socialising area (a big gazebo) and other cyclists to share experiences with. Fresh croissants and other treats every morning directly to the site (8am). Camping Tost Aven is also the home of Breton Bikes (see opposite).

Bike Shops

🚲 *If' Vélos*
1 route de Gouarec, Plouguernével,
06.80.88.79.93   jf.frelin@orange.fr
(4km from Gouarec)
🚲 *Breton Bikes*
02.96.24.86.72
www.bretonbikes.com (for cycling
holidays, hire, mild tinkering and
occasional spare parts, though not sales
or serious repairs).

Gouarec

Gouarec is a pretty village with an excellent
water feature in the form of the Nantes-
Brest canal meeting the river Blavet.
There's a supermarket, within five minutes
walk of the campsite, plus bakers, bars
and restaurants. The centre is Napoleonic
and a real picture with several magnificent
houses.

© Emmanuel Berthier

Just after Gouarec the route passes through some lovely countryside north of Lake Guerlédan (see following page)

TOTAL DISTANCE / ELEVATION: **55 km / 421 m ascent** | 34 mi / 1381 ft ascent

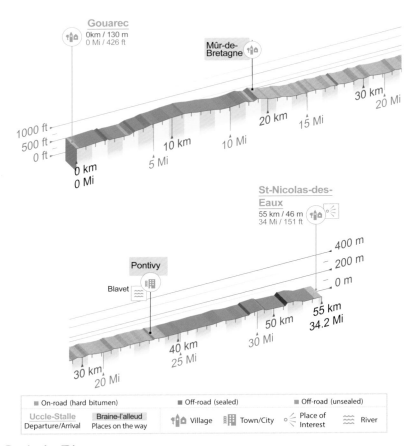

■ On-road (hard bitumen)	■ Off-road (sealed)	■ Off-road (unsealed)		
Uccle-Stalle Departure/Arrival	**Braine-l'alleud** Places on the way	⌂ Village	⊞ Town/City	○ Place of Interest ≈ River

Carhaix-Plouguer

This is a hilly town with everything you need in terms of provisions and supplies. The campsite and other amenities are very well signposted and there's a lively outdoor market on place de la Mairie, just a short hop from the tourist office. In the late 19th century Carhaix was the hub of a wagon wheel of newly built railway lines, some of which are now greenways (going north-west to Morlaix, east to Loudéac and south to Rosporden) which may explain why the town has more significance for cyclists than it does for other visitors.

Lac de Guerlédan

The Lac de Guerlédan is Brittany's biggest lake. Created in the 1920s along with the dam to provide hydro-electric power, it's a haven for watersports enthusiasts. There are boat hire, water skiing, boat trips and a hotel restaurant at Beau Rivage on the north bank and the forest of Quénécan to the south is known as "Swiss Brittany". The abbaye de Bon-Repos, a one-time Cistercian abbey is at the canalside at the western end of the lake and your route goes right past it. If you haven't had enough of cycling, there's a mountain bike centre with a choice of 12 tracks on the lake.

Day 3 Ride Notes

A nice mixture of greenways and pleasant roads makes for a varied and enjoyable day's riding. Go east on the signed V6 along the Nantes-Brest canal towards Mûr-de-Bretagne on the fast, evenly surfaced towpath. At 6km (ecluse Bon Repos) the V6 leaves the canal and swings steeply uphill to the left for a 1.5k climb on a quiet road (ignore the signed footpath to your right through the woods). Atop the hill go left onto the N road and almost immediately second right, up a tarmac track to rejoin the traffic-free trail.

Stick with the V6 signs through Caurel and on to Mûr-de-Bretagne (19km), which makes a good pit-stop before following road signage for the next section. The trail runs into Mûr-de-Bretagne down rue de la Gare by the old station. Go left here to meet the D35 (town centre up to the left). Your onward route goes right towards St. Aignan. 2.7km out of Mûr-de-Bretagne cross the Nantes-Brest canal and the River Blavet and briefly join the D18 for 0.7km before turning left onto the D156 to Pontivy. The last 3km into Pontivy is on the D764, so take care as you ride into town. Bustling on the Blavet, Pontivy makes a tempting hotel stop if you've had enough of camping, though the next 16km

along the river path to the next campsite, going south to the even more welcoming St-Nicolas, is perhaps the highlight of today's ride. Once you arrive at St-Nicolas, cross the River Blavet and follow the sign up the short, steep hill, arcing right into the entrance of the elevated expanse of Camping Le Clos Blavet. To get back down to St-Nicolas from the campsite on foot, there's a footpath from the campsite.

Accommodation

Le Rohan
90 rue Nationale, Pontivy
02.97.25.02.01 www.hotelpontivy.com

Le Rando'Plume
rue du Presbytère
56310 Bieuzy-Les-Eaux (west of the trail at St-Nicolas-des-Eaux)
Tél : 02.97.28.81.60

Camping Le Clos du Blavet
Bieuzy-les-Eaux
02.97.51.83.07 www.closdublavet.com

Bike Shops

Cycles du Blavet
5 rue Albert de Mun, Pontivy
02.97.25.03.46 belleccycles@orange.fr

Waterside riding:
Nantes-Brest canal at the abbaye de Bon Repos (below left) and along the River Blavet (below right) and at Pontivy (right).

© Rob Glover Creative Commons

© Ben Quintana Creative Commons

| Day 4 | St-Nicolas-des-Eaux → Erdeven or Quiberon |

TOTAL DISTANCE / ELEVATION: **79 km / 813 m ascent** | 49 mi / 2667 ft ascent

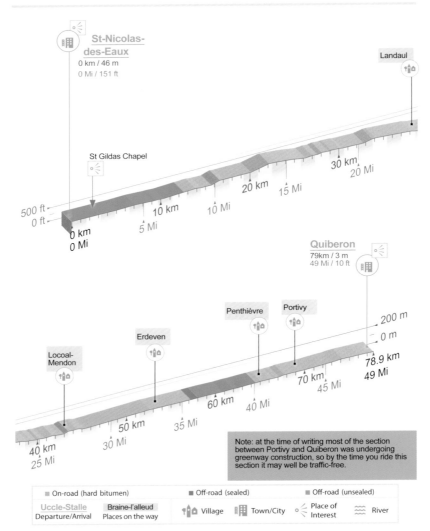

St-Nicolas-des-Eaux
0 km / 46 m
0 Mi / 151 ft

Landaul

St Gildas Chapel

500 ft
0 ft

30 km
20 Mi

20 km
15 Mi

10 km
10 Mi

5 Mi

0 km
0 Mi

Quiberon
79km / 3 m
49 Mi / 10 ft

Penthièvre

Portivy

200 m
0 m

Erdeven

78.9 km
49 Mi

Locoal-Mendon

70 km
45 Mi

60 km
40 Mi

50 km
35 Mi

40 km
25 Mi

30 Mi

Note: at the time of writing most of the section between Portivy and Quiberon was undergoing greenway construction, so by the time you ride this section it may well be traffic-free.

■ On-road (hard bitumen)	■ Off-road (sealed)	■ Off-road (unsealed)
Uccle-Stalle / Departure/Arrival	Braine-l'alleud / Places on the way	⛪ Village 🏢 Town/City ⊙ Place of Interest ≋ River

Day 4   Ride Notes

Unlike the previous three days this route is wiggly, but it's worth it for the diversity of riverside calm, quiet roads and downhill rolls towards the beach campsite at Erdeven. The route itself is not an official signed greenway but is endorsed by local cycle touring organisations such as Breton Bikes. To get started, freewheel down into St-

Nicolas, cross the bridge, turn right along the river Blavet path, shortly passing the remarkable Chapel of St Gildas (see pg 13) and follow the even surface as far as St. Adrien. At the bridge at St. Adrien, just before the rail bridge which is visible further downriver, turn left, leaving the Blavet behind. At the T-junction turn right and follow the road until it forks. Go right here, following the rusty sign to Bubry. The

Blavet now runs audibly and visibly below you on the right as you take the high road. At the next T-junction (5km), go right onto the D3, signed to Quistinic. Follow this for 500 metres and turn left onto the D172 towards Kergonan. The road soon crosses the river and at the next T-junction turn right and follow the sign to Kergonan, downhill on the D724. Continue along this large, quiet road for another 1.5km as it swings left, then take an acute left hand turn at the small, floral, triangular traffic island. This runs down onto a smaller, quieter road. Ride under the main road to a crossroads where you should head straight on, signposted to Gonec. Turn right at the next 'STOP' sign junction, then immediately left, signed to Kergueven. After another 2km take the right fork to Veihuen, then after another 2km turn left at the unsigned crossroads (there's a farm building in front of you) and ride on to Malchappe. This section meanders through some delightful, gently undulating countryside and there's hardly a car to be seen.

From Malchappe turn right and head for Landévant on the D24. 1km further on, go left, signed for Keridano. After 2 more km at the crossroads, go right (signed for Chanco) and go past a little chapel. At the next T-junction turn right, then immediately left and follow a road with a 'Sauf Livraison' sign for 2km until you reach a junction. Turn right here onto a comparatively busy, though downhill road and follow it into Landaul. Stay on the D16 through the village and onwards to Locoal-Mendon. 2km beyond Locoal-Mendon look for a left turn, signed for Le Cleff, and follow that onto a quieter road. At the next crossroads turn right past a house with (at time of writing) two fake swans on its gatepost, then very shortly turn left at the next crossroads. 2km further on at the junction with the busy road go left for 200m, then turn first right. Follow the quiet road round to the right and seek signs for Erdeven. Ride into town and follow signs for La Plage Camping, which is a couple of kilometres further on in Kerhillio. En route you'll see plenty of other campsites, but the beachside location is expansive, inexpensive and has shops, including one for bikes, plus other facilities (like the sea, for example). If you want to cycle on to the more touristy (in summer at least) - though truly spectacular - Quiberon peninsula then

head east along boulevard de l'Atlantique, picking up the roadside cycle lanes which accompany you for around 900m until the bend at Keravel where you pick up V5 signs on the off-road track, signed Plouharnel and Quiberon. Follow the signed track for around 2.7 km, past Ste Barbe village to emerge where the D768 crosses the railway line and join the excellent roadside track, heading south towards Quiberon. At Penthièvre the cycle lane swings right and joins boulevard de l'Ocean, which re-emerges on the D768 further south. Continue on the 768 into Kerhostin and here turn right onto rue de Sombreuil. This leads onto av de la Groix then av de la Mer, turning right in quick succession to head up rue de Port to emerge at the lovely harbour in Portivy. Head back inland up rue de Renaron to the small roundabout and right up route du Fozo, signed Côte Sauvage. Keep right at any junctions to touch the coast in several places - taking in magnificent scenery along the way. Meet the D186^A about 4km after the harbour at Portivy and turn right for Quiberon. This wide and fast road is relatively quiet as the Côte Sauvage scenery of rocky inlets battling with an often choppy sea tends to keep the sunbathers and swimmers away (they flock to the gorgeous east coast beaches) - and so it makes for a magnificent cycling entry into Quiberon (note there is a less scenic but traffic-free option inland). At the first roundabout on the edge of Quiberon the village centre is signed up to the left but a more panoramic ending lies ahead; the seafront and its many eating and accommodation possibilities and the lovely panorama of 'La Grande Plage' - the big beach.

Accommodation

Plenty of accommodation in Quiberon, though it may be booked out in summer.

Au Bon Accueil
6 quai de Houat
Quiberon   02.97.50.16.28
Good budget option
Several campsites mainly to the northeast around St-Julien plage, only 2km from your finish on Quiberon's front.

Bike Shops

Several bike shops on the streets to the east of rue de Verdun

Erdeven

Erdeven is a quieter option than Carnac, which attracts plenty of megalith hungry tourists.
Quiberon too is busy in summer. Erdeven and its dune dominated suburb Kerhillio are ideal
spots for a relaxing night on the beach and contemplating whether to continue your journey
down the coast, visit the alignments at Carnac, explore the beaches and summer tourism of
the Quiberon peninsula or return to Roscoff.

The Quiberon Peninsula

Quiberon itself is a well-known beach resort. What it lacks in architectural grandeur it more
than makes up for with its huge swathe of bathing beach and its jolly cafes and shops. Port
Maria is the fishing harbour and there are plenty of fish restaurants to choose from. The
best shopping area lies between the train station and the port (town plan on accompanying
waterproof map).

In summer the presqu'Île de Quiberon is packed with tourists exploring the peninsula's fine
beaches and taking boat trips to Belle-Île (for cycle routes here see page 171). Be aware the
Côte Sauvage on the western side is the scene of many drownings (though you'll be quite
safe if you opt for some sea-kayaking or surfing lessons at the tiny coastal village of Portivy).
In total contrast the eastern side of the peninsula houses safe beaches of soft white sand.

In July and August the tourist train known as the *Tire Bouchon* (corkscrew) heads north from
Quiberon to Auray.

If it's not the height of summer a bike trip to Belle-Île would cap your coast to coast ride
wonderfully. If time is not scarce you might want to try out the *Boucle de Quiberon*; a signed
15km walking and cycling route that starts in Quiberon on boulevard Chanard and visits the
interesting little Port Haliguen on the east coast as well as the west-coast cliffs, using some
traffic-free parts of the *La Littorale* , Brittany's long distance cycle route around its southern
coast (currently only tiny portions are available, this section being one).

© JF Gornet Creative Commons

Quiberon's attractive seafront is the relaxing ending for your Brittany Coast to Coast ride

© Brian Smithson Creative Commons

Although a magnet for crowds of tourists, it is difficult not to be impressed by Carnac's 3000 or so standing stones, thought to have been erected around 3300 BC. They are found just to the east of the Quiberon peninsula.

Around the Cotentin

Route Info

Around the Cotentin

You have plenty of options here; an easygoing 5 day circuit or a slightly more demanding 8 day tour. Both rides take advantage of the fact the Cotentin peninsula packs a lot of scenery into a small area; expansive beaches, towering dunes, fertile rolling countryside with barely a soul to be seen and beautiful river valleys.

A new signed route for 2012, the Petit Tour de Manche, will run south through the peninsula, so you will also see signs for this (for more details see pg 8).

Grade MEDIUM

Start / Finish   Cherbourg

Route Length

5 day loop 208 km / 129 miles
8 day loop 320km / 199 miles

Length of Suggested Days

27-50km / 17-31 miles
Day lengths are very short to suit slower riders - consecutive days are easily combined to reduce the length of the tours.

Route Surface & Signing

5 day tour = 20 % off-road
8 day tour = 19 % off-road
The national green and white cycle signage is common along the many greenways and minor road routes but on many of the sections you might also see Petit Tour de Manche signing and in time Tour de Manche signing (see pg 8).

Access to Cherbourg

 Brittany Ferries Sailings from Poole and Portsmouth
www.brittany-ferries.co.uk
Irish Ferries Sailings from Rosslare
www.irishferries.com
For access to Cotentin west coast ports from the Channel Islands see:
www.manch-iles-express.com
www.vedettesducotentin.com

 SNCF Intercity trains from Paris St-Lazare via Caen.
www.voyages-sncf.com

i Offices

Cherbourg, 2 quai Alexandre III
02.33.93.52.02
www.cherbourgtourisme.com
Barfleur, 2 rond point Le Conquérant
02.33.54.02.48   www.ville-barfleur.fr
St-Vaast, 1 place du Gal de Gaulle
02.33.23.19.32 www.saint-vaast-reville.com
Carentan, bd de Verdun
02.33.71.23.50   www.ot-carentan.fr
St-Lô, 60 rue de la Poterne, Plage Verte
02.14.29.00.17
Coutances place Georges Leclerc
02.33.19.08.10 www.tourisme-coutances.fr
Hayes-du-Puits 5 rue Emile Poirier,
02.33.46.01.42
Carteret place Flandres Dunkerque
02.33.04.94.54
OR
10, rue des Écoles, Barneville-Carteret
02.33.04.90.58 (about a mile from Carteret itself).
Briquebec 13 place St Anne
02.33.52.21.65
www.officedutourisme-briquebec.com

Your ride down the east coast provides huge variety, from lovely fishing ports such as Barfleur and St-Vaast-la-Hougue to sandy estuaries, like that seen here, to the marshlands on your approach to Carentan

Huge sweeps of beach on the Cotentin's west coast mean enough space for everyone. This particular stretch is near Surtainville (see Day 7).

Don't Miss

Utah Beach and D-day History

It's hard to imagine the scenes here in June 1944 as countless US troops and vehicles came ashore in the face of a German artillery onslaught, though the postcards showing scenes of the landings give some idea.

A recently expanded museum gives you plenty of detail about the landings that signalled the start of the end of WWII.

St-Vaast Seafood

A fine harbour is backed by numerous seafood outlets selling everything from fresh fish to ready to eat, sumptuous delicatessen style snacks.

Swamplife Galore

Just south of St-Vaast you enter the regional park of the 'Marais du Cotentin et du Bessin' - or the Cotentin and Bessin marshes, and don't leave it until just before St-Lô. This means easy, flat cycling country and wide vistas over marshes packed with wildlife. To get the full picture visit the Maison du Parc, en route just north of Carentan (Day 2).

West Coast Beaches

Even at the height of summer you can escape the crowds on these vast swathes of beach that line miles and miles of coast north of Carteret, backed only by tiny villages and some monster-sized sand dunes. Without doubt some of the finest, if not the finest beaches in Normandy.

Day 1   Cherbourg → St-Vaast-la-Hougue

TOTAL DISTANCE / ELEVATION: **43 km / 416 m ascent** | **27 mi / 1365ft ascent**

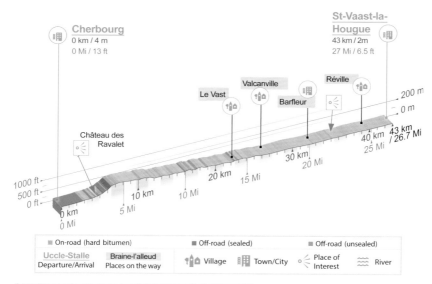

Cherbourg
0 km / 4 m
0 Mi / 13 ft

St-Vaast-la-
Houge
43 km / 2m
27 Mi / 6.5 ft

Le Vast
Valcanville
Barfleur
Réville

Château des Ravalet

200 m
0 m

43 km / 26.7 Mi
40 km / 25 Mi
30 km / 20 Mi
20 km / 15 Mi
10 km / 10 Mi
0 km / 5 Mi
0 Mi

1000 ft
500 ft
0 ft

- ■ On-road (hard bitumen)
- ■ Off-road (sealed)
- ■ Off-road (unsealed)

Uccle-Stalle	Braine-l'alleud						
Departure/Arrival	Places on the way	▲▦△ Village	▦ Town/City	○≶ Place of Interest	≈≈ River

The village of Le Vast is a great stopping off point in the lovely Val de Saire

Day 1 Ride Notes

The route out of Cherbourg for those arriving by ferry is a piece of cake - wide cycle lanes run along the boulevard Maritime; off the ferry head right for the short hop into town or left to pick up the outward route.

Once on the outward route, at the end of boulevard Maritime jink right onto rue Aristide Briand and immediate left onto the cycle lane along boulevard des Flamands before hitting boulevard de la Manche and heading right, away from the sea into the Tourlaville area.

Simply follow this road for about 1.8km, losing the cycle lanes and crossing over rue Gambetta onto boulevard du Cotentin. Here take the signed route down Chasse á Eaux and right again on the path by a beck to pass under the thundering N13. Carry on to emerge in open countryside, then bearing left to bring you to the superb Château des Ravalet.

The route bears left to meet the D63 and right onto it. Simply follow this steadily climbing road for some 4.5km to turn left onto the minor D413, signed Gonneville. Follow this road all the way to the D120 and go right.

It's then simply a matter of following D120 signs along the quiet, bucolic Val de Saire road all the way to the village of Le Vast where there's a great grassy picnic spot by the river. Keep the Saire river on your right, following the D25 to Valcanville and on to the working - yet tourist-orientated harbour at Barfleur's small and lively centre.

Pick up the D1 south along the coast which carries a bit heavier traffic - especially at rush hour and particularly at peak holiday season - but it takes you over a spectacular little bridge near Réville / Jonville, where the Saire river broadens out into a marshy sandscape. A long straight run in to St-Vaast-la Hougue arrives in the heart of the port village - an impressively-sized and busy harbour with the accent on pleasure rather than fishing as was the case at Barfleur.

Accommodation

A Napoleon
14, place de la République, Cherbourg
02.33.93.32.32   www.hotel-napoleon.fr

Chimène
131, rue du Val de Saire, Cherbourg
02.33.43.12.23   www.hotel-chimene.com

Beauséjour
26, rue Grande Vallée, Cherbourg
02.33.53.10.30 www.hotel-cherbourg.net

Camping Collignon
rue des Algues - Espace Loisirs
Collignon, Cherbourg
02.33.20.16.88
camping-collignon@wanadoo.fr

L'hôtel des Fuschias
18 rue marechal Foch, St-Vaast
02.33.54.42.26   www.france-fuschias.com

La Gallouette
1 place General de Gaulle, St-Vaast
02.33.54.20.57 www.lagallouette.com

Bike Shops

Cotentin Cycle Marc
41 rue Gambetta, Cherbourg
02.50.97.19.12

Kerhir Jean-Charles
31 boulevard Schuman, Cherbourg
02.33.53.04.38

Crabs for sale at Barfleur harbour

Cherbourg

Your approach to the city centre might not be greatly encouraging - outside the centre major roads dominate - but the quiet pedestrian old centre hides itself away effectively from the traffic. The main tourist draw is the Cité de la Mer - as the name suggests, featuring everything to do with the sea, including many aquaria and a nuclear submarine, housed partly in a beautiful Art Deco former ferry terminal. But there's also plenty of sea-based activity outside of such official tourist attractions, based around one of the biggest fortified harbours in the world - part of Napoleon's legacy. The innermost harbour has the impressive Roule Fort as a backdrop, the fort now housing the Museum of Liberation. The small pedestrian centre, located behind the tourist office is certainly worth a ramble and is packed with cafes and features a lovely theatre building. And 15 minutes of largely traffic-free cycling and the open

countryside greets you at the sumptuous Château des Ravalet - one of the finest municipal parks you are likely to see anywhere.

Roule Fort now houses the Museum of Liberation

St-Vaast-la-Hougue

St-Vaast has a more sizeable harbour than its northerly neighbour Barfleur, accommodating an impressive array of cross-channel yachts, a handful of fishing vessels and several old military fortifications from the days of Louis XIV (designed by one of his chief military advisers, the well-known Vauban). Fort de la Hougue is one of the most impressive. There's also an impressive array of fresh seafish, as well as restaurants and delicatessens using it. Just offshore lies the virtually uninhabited island of Tatihou and it's possible to walk across to it at low tide, negotiating local oyster beds on your way. There is a small information centre there and a maritime museum.

St-Vaast-la-Hougue's harbour is a fascinating place to stroll

For mapping see separate fold-out map

Château des Ravalet and park are only a short ride from Cherbourg's ferry terminal - but a world away from its traffic and noise.

Day 2   St-Vaast-la-Hougue → Carentan

TOTAL DISTANCE / ELEVATION: **50 km / 189 m ascent** | **31 mi / 310ft ascent**

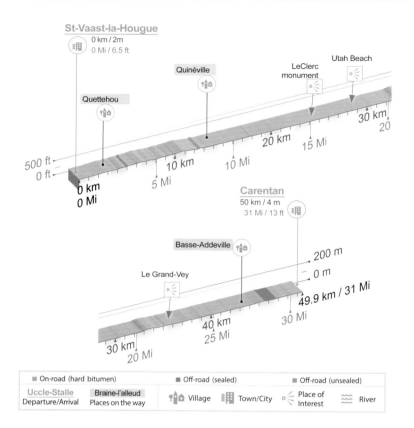

■ On-road (hard bitumen)		■ Off-road (sealed)		■ Off-road (unsealed)	
Uccle-Stalle Departure/Arrival	Braine-l'alleud Places on the way	†⚐ Village	🏢 Town/City	○⋜ Place of Interest	≈≈ River

Day 2 Ride Notes

From the centre of St-Vaast follow the D1 to the workaday town of Quettehou, where you pick up the D14 to Morsalines. These are quite fast roads but you soon lose much of the inter-town motor traffic by heading left onto the D421 to the delightful coastal village of Quinéville. Here you pass a lovely little natural harbour and pick up cycle route signs through back streets to pick up the D421 coast road keeping an eye out for the Memorial museum dedicated to detailing life under the occupation. It's now an easy, breezy ride along the coast, heading through tiny Ravenoville-Plage (little traffic on this stretch out of holiday season and weekends). Pass the LeClerc monument detailing the exploits of this crack French troop regiment.
From the D-day museum at Utah

beach carry on paralleling the coast to the south (the quiet D329, which skirts the coastal Beauguillot nature reserve). Swing right and pass through the hamlet of Pouppeville then left at the next junction into Le Grand-Vey - home to Chez Roger restaurant and Baie des Veys camping. (Heading right after passing through Pouppeville will allow you a there-and-back visit to the fascinating village of Ste-Marie-du-Mont, the first settlement to be liberated after the D-Day landings and full of the history of 1944, including two museums and very dramatic info plaques on the US-German hand to hand fighting). Follow the dead flat road for another 7km of quiet marshland scenery before bearing right to tiny Basse Addeville, bending left by the old waterpump. Very soon down to your left is the lovely Bellenau Château and gardens (see the fascinating info plaque on its history - open selected days or by appointment). Pass under the E46 motorway then take the very first minor left and next right to meet the main D913 and head left, passing the Maison du Parc on the right (good information about the Bessin marshland you have just passed through and organised boat trips). On the edge of Carentan come to a roundabout, where you go straight across. About 250m after the roundabout turn left into a small industrial estate (Blactot). This looks an unprepossessing entry to Carentan - but pass the high walls of the cemetery on the right and continue on rue de l'Aubrevoir to arrive in the main square, place Vauban.

Accommodation
Hôtel L'Escapade
28 rue du Dr Caillard, Carentan
02.33.42.02.00
www.hotelrestaurantescapade.com
Just off place Vauban and by the train station

Hôtel Vauban
7 rue Sébline, Carentan 02.33.71.00.20
levaubanhotelcarentan@yahoo.com
Good value rooms

La Baie des Veys
Le Grand-Vey
02.33.71.56.90
www.campinglabaiedesveys.com

Camping le Haut Dick
30 Chemin de Grand Bas Pays
Carentan 02.33.71.56.90
www.camping-lehautdick.com
Beautifully located site on the edge of town by the canal.

Bike Shops
Sebastien Masieu
12 rue Ste Marie
Quettehou
02.33.43.63.18
Saint Louis
31 rue Holgate, Carentan (south of the train station)

Carentan - Capital of the Marais
Carentan is a delightful small town at the heart of the Normandy Marais - an extensive area of marshland still used for grazing cattle and racehorses which are run at countless small racecourses across the region. It is also a favourite haunt of countless birds (including thousands of migrating ones) and was designated a regional nature park in 1991.
The town has a delightful old centre, especially in the areas around the place de la République, the town church and the grand town hall. The old commercial port is now a marina and the canal towpath is a nice stroll to the edge of the marshes.

Quinéville, a lovely introduction to the coast road down to Utah beach

Day 3 | Carentan → St-Lô

TOTAL DISTANCE / ELEVATION: **48 km / 347 m ascent** | 30 mi / 216ft ascent

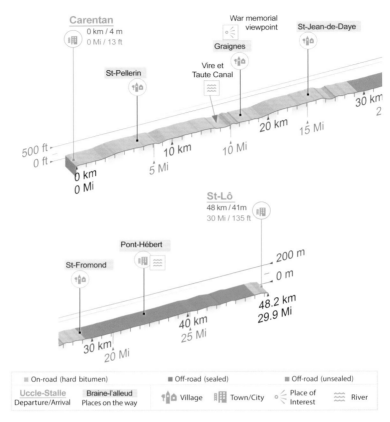

Carentan
0 km / 4 m
0 Mi / 13 ft

St-Pellerin

War memorial
viewpoint

Graignes

Vire et
Taute Canal

St-Jean-de-Daye

500 ft
0 ft

0 km
0 Mi

5 Mi

10 km

10 Mi

20 km

15 Mi

30 km

St-Lô
48 km / 41m
30 Mi / 135 ft

Pont-Hébert

St-Fromond

200 m

0 m

48.2 km
29.9 Mi

30 km
20 Mi

40 km
25 Mi

■ On-road (hard bitumen)	■ Off-road (sealed)	■ Off-road (unsealed)
Uccle-Stalle Departure/Arrival	**Braine-l'alleud** Places on the way	↑🏠 Village 🏢 Town/City o≷ Place of Interest 〰 River

Resting by the Vire et Taute canal. The towpath cuts around 14,5km (9 miles) off the day's ride, but is grassy, slow and rather bumpy.

Day 3 Ride Notes

(Off-road short-cut for mountain bikes along the Vire / Taute canal would shorten the day's ride to around 21 miles / 34km - the path is grassy and narrow and bumpy in some places).

Though heading for inland Normandy where you start to get the first whiff of the more serious hills that lie to the south, you won't find many easier days touring than this, as the route barely climbs above 50m, and after St-Fromond it's a dead flat riverside path all the way to St-Lô - this is generally good quality crushed stone path (though occasionally a bit rough), but a minimum of touring tyres are recommended.

From Carentan the route is well-signed once you have picked up the scent; from place de la République head down rue du Château and follow it to cross over the river. At the roundabout in the suburb of St-Hilaire-Petitville meet a roundabout and pick up the signs for the cycle route.

From here you are on lovely country roads through the village of St-Pellerin, following cycle signs for St-Jean-de-Daye and St-Lô. A major new road in the area was being built at the time of writing but the route should be well-signed over new minor road bridges to bring you over the Vire and Taute canal / river.

After the canal crossing we briefly head off the main signed route, following signs for Graignes on the D89. Follow memorial/viewpoint signs along the D389[E2] to climb to a large war memorial with a nearby viewing platform over the marshes. Descend to the centre of Graignes with its unusual concrete church, picking up the D57 then the D389 signed St-Jean-de-Daye. Following more virtually deserted country roads along the signed route to St-Jean-de-Daye (with its full complement of the usual shops and WWII monuments and plaques) jink right then left across the main N road and pick up cycle route signs for St-Fromond / St-Lô.

Having followed cycle route signs to St-Fromond head over the bridge over the Vire and almost immediately turn right onto the greenway alongside the Vire, for a superb riverside ride. The riverside track briefly leaves the river onto a minor road but then it hugs the river banks all the way to St-Lô. There's a great picnic spot at the locks (complete with fish ladder) north of Pont-Hébert, where the path swaps banks (you need to cross the main road bridge here) before an increasingly picturesque run into St-Lô, where you join a riverside road which can be followed all the way to the train station. The town centre lies beyond the pretty canalised river, inside the ramparts up to your left, whilst the main route continues on the road past the station (D900 for Agneaux).

Accommodation

Amoric Hôtel
15 rue de la Marne - St-Lô
02.33.05.61.32 www.contact-hotel.com

Bike Shops

Sarl 14
1 bis boulevard de la Dollée
St-Lô

Cyclepath along the Vire river - a rural idyll

Day 3a Carentan → Carteret

TOTAL DISTANCE / ELEVATION: **48 km / 248 m ascent** | **30 mi / 814ft ascent**

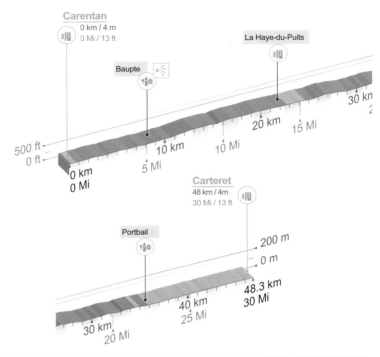

■ On-road (hard bitumen)	■ Off-road (sealed)	■ Off-road (unsealed)
Uccle-Stalle Departure/Arrival	**Braine-l'alleud** Places on the way	👫🏠 Village 🏢 Town/City ⊙ Place of Interest ≈ River

Crossing the estuary over the lovely bridge at Portbail

Day 3a Ride Notes

The greenway between Carentan and La Haye-du-Puits is wide and flat and passes through open countryside in the heart of the Bessin marshland, with several good viewpoints over it - notably leaving Carentan and from the bridge at Baupte. The start of the greenway is near Carentan centre but rather hidden away on the southern side of the railway line on rue de la Guiguette.

The surface is a rather disappointing red crushed stone with largish chunks of stone and patches of gravel that are more of an irritant than a serious hazard (though at a minimum bikes should have touring style tyres).

At La Haye-du-Puits there is a break in the old rail line - well signed via minor roads in the area of St-Symphorien-le-Valois. Shortly after rejoining the greenway it splits in two, and you opt for the left-hand option signed for Portbail, Baudreville and Barneville-Carteret. Thankfully the surface is much improved - now well-compacted, almost resembling concrete in the dry.

The greenway ends short of Portbail centre, where you pick up signs for Portbail and Barneville-Carteret, crossing the D15 almost immediately after leaving the greenway, onto a minor road. Similar signing soon leads onto a sandy track, with great views across the estuary and dunes, coming back onto tarmac and into Portbail's small centre. Head left over the lovely many- arched bridge crossing of the estuary.

The route bends right past a small harbour and sailing school before heading inland 90 degrees up a small road, signed to Barneville-Carteret.

Shortly head left onto rue Roze and right onto avenue Pasteur. The route is generally well-signed for Barneville-Carteret and St Georges-de-la-Rivière at various junctions (head straight across at any unmarked crossroads). Signs for St-Georges-de-la-Rivière are replaced by ones for St-Jean-de-la-Rivière (both are just north of the main signed route). You pick up the GR223 hiking route just east of Carteret, and follow it left at a right hand bend, and left at another right hand bend to cross a small stream using rue des Prés Salés on a tiny bridge. Finally, head left onto smooth tarmac then jink left and right over a small roundabout to approach Carteret centre along a fine seafront ride.

Accommodation

Hôtel Le Cap
promenade Abbé Lebouteiller, Carteret
02.33.53.85.89   www.hotel-le-cap.fr
Lovely location on the front.

Bar-Restaurant La Plage
63 av de la Mer, Carteret Plage
www.hotel-restaurant-barneville-plage.fr
02.33.53.85.75

Camping le Pré Normand
50270 Saint-Jean-de-la-Riviére
02.33.53.85.64
www.pre-normand.com
Large family orientated site and rather pricey - but handily next to the route.

Camping le Bocage
4 rue du Bocage, Carteret
02.33.53.86.91 - 02.33.04.35.98
Lovely site on the edge of Carteret, just behind the church.

A short track section gives great views coming into Portbail

Day 4   St-Lô → Coutances

TOTAL DISTANCE / ELEVATION: **37 km / 568 m ascent** | 23 mi / **1863ft ascent**

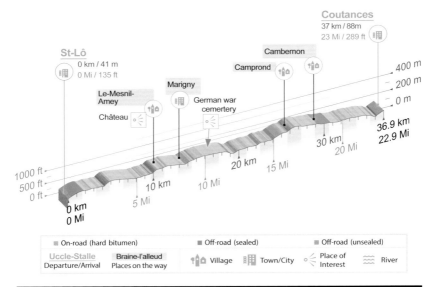

The German war cemetery near Marigny is the final resting place of over 11,000 war dead

Day 4 Ride Notes

For much of this day's ride you use very quiet and very beautiful country lanes deep in the Normandy countryside. From the road in front of the train station in St-Lô pick up the D900 signed to Agneaux, which climbs on a rather busy road initially, heading over a roundabout, though you soon pick up the excellent road-side cycle lane through the modern suburb of Agneaux. After bearing right at a roundabout for Hébécrevon (D900) look out shortly for a left turn signed La-Chapelle-en-Juger then immediate right. Head over the massive E3 main road on this very quiet country road. Stay on the D149 over a couple of minor crossroads, following La-Chapelle-en-Juger signs and across the D77. Shortly take the first unmarked left split.

You soon pick up cycle route signs (green cycle on white) to come to le Mesnil-Amey, with its grand château and church. Follow cycle route signs into the sizeable village of Marigny with its plethora of the usual village services. Head north out of Marigny on the D29 to visit the German war cemetery on the right, where a staggering 11,000 soldiers are buried. Head back to the D29 and straight across on the D341 signed to Le Lorey. Keep following Le Lorey signs (crossing the tiny Lozon river as you go). Go straight through Le Lorey and follow the D341 to Camprond. Pass the church on the left to come to the D52. Go left and immediate right still on the D341

for Cambernon and Coutances. Ignore minor turnings in Cambernon and after a look round this attractive little village head south on the greenway to its end at the DANGEROUS AND FAST D972. Very carefully head left then right over this road following signs for the GR221 walking route. Cross over the railway twice before picking up the D99. Just before the D99 crosses back over the railway on a bridge with grand views towards Coutances head right (you're in tiny St-Pierre-de-Coutances) to descend steeply on rue de la Galaicière, climbing towards the town centre on rue Ernest Hulin. Meet a main road and go right. Head over a roundabout (signed Centre Ville) then shortly look for a small walkway through trees up to the left and follow it up the hill through a warren of streets to come to the main street with its unmissably massive yet graceful cathedral.

Accommodation

Hôtel Le Parvis
18 place du Parvis Notre-Dame, Coutances
www.hotel-restaurant-taverne-du-parvis.com
02.33.45.13.55

Camping les Vignettes
rue de St Malo (D44)
02.33.45.43.13
Well-equipped municipal site little more than 0.5 miles from the town centre. It's on the main D44 and a short climb west up it will allow you to rejoin the route to La-Haye-du-Puits at the roundabout

St-Lô

St-Lô was one of the most heavily bombarded places in the battle for Normandy and today still bears the alternative name 'The Capital of Ruins' (in one attack over 1,000 bombs were dropped in 20 minutes). The Cathedral of Notre Dame was reconstructed incorporating modern materials and building styles alongside the original. The main square also features a rather strange 1950s concrete viewing point and you can also find the old prison gate, commemorating the WWII victims of the Nazis, from French resistance members to those deported east. Despite the sombre reminders of the past, St-Lô is a lively and attractive town today, the centre lying on a rocky hilltop, above impressive ramparts themselves rebuilt after WWII. The ramparts can be seen as you enter the town beyond a pretty section of canalised river which lies in front of the train station. Most town's hotels are grouped near the station.

Day 5 **Coutances → La Haye-du-Puits**

TOTAL DISTANCE / ELEVATION: **48 km / 427 m ascent** 30 mi / **1401 ft ascent**

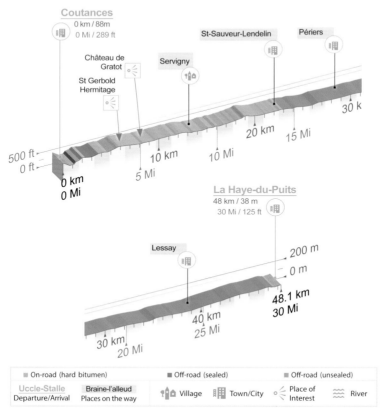

On-road (hard bitumen)	Off-road (sealed)	Off-road (unsealed)

| **Uccle-Stalle** Departure/Arrival | **Braine-l'alleud** Places on the way | 🏘 Village | 🏢 Town/City | ⊘ Place of Interest | 〰 River |

Coutances

Dominated by the towering, hilltop gothic cathedral of Notre-Dame, Coutances certainly exudes class, from its large, formal square in front of the cathedral to the luxurious public gardens just to the west and down the hill on your cycle route out of town. The cathedral's twin spires tower 255ft above the very compact town centre and the building was miraculously untouched by the intense bombing of June 1944 in the area.

The grand towers of Coutances cathedral contemplated from the public gardens

Day 5 Ride Notes

After a twisting, turning section on flatter roads north of Coutances this section rejoins an easy railpath to enjoy all the conveniences of a French market town at La Haye-du-Puits.

In Coutances head behind the Hôtel Le Parvis and left then right to drop steeply down past the public gardens. At the next junction pick up signs for St-Malo-de-la-Lande (D44). Shortly head left onto rue des Piliers, a quiet shortcut to the D44 again where you head left then right onto rue de la Broche. You pass through tiny L'Ecoulanderie and bear left at a split, now firmly in the heart of the countryside. On seeing the large road bridge ahead turn left before it and descend to a roundabout on the D44. Through the car parking area on the far side head right to pick up good quality cycle lanes. Head over the next small roundabout then turn right at the next roundabout signed Château de Gratot. Split left following château signs then straight across signed Hermitage St Gerbold to visit this remarkable site. Head back to the D244 and past the Château de Gratot on your right (impressive castle remains, visitable for a small fee). By the mairie go right up route de la Feu Ferme. At the T-junction on the edge of Brainville go right then left at the next T-junction, on the D74, picking up cycle route signs. Follow cycle route signs and signs to Servigny, soon crossing the

main D2. Head up the D534, ignoring minor turnings, then leave the official cycle route to turn right onto the D393 (towards D971) and follow signs for it past a large pond. Turn left signed for Les Roques and Rome, amongst other farmsteads. Just past La Petite Violette Est hit a T-junction and go right. Take the next left signed for the D434 (le Rouillais). Just coming into le Rouillais turn right at the split, to pass a dead end on the right. Cross an unmarked crossroads and left up the main D971 into St-Sauveur-Lendelin's centre. Take the second turning signed Périers and Carentan, passing the church and picking up the greenway by the old station, heading north on it towards Périers and Lessay. It's now an easy ride on the gravel of this railpath all the way to La Haye-du-Puits, though the centres of Périers and Lessay (with its impressive abbey) are certainly worth short detours off the path.

Accommodation

Le Colquin
1 rue du Calvaire, La Haye-du-Puits 02.33.46.10.33 or 06.04.03.83.38
Camping Etang des Haizes
43, rue Cauticotte, Saint-Symphorien-le-Valois, La Haye-du-Puits 02.33.46.01.16 www.campingetangdeshaizes.com Large family orientated site with mobile homes to rent in high season

A Hermit's Life - the tale of St Gerbold

About 3 miles on the route out of Coutances in a suitably well-hidden and tranquil location deep in the Normandy countryside where you'll find a tribute to a most peculiar medieval character.

St Gerbold, so the legend has it, was at the centre of an extraordinary chain of events, involving the spurned advances of a female aristocrat, a millstone, a ring swallowed by a fish and a dysentry epidemic.

Even though St Gerbold never lived in the area the hermitage was built in his honour.

Ponder a hermit's life north of Coutances

Day 6   La Haye-du-Puits → Carteret

TOTAL DISTANCE / ELEVATION: **27 km / 97 m ascent** | 17 mi / 318 ft ascent

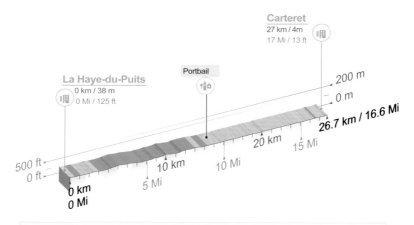

■ On-road (hard bitumen)		■ Off-road (sealed)		■ Off-road (unsealed)	
Uccle-Stalle Departure/Arrival	**Braine-l'alleud** Places on the way	♦♦♦ Village	▦ Town/City	○⟨ Place of Interest	≈≈ River

Day 6 Ride Notes

See Day 3a for ride notes.

Accommodation See day 3a entries

Route des Caps

Actually a driving route, using mainly quiet roads and linking Cherbourg with Carteret via the Cap de La Hague, the extreme north-western tip of the Cotentin peninsula. We follow signs for it from just north of Carteret all the way to Cap de Rozel. The Caps in question - small, cliff-like promontories, are worth a scramble off the road route (usually using the GR223 hiking route) for magnificent views along this very wild stretch of coast.

Cap de Carteret - worth the effort!

Route des Caps sign near Surtainville

Day 7	Carteret → Briquebec

TOTAL DISTANCE / ELEVATION: **36 km / 652 m ascent** | 22 mi / 2139 ft ascent

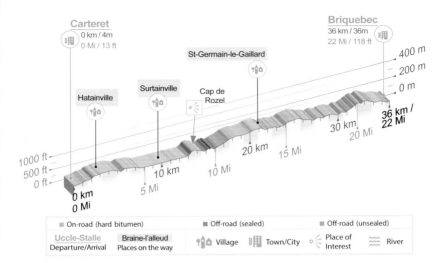

■ On-road (hard bitumen)	■ Off-road (sealed)	■ Off-road (unsealed)
Uccle-Stalle Departure/Arrival	Braine-l'alleud Places on the way	⌂ Village · ⊞ Town/City · ○ Place of Interest · ≈ River

Day 7 Ride Notes

Find Le Carteret restaurant in Carteret and bear left, signed Hatainville, passing Le Bocage camping on the right. Follow Hatainville signs into the village itself and bear right there onto the D242. Take a left onto the D201 to Baubigny, descending to la Vallée . You have now picked up very obvious signs for the driving route 'Route des Caps', as you rise and fall on this very minor road paralleling the sea. Pass Camping Bel Sito, being guided by the Route des Caps signs, with fantastic views over the dunescape hereabouts. The signs guide you through Hameau Béghin and into Surtainville on the D117. Here pick up the D66 for le Rozel following Route des Caps signs to climb steeply to the D62. The amazing headland of Cap de Rozel is worth a detour left at the D62 (signed 'la mer'). The GR223 hiking route actually climbs up to the left off this road with amazing views over long stretches of beach to the north and south.
Turn round and head inland on the D62 to the main D650. Head right (TAKE CARE - FAST TRAFFIC) shortly taking the first left to St-Germain-le-Gaillard. Head straight across by the minimarket here, on the D62 towards Grosville then very shortly, just out of the village, split right. Follow signs for Bernay and pass through

it to come to Longueville, picking up signs to the D23 along the D317. At the next set of junctions by the small wooden bus shelter follow signs for Hameau l'Abbé on the D331. Ignore the D367 on the left, following signs to la Croix Morain. Head left on the main, fast D66 to Briquebec and follow it all the way to this lovely market town.

Accommodation

🏨 *Hôtel le Donjon*
2-4 place Sainte Anne, Briquebec
02.33.52.23.15
www.hotel-restaurant.hotel-le-donjon.fr
🏨 *Monsieur Albert Simon*
route de Carteret, Briquebec
02.33.52.35.13

Bike Shops

🚲 *E. Lecarpentier*
38 rue Frères Fremines, Bricquebec.
02.33.52.24.89

Day 8 | Briquebec → Cherbourg

TOTAL DISTANCE / ELEVATION: **31 km / 435 m ascent** | **19 mi / 1427 ft ascent**

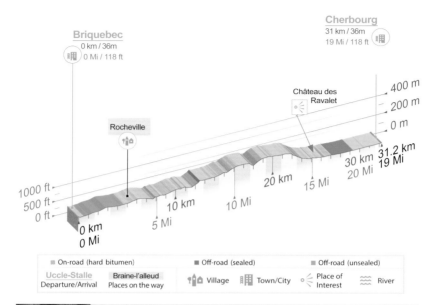

On-road (hard bitumen)		Off-road (sealed)		Off-road (unsealed)	
Uccle-Stalle Departure/Arrival	**Braine-l'alleud** Places on the way	Village	Town/City	Place of Interest	River

Briquebec's impressive castle

Day 8 Ride Notes

The greenway north from Briquebec is found on your way in - about 0.4km before the town centre. The greenway stops just a stone's throw from the little village of Rocheville where you pick up on-road bike route signs, heading on very quiet rural roads into the greenness of rural Normandy. In a little over a mile you cross the main rail line that heads north to Cherbourg and in about 600m turn left onto a very minor road through Hameau Baudry.

At the D62 jink right then left onto the D262^{E1} to continue in rural tranquility. Just on the far side of the hamlet of rue És Vésques turn left up route du Petit Vivier and follow this road over the D262 and on the quietest of quiet roads, following signs for a couple of kilometres (Brix is just to the west of this section if you need a cafe or food stop) to meet the D119 and left, crossing a bridge and heading immediate right onto route du Pont d'Aumaille.

In just under a km this crosses the hugely busy N13 - the main transport artery for the peninsula. Thankfully you are on the quiet route du Mont Hébert before bearing left onto route des Tuileaux. This meets the D56 where you jink right then left to pick up route de la Brûlette. This skirts the N13 before plunging off into quiet

countryside again and a lovely wooded section brings you to a right turn up the D322 for Mesnil-au-Val, some 2.75km after joining route de la Brûlette, which you take. In another 1.7km ignore the right split on the D413 to Mesnil-au-Val. Stay on this D322 to cross the D122, following signs for Tourlaville. Simply follow this road all the way to Château des Ravalet. Almost past the château jink left and stay on tarmac to head right to retrace your outward route through Penesme on route des Sourds, as described on page 29, heading under the thundering N13 and left onto Chasse à Eaux and right onto boulevard du Cotentin. Once at the ferry entrance in Cherbourg you may want to head for the town centre. Carry on on the cycle lanes to the roundabout, following signs for Cherbourg Centre. At the next main crossroads bear right with splendid views over inner and outer harbours on a little bridge. The town centre lies ahead.

Accommodation & Bike Shops

See Day 1 - Cherbourg to St-Vaast-la-Hougue

Arriving just too late for the market at Cherbourg's attractive place Général de Gaulle

St-Malo - Mont-St-Michel Circular

Route Info

St-Malo - Mont-St-Michel Circular

This 5 day ride is a gentle, easily accessible introduction to Brittany with short day ride lengths (the trip is easily made into a 3 or 4 day trip if you are in a bit more of a hurry). Beginning and ending at fortress St-Malo you'll hug the River Rance on good quality riverside tracks, wander from village to village and make a brief foray into Normandy. The final leg brings you back west along the coast from the ever popular Mont-St-Michel.

Grade EASY

Start / Finish St-Malo.

Route Length 211km / 131 miles

Length of Suggested Days
30.5-71km / 19-44 miles
Day lengths are fairly short to suit slower riders - consecutive days are easily combined to reduce the time of the tour.

Route Surface & Signing
46% off-road
Quiet roads plus some good quality tracks, railpaths and towpaths. Signage is the usual green and white design but with regional routes indicated (see pg173 for more detail); V3 and V2 share the route between Dinard and south of Dinan, where V3 splits off and you carry on, on V2. From Montreuil-sur-Ille you will be using a minor road route officially known as VD4 (though often just signed with the green and white cycle signs). Route designation becomes less coherent after Pontorson and at the time of writing was confused from Mont-St-Michel to St-Malo. Officially this will be Brittany regional route V4 along the north coast, but was not fully in place when we rode the route. All this may well have changed by the time you ride the route - see *Petit Tour de Manche*, pg 8, which you should come across signs for.

Access to St-Malo

Ferries from Portsmouth
www.brittany-ferries.co.uk
Ferry from Dinard (April to October), every 40 minutes (www.compagniecorsaire.com). The ferry accepts bikes.

SNCF Trains to St-Malo from Paris Gare Montparnasse
www.voyages-sncf.com

i Offices
Saint-Malo esplanade Saint-Vincent, 08.25.13.52.00 www.saint-malo-tourisme.com
Dinan place du Guesclin, 9 rue de Château 02.96.87.69.76 www.dinan-tourisme.com
Hédé At the mairie (Town Hall) 02.99.45.46.18
Bazouges-la-Pérouse
2, place de l'Hôtel de Ville 02.99.97.40.94
Antrain Best visit Bazouges for a full information service, though the town hall here can help with internet access
Mont-St-Michel, inside the main gate on the island, www.ot-montsaintmichel.com
Cancale 44 rue du Port 02.99.89.63.72 www.cancale-tourisme.fr

Don't Miss

Walking St-Malo's Ramparts
It's 1754 metres once around the walls of St-Malo. They date from the 18th century and the path runs the circumference of the old town, via turret and step (don't take your bike) and overlooks the labyrinthine streets, the harbour, Dinard and the Île de Cézembre out to sea (from which St-Malo was bombarded during WWII).

An outdoor swim at Piscine Les Pommiers, Lehon
Fabulous setting for a few lengths in the 25m by 15m 'pool of apples' before you switch to cycling and head off down the canal. This is a peach of a pool, found in the shadows of the Lehon Abbey, open all year round,though not early mornings. 02.96.39.21.00

The Eleven Lock Staircase
'Les Onze Ecluses', compensation for Hédé's hillside location, run along the 3km stretch of the Canal d'Ille et Rance between Hédé and Montreuil-sur-Ille. Whilst the staircase may slow boaters down considerably, it enlivens the first half hour of the day's ride.

Giving Mont-St-Michel back to the Sea
Previously you had to cycle down the causeway road along with day-trippers' cars to this Benedictine Abbey atop the islet. By 2014 a new dyke and car-free 'bridge on stilts' will be in place along with a shuttle service and the old causeway - one cause of the silting up of the estuary - will be demolished. The overall aim is to get the sea flowing around the Mont once more. As yet plans for bike access are unclear! www.projetmontsaintmichel.fr for updates

Mont-St-Michel may be one of the most recognisable silhouettes in the world, whether seen from near or afar. Indeed, it's probably the second most iconic building in France after the Eiffel Tower.

Day 1	St-Malo → Dinan

TOTAL DISTANCE / ELEVATION: **30.5 km / 269 m ascent** | 19 mi / **882ft ascent**

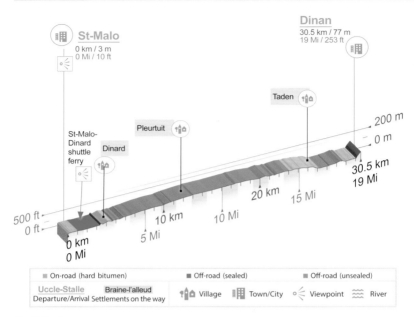

■ On-road (hard bitumen)	■ Off-road (sealed)	■ Off-road (unsealed)
Uccle-Stalle **Braine-l'alleud** Departure/Arrival Settlements on the way	♦♦♦ Village ▦ Town/City	○⧏ Viewpoint ≋ River

St-Malo

As far as this imposing ancient walled city is concerned, you're either in (intra-muros) or out (extra-muros). Over three quarters of the citadel was left in ruins in WWII and has since been rebuilt in the 17th-18th century style. Intra-muros the labyrinthine streets are best experienced on foot (distances are short and the cobbles are bike-unfriendly). Look out for the 12th century St. Vincent's Cathedral and the House of Quebec, built to celebrate the 450th anniversary of Canada's discovery by Jacques Cartier (who died in St-Malo in 1557). Looking outwards from the ramparts, the ferry terminal is adjacent to the main gates of the town. To the east the suburbs of

Courtesville, Rochebonne and Paramé are lined with expansive beaches, plenty of mid-range hotels and the option of the town Youth Hostel.

Don't miss a walk around St-Malo's ramparts

Day 1 - Ride Notes

The voie verte from Dinard to Dinan is a flat, quiet, pleasant cinch, though finding its starting point is tricky.

Your route from St-Malo to Dinard depends on the time of year you arrive; from April to October it's easiest to hop over the water to Dinard on the seasonal shuttle ferry which leaves every ten minutes. Coming off the St-Malo ferry (docks at Terminal du Naye) the shuttle boats are left at the first roundabout, following Intramuros signs, just off esplanade de la Bourse on the left.

During low season cycle south out of St-Malo, following signs for the Barrage de la Rance, turning right 6km from St-Malo to cross the barrage for some 750m. A path accompanies the barrage and protects you from the traffic, though you'll have to negotiate busy and fast dual carriageway traffic before and after the crossing. Over the barrage bear right onto the D114. At the next major junction in just under 2km go right for 'centre ville', picking up the route described below at the tourist office.

If arriving by shuttle ferry ('vedette') head along the quay in Dinard and right onto avenue George V, swinging left onto Georges Clemenceau and Président Wilson. The tourist office is signed up to the left on Boulevard Féart, which is also your route to the greenway. After about a third of a mile turn right onto rue Émile Barra and continue onto rue de la Gare. After another third of a mile go left onto place de Newquay and shortly on your right look for the greenway. At the time of writing the greenway was on wasteground that looked to be due for redevelopment, so this direction could change.

Despite being hidden away, you'll find the greenway to be a good quality track, passing through the village of Pleurtuit, whose busy little centre is just off the track to your left, past Jean-Michel Rault's cycle shop. At Pleslin-Plouër, the old station is now a gîte d'étape - see rando. abri.free.fr for this and the one down the path in St-Samson-sur-Rance. Near Pleslin-Plouër is Champ des Roches, 65 four thousand year old standing stones. The greenway ends at a tiny rural road where you head left, over a level crossing on what is signed as a 'route partagée' or shared route. Bear right at the next crossroads and left and next, onto a busier road with cycle lanes. Head across

a roundabout into Taden's beautiful old centre with the handy Bar du Manoir. By the church head right down rue des Grèves. Bend left and right and descend on rue des Marières to the greenway along the banks of the River Rance. Head right on this good quality crushed stone path. In about 1.3 miles you join the D12, keeping the river on your left and enter Dinan. At the lovely old bridge head up rue du Petit Fort, climbing steeply on its cobbles as it becomes rue du Jerzual. Dinan's busy and touristy - though very attractive - centre is then off to the left down the main drag of rue d'Horloge. This final section along the river and into Dinan is a real highlight.

Accommodation

🛏 *Centre Patrick Varangot (youth hostel)*
37 av du Père-Umbricht, Paramé, St-Malo
02.99.40.29.80 www.centrevarangot.com

🛏 *Hôtel Nautilus*
9, rue de la Corne de Cerf, St-Malo
02.99.40.42.27   www.lenautilus.com
Well-priced option within the walled town

⛺ *Camping Municipal de la Cité d'Alet*
allée Gaston Buy, St Servan, St-Malo
02.99.81.60.91 / 02.99.21.92.64
Nearest site to St-Malo with a dramatic headland location southwest of St-Malo

🛏 *Hôtel Beaurivage*
place du Général de Gaulle, Dinard
02.99.46.14.34   Only 500m from the route and so a better option than St-Malo if you want an early cycling start

🛏 *Hôtel de la Tour d'Horloge*
5 rue de la Chaux, Dinan   02.96.39.96

⛺ *Camping Municipal*
103 rue Châteaubriand, Dinan
02.96.39.11.96 By the western ramparts

Bike Shops

🚲 *Cycles Lebourg* 76 rue de la Marne, St. Servan, St-Malo, 02.99.82.61.51

🚲 *Electra Breizh*
5 bis av John Kennedy, Paramé, St-Malo, www.electra-breizh.fr (near youth hostel)

🚲 *Breiz Cycles* 8 rue St. Enogat, Dinard, 02.99.46.27.25
www.breizhcycles.com (closed Mondays)

🚲 *Garage Jean-Michel Rault*
31 rue Brindejonc-des-Moulinais, Pleurtuit, 0199884562 (visible from the voie verte – to the left)

🚲 *Cycles Gauthier* 15 rue Deroyer, Dinan, 0296850760 (near railway station)

Day 2   Dinan → Hédé

TOTAL DISTANCE / ELEVATION: **38 km / 327 m ascent**   23.5 mi / 1073 ft ascent

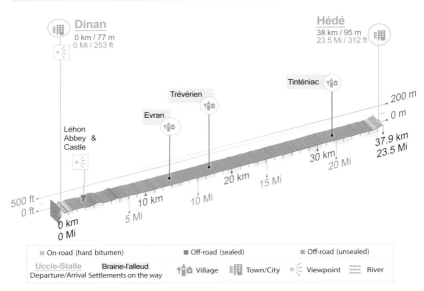

On-road (hard bitumen)	Off-road (sealed)	Off-road (unsealed)

| Uccle-Stalle   Braine-l'alleud | ↑🏠 Village | 🏢 Town/City | ∘≶ Viewpoint | 〜 River |
| Departure/Arrival Settlements on the way | | | | |

Good quality path by the River Rance

Day 2 Ride Notes

Apart from the plunge down from Dinan and the final ascent into Hédé, this is a meandering riverside path of a day. Retrace your route into Dinan and cross over the lovely bridge to pick up the towpath on your right. Follow it for 2.8km before swapping banks, skirting Léhon, with its impressive castle ruins and abbey in the valley (on your left). Take the road beside the Canal d'Ille et Rance for 800m, then the route turns onto the towpath again, hugging the canal all the way to Hédé. It's peaceful pedalling throughout, passing through Evran (swap sides here), Trévérien and Tinténiac. After around 34km leave the canal by the road on the right to climb into Hédé.

Accommodation

La Maison du Bienêtre B&B
12, rue Jean Boucher, Hédé
02.99.45.47.08
contact@enforme-naturellment.com
Hostellerie du Vieux Moulin
La Vallée des Moulins, Hédé
02.99.45.45.70 www.logishotels.com
Camping Aire Naturelle Municipale
La Magdaleine, Hédé
02.99.45.46.18

Dinan

With one foot in the River Rance, the old, walled section of this split level town towers 250ft up, fortified by 2650 metres of ramparts (the longest in the region). Settled by monks in the 9th century, medieval Dinan is worth the short, winding ascent and has plenty of commerce and accommodation. Inside the ramparts you'll find a mix of modernity and leaning, timber dwellings circa 1400. More recently, Dinan hosted the start of a Tour de France stage in 1995.

© Iain G Creative Commons licence Iain G

Dinan's old bridge heralds your arrival at the foot of its winding medieval streets

Hédé

The short climb into town from the canal offers a good view of the ruins of the town's 13th century castle. Historically, Hédé's existence owes much to the canal itself. The Musée de la Maison du Canal will regale you with knowledge about life on the canal in days gone by (02.99.45.48.90). Although the town itself is a good place to stock up on supplies, accommodation is in fairly short supply. That said the guesthouse listed above is not only one of the best found on the trip (book early), but is also run by a physiotherapist should aching muscles be a problem....

Day 3   Hédé → Antrain

TOTAL DISTANCE / ELEVATION: **44 km / 455 m ascent** | **27.5 mi / 1493 ft ascent**

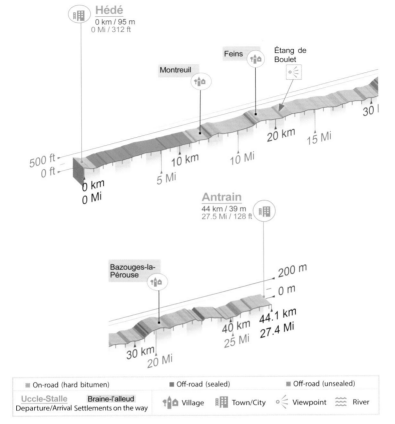

| ■ On-road (hard bitumen) | ■ Off-road (sealed) | ■ Off-road (unsealed) |

| Uccle-Stalle | Braine-l'alleud | 🛈🏠 Village | 🏢 Town/City | ○ Viewpoint | 〰 River |
| Departure/Arrival | Settlements on the way | | | | |

Day 3 Ride Notes

After two days by the Rance, today's ride undulates a little and reacquaints you with traffic from time to time, albeit a smattering on the signed cycle route between Montreuil-sur-Ille and Antrain, as you hop from village to village on quiet roads.

From Hédé's centre retrace your route out of town to split right onto the D87 signed Bazouges-sous-Hédé and at the canal turn right before the bridge over it onto the towpath. Follow the towpath for around 10km (swapping to the opposite bank after 6km) and head left onto the D221, down into Montreuil.

Cross the railway tracks and sweep left, signed as the D12 towards Feins. Very shortly turn left, up rue Docteur Lemoine. This tiny, deserted rural road heads through the hamlets of la Pfiffaudière and le Petit Boulet before splitting right at a fork, to pass through another hamlet, le Boulet Prioult. Ignore two tiny roads off to the right and follow through la Lande Perrine and into the town of Feins. Bear left onto the D12 on the outskirts of the town. By the church bear left onto the D20, signed Dinge and Combourg. Very shortly head right down rue de Noyan and left again, to follow the D91 out of town.

At a staggered crossroads just carry on ahead (camping municipal signed down to the left and St Rémy on the D12 to the right). Simply follow the whisper-quiet D91 for around 7.3km, ignoring minor turnings, to come into Marcillé-Raoul. Here head for the pencil-like church spire and head straight across a crossroads with a handy collection of shops, staying on the D91, signed Bazouges-la-Pérouse. Just follow the D91 for another 4km or so, before a very minor turn left, marked only by green and white cycle signs, takes you on the tiniest of roads to meet the D796. Go right onto this fast and very straight road into Bazouges-la-Pérouse. Here pass the church up to the left but very shortly turn left up rue de Mairie, passing the centre over to left, and continuing on to rue des Forges to drop down to a crossroads on the edge of town. Head straight across onto the D91 again, signed Vieux-Viel. After about 1.5km split right onto the C202, signed la Fontenelle. Follow the cycle signs through a series of tiny roads for the next 2.4km to emerge at the more major D313 to turn left onto it. In about 0.5km turn right, onto another set of tiny roads, following cycle route signs for the next 2.7km, to cross the D155 on the edge of Antrain. Head into its centre by simply following straight across several junctions and down ruelle des Fossés onto the central rue de Couesnon.

Accommodation

La Maison de Claire
2, rue de Couesnon, Antrain,
02.99.98.43.76
claire.perrin5@wanadoo.fr
Evening meals available
La Cour Horlande
25, rue de Pontorson, Antrain
02.99.18.09.74
www.lacourhorlande.com
Camping Municipal
avenue Kléber, Antrain
02.99.98.31.09 antrain@wanadoo.fr

Antrain

On the river Couesnon, this smallish town has all you need for a stop-over, with a couple of restaurants, shops, street market (Tuesday morning), an enormous supermarket and guest houses. Information for tourists is not especially easy to find, although the Town Hall (rue de l'Eglise, 02.99.98.31.09) will help if you're looking for internet access (as well as being a Job Centre if you're really serious about the place).

The spectacular lock staircase near Hédé

TOTAL DISTANCE / ELEVATION: **30.5 km / 83 m ascent**   19 mi / 272ft ascent

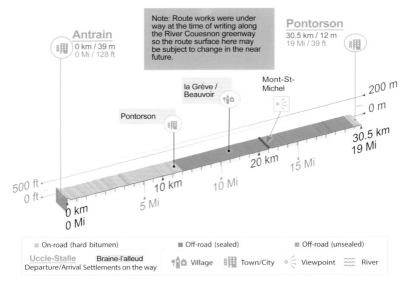

On-road (hard bitumen)	Off-road (sealed)	Off-road (unsealed)

Uccle-Stalle   Braine-l'alleud
Departure/Arrival Settlements on the way   ⛪ Village   🏢 Town/City   ⌖ Viewpoint   ≈ River

Day 4 Ride Notes

There are two signed cycle routes north of Antrain - we take the most direct to Pontorson before a there and back trip alongside the Couesnon river to one of France's premier tourist destinations, Mont-St-Michel.

In Antrain head down rue de Couesnon which becomes rue de l'Église. At the busy junction at the end of here go immediate left onto rue de Pontorson and head downhill to cross the pretty river Loisance and left at the T-junction. Almost immediately turn left up the quiet street known as La Gare.

Follow cycle route signs on this extremely quiet road route for some 10km to enter Pontorson by a small industrial estate on your left. Head left at the junction here, then right to pass under a rail bridge. At the next junction head right then immediate left, to come to Pontorson's busy main street. Head left onto it and at the roundabout go right up the D19, signed Mont-St-Michel. Very shortly head left up Cours de la Victoire, bearing right. After a short while this runs alongside the river as a newly laid track.

It's now a matter of following the river for some 7.8km to emerge at the causeway to Mont-St-Michel, using the roadside cycle route to visit this incredible location (best done when the coach parties have departed at the end of a long summer's day). There are a few often pricey accommodation options so you may well wish to head back to more mundane Pontorson for a wider range of eating and sleeping options.

Mont-St-Michel

Although attracting more than 2 million tourists annually, this abbey still lives up to its sobriquet of 'the wonder of the west'.

Built on a granite island, the abbey itself crowns the rock and was built between the eighth and sixteenth centuries. Many of the hotchpotch of surrounding houses at the base were later additions.

The whole ensemble takes the shape of a series of fortified courtyards (the island was never successfully besieged) leading to the busy Grande Rue and to the heavy fortifications of the abbey itself. For the new access scheme see its Don't Miss entry at the start of the chapter.

Accommodation

La Tour Brette
8 rue de Couesnon, Pontorson
02.33.60.10.69
www.latourbrette.com

Hôtel Restaurant Au Jardin Saint
Michel 37 rue de la Libération,
Pontorson
02.33.60.11.35   www.aujardinstmichel.fr
Though accommodation on the
Mont itself is often fully booked and
overpriced there are options for staying
at or near Mont-St-Michel if you want
to wander around when the daytrippers
are gone.

Du Guesclin
One of the more reasonably priced
hotels on the Mont. Part of the Logis
chain 02.33.60.14.10
www.hotelduguesclin.com

There are a group of 4 modern
chain style hotels on the mainland
before the crossing. A bit of a

tourist trap but handy for visiting the
monastery when the daytrippers have
disappeared:
Hôtel Formule Verte 02.33.60.14.13
Hôtel Vert 02.33.60.09.33
Hôtel Mercure 02.33.60.14.18
Le Relais du Roy 02.33.60.14.25
All at www.le-mont-saint-michel.com

Camping Haliotis
Chemin des Soupirs, Pontorson
'Luxury' site that isn't that much
cheaper than the cheapest rooms in
Pontorson! 02.33.68.11.59
www.camping-haliotis-mont-saint-
michel.com

Camping aux Pommiers
28 route du Mont Saint Michel, Beauvoir
02.33.60.11.36
www.camping-auxpommiers.com

Bike Shops

Couesnon Motoculture
1 bis rue Couesnon, 50170 Pontorson,
02.33.60.11.40

Mont-St-Michel can be spectacular from the inside as well as the outside

Day 5   Pontorson or Mont-St-Michel → St-Malo

TOTAL DISTANCE / ELEVATION: **68 km / 392 m ascent** | **42 mi / 1286ft ascent**

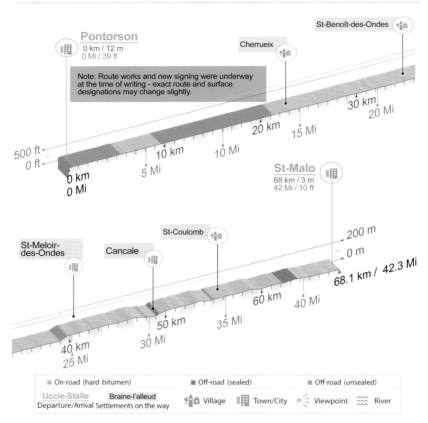

Note: Route works and new signing were underway at the time of writing - exact route and surface designations may change slightly.

On-road (hard bitumen)   ■ Off-road (sealed)   ■ Off-road (unsealed)

Uccle-Stalle   Braine-l'alleud   🏠 Village   🏢 Town/City   ○ Viewpoint   〜 River
Departure/Arrival Settlements on the way

Day 5 Ride Notes

NOTE: At the time of writing this section was being integrated into the Petit Tour de Manche (see pg 8 for more detail) and so this is a somewhat provisional route description; comprehensive signing on the exact final route alignment was still being put in place, but these abbreviated directions should help you find what should be a well-signed and attractive flat coastal route until just south of Cancale, after which it becomes hillier. From both Pontorson and Mont-St-Michel there will be signs leading across the polders marshlands to the west of the River Couesnon greenway. You ride away from Mont-St-Michel or Pontorson using tracks and quiet roads to link to a greenway that runs atop an old dyke and heads towards the sea, to spill you back onto public roads near

the lonely little chapel of Ste-Anne. Through Le Lac enter small, pretty Cherrueix from where you follow the D797 and after Le Vivier-sur-Mer the D155. Plans for a traffic-free cycle lane are still at an early stage, so unfortunately you are obliged to follow the rather busy road.

About 1.6km after St-Benoît-des-Ondes you head away from the coast using tiny back roads via St-Meloir-des-Ondes, turning left at the go-karting track. There's a short, steepish climb and at the cross-roads head briefly right before going left for 600m to the junction with the D76.

Here signs will take you to the outskirts of the rather unprepossessing St-Méloir-des-Ondes before swinging you sharply right just before the towering spire of the church. 500m further on and you are back on the D155, which you cross, taking the lane round the back of the tiny hamlet of Haute Ville before heading left along for 2.5km up to Les Hauts Champs.

At the cross-roads, a signed loop to the east lets you visit Cancale whilst your final progress westwards uses mainly quiet roads via St-Coulomb, Rotheneuf and the St-Malo suburb of Paramé, using the D201, D155 and D137 in turn. You will pick up the dedicated cycle lane just after Le Minihic, as you approach the mighty sweep of beach that goes all the way down to St-Malo bay. The route takes you past the walls of St-Malo Intramuros and down to the ferry terminal.

Accommodation & Bike Shop Listings - see Day 1

Creative Commons licence Sam Romilly

There can be no doubt what the main industry in Cancale (above) is; as well as being sold everywhere the town's obsession with shellfish is also well documented in the local museum. You'll see the small fishing fleet at the smart port of La Houle as the cycle route passes right along the busy little front, lined with eateries and hotels, before climbing to Cancale's main square.

The coastline around St-Malo (below) is great for walking and bike riding, with fascinating views around every twist and turn. Here is Saint-Servan just to the south of St-Malo with its lovely harbour and the Tour Solidor housing models of ships and boats.

© Creative Commons licence Charlie Dave

Avenue Verte & Seine Valley
Dieppe - Paris - Le Havre

Route Info

Avenue Verte & Seine Valley
14 days of moderate mileages mean this is a relaxing three week trip if combined with a break of a few days in Paris. It could easily be split into several shorter tours (see Route Length below).

From Dieppe to Paris's emblematic Notre-Dame cathedral you are following part of the signed Avenue Verte, which in its entirety links London to Paris and offers a much longer western option via Beauvais and Senlis (see pgs 192-3 for eastern option). The harder days come after the end of the wonderfully-surfaced and maintained traffic-free railpath between Dieppe and Forges-les-Eaux (though an extension of the traffic-free trail was promised to Gournay-en-Bray for 2013 and further in the future into the heart of Dieppe as well as westwards to Beauvais).

An undulating, quiet agricultural landscape, the Pays de Bray, is crossed on minor roads leading to the attractive market town of Gournay. Then it's easier cycling down the Epte valley to castle-dominated Gisors and another fine railpath leading to the rolling hills and protected landscape of the area known as the Vexin. At this point you can opt to miss out Paris all together, shortcutting to Vernon and returning to the coast at Le Havre along some wonderful stretches of the Seine.

If Paris is your goal, hop across the Vexin on tiny roads and agricultural tracks (dry weather only - road alternatives available) to its outskirts. Much of the riding into the centre from here is surprisingly traffic-free. Retrace your tracks by bike or train, to find yourself downstream on the Seine again at Vernon. The Seine dominates your journey from here to the coast, whether it's overlooked by Richard I's enormous castle, criss-crossed by lovely local ferry boats, spanned by truly massive, elegant suspension bridges or hemmed in by white chalk cliffs. City attractions are provided by the medieval centre of Rouen and the futuristic feeling cityscape of Le Havre with a dash of ancient splendour at Honfleur.

Grade MEDIUM

Start / Finish   Dieppe / Le Havre.

Route Length   Numerous route options; a Dieppe-Paris-Le Havre round trip (with a train hop from Paris to Vernon) would be 504km / 312 miles. Dieppe to Notre-Dame at the heart of Paris is around 236km / 146 miles, from where you could take the Eurostar back to London. The option avoiding the spur route into Paris altogether (i.e. Dieppe to Le Havre via Vernon) would come to 430km / 267 miles.

Length of Suggested Days
27.5-45km / 17-28 miles
Very comfortable daily distances mean plenty of time for exploration off the bike or the possibility of reducing the 14 day trip by several days (though with minimal sightseeing).

Route Surface & Signing
37% off-road currently, mainly on the Avenue Verte from Dieppe to Paris, with more in the pipeline. Predominantly quiet roads, but with two tarmaced traffic-free paths - the Avenue Verte south of Dieppe and Gisors-Gasny traffic-free trail. Elsewhere traffic-free sections are the product of the developing network in towns and cities meaning you can avoid really heavy and unpleasant road traffic in such areas as western Paris and Rouen (though be ready for small sections of heavier traffic).

For signing along the Avenue Verte between Dieppe and Notre-Dame, Paris see photos opposite.

It's worth noting that there are plans for a signed touring route - the Véloroute du Val de Seine - to link Rouen and Le Havre, following the river much of the way. In 2012 the only part in place was the traffic-free riverside path south-west of Villequier. However, in years to come you may find new signed, traffic-free sections linking the destinations used by this route.

Access to Dieppe & Le Havre

Cross-Channel Ferries
Sailings from Newhaven to Dieppe and Portsmouth to Le Havre www.ldlines.co.uk Depending on timetabling, it may be quicker (though probably quite a bit more expensive) to take the train from Le Havre to Paris St Lazare (limited bike carrying services) and then the Eurostar back to London from Paris Gare du Nord.

i Offices
Dieppe pont Jehan Ango 02.32.14.40.60 www.dieppetourisme.com
Neufchâtel-en-Bray 6 place Notre-Dame 02.35.93.22.96 www.ot-pays-neufchatelois.fr
Forges-les-Eaux rue Albert-Bochet 02.35.90.52.10 www.forgesleseaux-tourisme.fr
Gournay-en-Bray 9 place d'Armes 02.35.90.28.34 www.ot-gournay-en-bray.fr
Saint-Germer-de-Fly 11 place de Verdun 03.44.82.62.74 www.ot-paysdebray.fr
Gisors rue du Général-de-Gaulle 02.32.27.60.63 www.tourisme-gisors.fr
Théméricourt (Vexin) Maison du Parc 01.34.48.66.10 www.parc-naturel-vexin
Maisons-Laffitte 41 avenue de Longueil 01.39.62.63.64

Saint-Germain-en-Laye 38 rue au Pain
01.30.87.20.63 www.ot-saintgermainenlaye.fr
Le Vésinet avenue des Pages
01.30.15.47.80 www.levesinet.fr
Bougival 10 rue du Général-Leclerc
01.39.69.21.23 www.tourisme-bougival.com
Saint-Denis 1 rue de la République
01.55.87.08.70 www.saint-denis-tourisme.com
Paris 25 rue des Pyramides. Also smaller
centres at Gare du Nord, Gare de l'Est and
Gare de Lyon train stations as well as at
Montmartre, Anvers and Porte de Versailles
(telephone numbers not publicised). See
locations on main Paris plan (separate map).
www.parisinfo.com
Giverny 70 rue Claude Monet
02.32.51.39.60 www.cape-tourisme.fr
Vernon 36, rue Carnot 02.32.51.39.60
www.cape-tourisme.fr

Gaillon 4 Place Aristide Briand
02.32.53.08.25
Petit Andely rue Phillippe Auguste
02..32.54.41.93
http://office-tourisme.ville-andelys.fr/
Pont de l'Arche 11 rue Jean Prieur
02.35.23.17.64
Rouen 25 place de la Cathédrale
02.32.08.32.40 www.rouentourisme.com
Duclair 227 avenue du Président Coty
02.35.37.38.29
Jumièges rue Guillaume le Conquérant
02.35.37.28.97 www.jumiegesinfotourisme.com
Caudebec-en-Caux
place du Général de Gaulle 02.32.70.46.32
Honfleur quai Lepaulmier 02.31.89.23.30
www.ot-honfleur.fr
Le Havre 186 boulevard Clemenceau

◻ **www.avenuevertelondonparis.com**
Interactive maps, downloadable GPS
routes, news and facilities and feedback /
photo area

Guide
Detailed Sustrans publication to the whole
500km of Avenue Verte route between
London and Paris, including the eastern
route option via Beauvais and the river
Oise.
Due spring 2013.
ISBN 978-1-901389-88-3

Avenue Verte signing between Dieppe and Paris. In Paris it follows the pink signs of the north-south route too (above left). Black and yellow (top right) means a temporary section.

Don't Miss

Paris's Doorstep Rural Retreat

Whilst Paris is world-famous the nearby area of rolling wheat fields, woods and mellow-hued villages known as the Vexin is little-known outside France. The remarkable estate at Villarceaux aside, it's the unspoilt villages featuring washhouses and dovecotes and often decorated with a distinctive design of cross that capture the imagination.

Cycle-friendly Paris

Under mayor Bertrand Delanoë's rule Paris has made huge cycle-friendly strides, its growing cycle lane network allowing the Vélib' hire bike scheme to flourish. All this in one of the world's most beautiful cities. There are fine views from the riverside cycle route.

Richard the Lionheart's Lookout

Towering above the Seine at Les Andelys, Château Gaillard is the embodiment of many people's idea of a medieval castle; seemingly impregnable and hugely imposing, allowing views of and being seen from the countryside for many miles around. And this is just the remaining outline after its destruction in 1603. Access best on foot and allowed from mid-March to mid-November.

Ride over the Seine to Honfleur

This ride over the Pont de Normandie bridge is not for the faint-hearted - it takes you steeply up above the Seine. Cycle lanes are narrow and unsegregated. If in doubt walk your bike across on the pavement! However, the views in fine weather are staggering from one of the world's biggest cable-stayed bridges.

Day 1 Dieppe → Neufchâtel-en-Bray

TOTAL DISTANCE / ELEVATION: **37.5 km / 160 m ascent** | 23.5 mi / **525ft ascent**

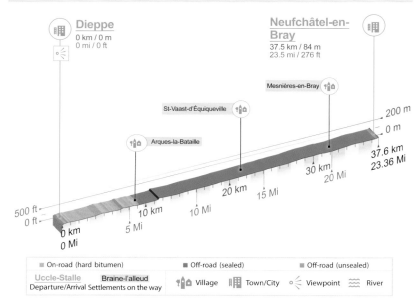

Dieppe
0 km / 0 m
0 mi / 0 ft

Neufchâtel-en-Bray
37.5 km / 84 m
23.5 mi / 276 ft

Mesnières-en-Bray

St-Vaast-d'Équiqueville

Arques-la-Bataille

200 m
0 m
37.6 km
23.36 Mi
30 km
20 Mi
20 km
15 Mi
10 km
10 Mi
5 Mi
500 ft
0 ft
0 km
0 Mi

■ On-road (hard bitumen) ■ Off-road (sealed) ■ Off-road (unsealed)
Uccle-Stalle Braine-l'alleud
Departure/Arrival Settlements on the way ♦ Village ■ Town/City ○ Viewpoint ≋ River

Day 1 Ride Notes

The hardest part is finding your way through Dieppe town centre as there is a one-way system for bikes which avoids the busy one-way system for cars. **Note:** There is a quieter, hillier, alternative route as shown on the map, though here we describe the quickest, though busiest route. In time it will be much improved, as the disused railway that reaches into the heart of Dieppe becomes converted into a cyclepath.

From the ferry terminal follow signs for "centre ville" and cross the harbour on a metal swing bridge, the Pont Colbert. Before crossing a second bridge turn left and follow the signs through the commercial harbour area. The road swings round to the right and brings you out opposite the railway station. Turn left before the station into a rather intimidating multi-lane one-way road – remember to keep right and take the first right into another industrial area beside the railway tracks. Pick up a cycle track and follow through the industrial estate, ending at a road where you turn right and cross a railway line at a level crossing. This is the old Dieppe to Forges-les-Eaux line, which is planned to become part of the Avenue Verte.

Turn left into Rue General Chanzy and carry on for 7km to Arques-la-Bataille, paralleling the old railway. You pass several cafes and hotels. The only thing to watch out for is a major roundabout where you may encounter some of the lorries coming from the ferry.

On entering Arques-la-Bataille there is a fork in the road with an imposing church in the background. Take the right fork following the D154 to Torcy. As you climb up a slight gradient into the centre of Arques, you will see the old château up on the hill above the village. Straight ahead in the village centre then bear left at the end of the square to go downhill. Arques is an attractive village with plenty of bars, restaurants and shops. Continue on the main road until you see a level crossing but turn right before you reach it, onto the start of the superb traffic-free path. The path winds through an attractive outdoor leisure park with many water-based activities, eventually joining the old railway beside a large industrial site. Continue for 24km on the fantastic smooth tarmac surface all the way to Neufchâtel. You can do this very quickly, but we recommend that you take your time and visit some of the attractive villages along the route, most very close to the old railway, just a minute or two to bars, cafes and the all-important "boulangeries". Many of the local businesses have signs up at the many minor road crossings to entice you to try their wares. One place worth a stop is the Guy Weber educational natural park just after the start of the railway path. This is free to enter and a great place for a picnic or a stroll beside the river Béthune .

You will not miss the magnificent château at Mesnières, which is on your left. There is more to the village than the château and it is well worth spending a while here. Just before the village look out for a small sign for "lavoir" to the left, where a narrow path leads to an enchanting well and shaded rest area.

In Neufchâtel the old station has been converted into a public space and is a useful jumping off point for the town. The town centre is not immediately obvious – if in doubt head for the church spire. There is a wide range of shops and services on offer and a few hotels too.

Accommodation

Hôtel de la Plage
20 boulevard de Verdun, Dieppe
02.35.84.18.28 One of many seafront hotels. Good price rooms. Secure garage.
www.plagehotel.fr.st

Hôtel Les Arcades
1-3 arcades de la Bourse, Dieppe
02.3584.14.12 www.lesarcades.fr

Camping Vitamin'
865 chemin des Vertus, Dieppe
02.35.82.11.11 www.camping-vitamin.com
Good quality site but a couple of miles out of town and up a steep hill.

Hôtel les Airelles
2 passage Michu, Neufchâtel-en-Bray
02.35.93.14.60
www.les-airelles-neufchatel.com

Hôtel le Grand Cerf
9 Grande Rue Fausse Port,
Neufchâtel-en-Bray   02.35.93.00.02
www.grandcerf-hotel.com

Bike Shops

Cycles Herbert
32-34 rue d'Ecosse, Dieppe
02.35.82.24.27

Cycles Herve Gourgand
32 bis, avenue Jean-Jaurès, Dieppe
02.35.90.01.14

Avril Cycles
11, Grande Rue Saint-Jacques,
Neufchâtel-en-Bray
02.35.93.13.28

The Avenue Verte between Dieppe and Forges-les-Eaux is a cycling safe haven for those of all ages. There are also numerous signed routes off it, using minor roads through the surrounding countryside.

Dieppe

Dieppe's centrepiece is undoubtedly its lively harbour which ensures a constant supply of fresh seafood to the restaurants that line it. A climb to the small chapel of Notre-

Dame-de-Bon-Secours lets you appreciate all the more the dramatic setting of the harbour, packed between cliffs. The château museum just to the west of the front is also a great viewpoint. The lovely seafront lawns are a good place for a stroll, or those with younger cyclists might want to visit the aquariums of Cité de la Mer.

Dieppe's harbour is at the heart of the town

Day 2   Neufchâtel-en-Bray → Gournay-en-Bray

TOTAL DISTANCE / ELEVATION: **43 km / 600 m ascent**   27 mi / 1968ft ascent

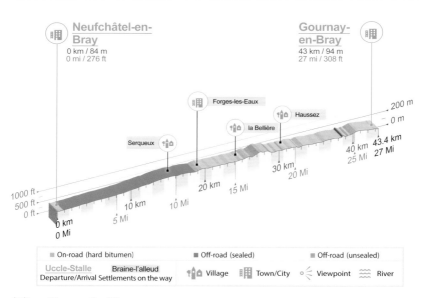

The Pays de Bray

A countryside of green, rolling hedge-lined dairy pasture and fruit farms is dotted with half-timbered agricultural buildings characterising what, in tourist terms at least, is the rural backwater of the pays de Bray. Of course, that makes it ideal cycling country with its lack of motor traffic and fine scenery. Cheese gourmets should look out for Coeur de Neufchâtel. The main towns of the area include Forges-les-Eaux, which gets it name from its reputation as a spa town, and Gournay-en-Bray with its sizeable market on Tuesday, Friday and Sunday mornings.

Day 2 Ride Notes

Continue on the traffic-free path, climbing gradually up the Béthune Valley to Beaubec-la-Rosière, where the railway path comes to an end at the main line railway (trains from Serqueux to Rouen and Paris). The route continues on a traffic-free path, crossing under the live railway. This emerges onto a road on Serqueux's outskirts. Turn right and prepare for the first hill after leaving Dieppe! Pass over the railway again then turn left onto another path (not well signed). Bear right where this becomes a narrow lane and cross over a main road into another green lane. This soon leads into a zigzag ramp onto another short section of railway path.

You have crossed the watershed between the Béthune and Epte valleys, so this section is delightfully downhill into Forges, but take care that you don't miss the yellow diversion signs for the town centre on the left. It is possible to continue to the end of the line where you will see an old station building and on your right the monumental gate of Gisors. Back to the diversion, follow the yellow signs through quiet residential streets. Turn right at a school to pass the imposing church down to rue de la Republique, where you turn left for the town centre.

The section from Forges to Gournay is very different to the railway path and younger children may find the ups and downs and twists and turns quite challenging. The route passes through an undulating landscape on minor roads, some with much poorer surfaces than the railway path. Although it does pass through a number of villages, there are very few facilities – this author did not see a single shop or café in 27km.

From the centre of Forges take the D915 for a short distance towards Gournay, then turn left at the Hôtel Le St Denis (rooms from 34 Euros) onto the rue de la Republique (D919). Cross the old railway then turn immediately right into a very quiet road which soon passes fields and farmhouses. Continue beside the railway line until you come to a T-junction, turn right, cross the railway then turn immediately left. This railway line is planned to form the extension of the railway path from Forges through to Gournay.

At the next junction turn left onto the D61 and cross the railway again at La Bellière. Continue on the D61 through Pommereux, climbing steadily to a crossroads where you go straight ahead. At the next junction take the right fork for the D120 to Haussez. You may be tempted by the sign to "Cidres Calvados", one of many in this region. The surface of this road is very poor so do take care, especially on downhill sections. In Haussez turn right and right again, then under the railway bridge and immediately left on a very quiet lane which crosses the river Epte then climbs steadily out of the valley to Ménerval, a small village with a huge church. Just before you reach the watertower turn left. This is one of the highest points on the route between Forges and Gournay and you can look forward to several km of downhill. Keep an eye out for the Avenue Verte sign as there is a sharp right then left that is easy to miss as you pick up speed down the D16 towards Dampierre-en-Bray. If you do miss this turn you will pick up the route again after the loop through Dampierre.

In the village centre turn right then left onto the D84. Turn right at the roundabout onto the D16 for Gournay, then turn left after a short distance to Cuy-St-Fiacre. Carry on through the village until the road joins the D916 to Gournay. This is one of the main roads into the town and can be busy, so you are advised to turn left to Cité St Clair. You will come to the signalled junction of the D916 with the N31 on the edge of the town centre. Proceed ahead on rue des Bouchers for the town centre. Gournay is a sizeable town with a wide range of facilities, including hotels, restaurants and a bike shop. Look out for the sign pointing to Hailsham 196km away. Hailsham in East Sussex is the twin town of Gournay and by happy coincidence is located on the Cuckoo Trail, which forms part of the Avenue Verte route in England.

Accommodation

Hôtel le Cygne
20 rue Notre Dame, Gournay-en-Bray
02.35.90.27.80   www.lecygne.c.la
Hôtel de Normandie
21 place Nationale, Gournay-en-Bray
02.35.90.01.08
www.hotel-normandie-gournay-bray.
federal-hotel.com

Day 3 Gournay-en-Bray → Gisors

TOTAL DISTANCE / ELEVATION: **39 km / 442 m ascent** | **24 mi / 1450 ft ascent**

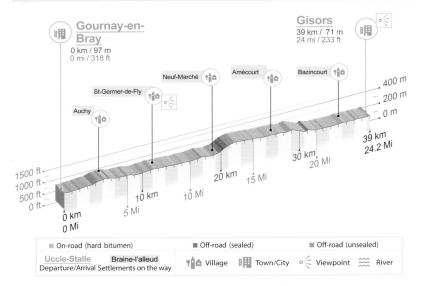

Legend:
- ■ On-road (hard bitumen)
- ■ Off-road (sealed)
- ■ Off-road (unsealed)

Uccle-Stalle | Braine-l'alleud
Departure/Arrival Settlements on the way | ⛪ Village | Town/City | Viewpoint | River

Day 3 Ride Notes

From the centre of Gournay, which features an attractive square with fountains, take the rue du Dr. Duchesne, heading east towards Ferrières. When the road becomes one-way east to west, take a right into a cul-de-sac. This is a no through road for motors but bikes can use the delightful boulevard des Planquettes, a tree-lined avenue. This path crosses the Epte on a footbridge then rejoins rue du Dr. Duchesne by turning left and right. Beware – this section of the road is still one-way but bikes are allowed.

Continue to the traffic lights at a busy intersection with the N31. Cross the main road and the railway line then immediately right on the D21. Continue past the Danone factory and you are soon in open countryside, with a steady climb through woodland to Bethel and Auchy. You are rewarded with extensive views across the valley and a pastoral scene with grazing cattle. At Auchy look out for a sharp right towards Orsimont and St-Germer-de-Fly. Continue until you meet the D104 and follow this all the way to St-Germer. The road twists and turns and there are some short steep climbs until you coast into St-Germer, which is dominated by the imposing abbey. Take care crossing the

N31 for a second time. Just before the N31 you will notice a short rise to meet the old railway line, which forms part of the long term plan for the Avenue Verte between Gournay and Beauvais.

St Germer is the junction for two branches of the current Avenue Verte route – at the main square keep right for Gisors and Cergy (or turn left for the alternative route via Beauvais - not covered in detail here but outlined on pgs 192-193). For Neuf-Marché don't be tempted to take the more direct route signed on the D104 but follow the Avenue Verte signs right at a small roundabout. You will be rewarded with a beautiful ride on quiet lanes heading gradually downhill close to the railway and the river Epte. Just outside Neuf-Marché you pick up the D104 once again and follow this for a short distance into the village and the traffic lights at the crossing of the busy D915. Neuf-Marché boasts a château, the Collégiale St Pierre.

After crossing the main road take the left fork signed to Les Flamands and Rouge Mare, which becomes a long steady climb past meadows and a wooded ridge. Do look back before you reach the top for a wonderful view down to Neuf-Marché and the Epte valley. Your efforts are rewarded with extensive views towards the Levrière valley and beyond and a superb ridge-top quiet road. On leaving Les Flamands take the left fork, although you have the option of a short diversion of 500 metres if you continue towards the Rouge Mare memorial. This is a curious sculpture in a delightful woodland setting.

Continue above the Epte valley through Amécourt, where you will pass the Domain du Patis, a large farmstead which has converted one wing for a small number of bed and breakfast rooms. The road falls gradually then steeply into the Epte valley, where it stays until it enters Gisors. In Amécourt follow the road round to the right then turn left on the D660 out of the village, passing the tiny Chapelle Sainte-Anne. After a short distance fork left then at the next junction turn left and follow the road round and down through woodland towards Serifontaine. If you need supplies you may wish to divert through this large village, otherwise carry on to Thierceville then join the D14 to Bazincourt and Gisors. At the bottom of the hill, don't be tempted to take the main road round to the left, but carry straight on and slightly right, up a gentle slope at the edge of the woodland. You may catch glimpses of the river Epte down to the left. In Thierceville turn right at a fine country house. At the crossroads at the edge of Bazincourt continue straight ahead on the D14. In Bazincourt you will find a large number of fine old cottages and farm buildings. Carry

on through the village and on towards Gisors, hugging the wooded edge of the Epte valley.

At the first major road junction in Gisors turn right. The official route goes straight ahead, but we recommend that you turn left for the classic Norman castle, which offers fine views over the old town and the church and a good place for a picnic.

Accommodation

Hôtel Le Moderne
1 place de la Gare, Gisors
02.32.55.23.51
www.hotel-moderne-gisors.com
Camping de L'Aulnaie
L'Aulnaie, Dangu
02.32.55.43.42
etangcampingdangu@orange.fr
About 4 miles beyond Gisors along the Avenue Verte.

Bike Shops

Pro Cycles Gisors
61 rue de Vienne 02.32.55.24.79
www.procyclesgisors.com

© RD Picard Creative Commons

The medieval castle at Gisors is remarkably well-preserved

Gisors

Located on the border of the Normandy and French Vexin areas, Gisors was the focus of struggles between the Duchy of Normandy and the kingdom of France in medieval times. The castle stronghold overlooking the city, built in the eleventh century on a motte, housed, according to legend, the treasure of the Templars. It faces the church of Saint Gervais-St. Protais, built in the twelfth century, which has the dimensions of a cathedral and a surprising mix of architectural styles.

Day 4 — Gisors → Théméricourt or Vernon

TOTAL DISTANCE / ELEVATION (THÉMÉRICOURT): **42.5 km / 406 m ascent** | 26.5 mi / 1332ft ascent

TOTAL DISTANCE / ELEVATION (VERNON): **41.5 km / 407m ascent** | 26 mi / 1335 ft ascent

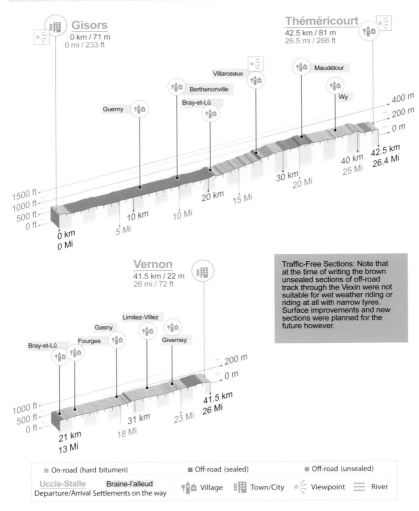

Gisors 0 km / 71 m — 0 mi / 233 ft

Théméricourt 42.5 km / 81 m — 26.5 mi / 266 ft

Villarceaux · Berthenonville · Bray-et-Lû · Guerny · Maudétour · Wy

Vernon 41.5 km / 22 m — 26 mi / 72 ft

Bray-et-Lû · Fourges · Gasny · Limitez-Villez · Giverney

Traffic-Free Sections: Note that at the time of writing the brown unsealed sections of off-road track through the Vexin were not suitable for wet weather riding or riding at all with narrow tyres. Surface improvements and new sections were planned for the future however.

Legend:
- On-road (hard bitumen)
- Off-road (sealed)
- Off-road (unsealed)
- Uccle-Stalle / Braine-l'alleud — Departure/Arrival Settlements on the way
- Village
- Town/City
- Viewpoint
- River

Day 4 Ride Notes

From Gisors town centre on rue de Vienne head south and you will soon pick up the Avenue Verte signs. Look out for the left turn into chemin Noir which is not easy to see and you join what appears to be a country lane. Continue downhill until you meet the bypass and cross carefully into the road opposite, which runs alongside the river Epte. Soon turn right onto the "voie verte de la vallee de l'Epte" on the old railway line to Gasny. You can see the old tracks on the bridge over the Epte to the left. This is a fairly new path and is not as well developed as the original Avenue Verte south of Dieppe. There are very few villages directly on the line, but at each road junction you will find a helpful sign to the nearest village, with an indication of the range of services available. The railway path is naturally very easy to follow and passes through woodland, open fields and is never far from the river Epte.

On the approach to Bray-et-Lû you will notice the old zinc factory, dominating the village. The railway path is cut by the road and a roundabout, where you need to turn back sharp left and immediately right into the village. Passing the factory you will notice a memorial with the date of 1837. A channel of the river Epte passes under the factory, suggesting it may once have been water powered. If heading to Vernon now pick up the Ride Notes in the opposite column marked *. If Paris-bound, at a roundabout go straight over and start the steady climb out of the Epte valley. At the next junction continue straight ahead on the D142 to Chaussy and the Parc Naturel du Vexin. This is a protected landscape of rolling hills, meadows, woodland and villages. You can't miss the church in Chaussy as it's built almost in the middle of the road! Continue up the valley to Villarceaux, where you can catch glimpses of the château behind the trees before it reveals itself. Turn left and climb steeply up the hill through woodland. At the top keep ahead and slightly right before descending gently. Continue uphill to a junction, now out of the Epte valley at a high point between Bray-et-Lû and Théméricourt. Turn left onto an unnamed road, which runs straight as far as the eye can see. At the next junction the sign points ahead onto a rough track. This is not a mistake, it is the official route. It is passable on a road bike when dry, but likely to be difficult in the wet. It is hard work and you might want to take an alternative on-road route (see Touring Routes map for options). Rejoin the road at Maudetour, where you turn right. Turn left at the church and pass the château on your right (a B&B). The official route turns right down a grass track, but we strongly recommend you continue on the road to Arthies. Take the D159 to Wy-Dit-Joli-Village, which is a fast gentle downhill stretch. Straight ahead through the village, with a wiggle right and left. At the last junction in the village keep right and out into open countryside. In Gadancourt straight across the first junction and right at the second. Another fast downhill leads to delightful Avernes. Unfortunately, the official route takes us away from the village centre, with a left turn at the Grande Rue and a right fork up rue de Clos Brigent. Continue straight ahead until the tarmac runs out and join a rough track. Take a left then right on farm tracks and continue until you meet tarmac roads in Théméricourt. You may prefer to take the D81 main road between Avergnes and Théméricourt to avoid these tracks. The Maison du Parc comprises an impressive château and an extensive public park. Not many facilities, but there are places to stay and at least one restaurant.

* Bray-et-Lû to Vernon option:

At Bray-et-Lû don't leave the greenway but continue on it until its end at Gasny. Cross a grassy area and car park to emerge at the southern end of the shop-lined main street to jink right then left up rue de l'Industrie. Follow this quiet road out of Gasny to rue de Vernon and head left to cross the D5 onto rue de la Treille. In front of the church at St-Geneviève-de-Gasny go left onto rue de l'Eau. Coming into Gommecourt wiggle left and right, staying on the Grande Rue before picking up the D200 on the right, signed Limetz-Villez.

In Limetz-Villez, shortly after the handy bakers, head right onto the D201, signed Giverny and Vernon. Head up to the busy and fast D5 which you turn left onto only briefly, before heading right past the hotel La Musadière and through the village of Giverny, home to Monet's house and garden and the Museum of American Art. In season it's awash with tourists and associated gift shops and cafes and all but deserted out of season. As you exit Giverney, just before the D5, head right onto the traffic-free trail. This ends at Vernonnet, where you follow signs to Vernon through backstreets then cross the bridge over the Seine into Vernon centre.

Accommodation

Chambres d'hôtes Le Pigeonnier
Château d'Hazeville RD81
Hameau de Hazeville
Wy-dit-Joli-Village 01.34.67.06.17
Hôtel Normandie
1 rue Mendès-France, Vernon
02.32.51.97.97 www.givernyhotel.com
Vernon Youth Hostel
28 avenue de l'Île-de-France, Vernon
02.32.51.66.48 - www.fuaj.org/vernon

The Vexin and Giverny

The Vexin is designated a Parc Naturel Régional with the aim of protecting its gentle landscapes, architecture and wildlife - as well as its human population who have been leaving the area steadily over the last few decades. You enter at Sagy and head through the Parc Naturel encountering a string of small, delightful villages using a mix of minor roads and tracks (dry weather only for the tracks at the time of writing - upgrading and new off-road routes were in the pipeline though). The museum of the Vexin is housed in a lovely château at Théméricourt.

By contrast, Giverny is something of an international tourist trap, the hordes flocking in coach loads to Monet's house and garden as well as the associated Museum of American Art. Monet's garden, complete with water-lily pond, is indeed spectacular, but Vernon is a better stopover than tiny Giverny, in practical if not aesthetic terms, with its plethora of cafes, restaurants and hotels.

The Seine often forms a beautiful southern boundary of the Vexin Parc Naturel Régional

The cycle track between Giverny and Vernon

For mapping see separate fold-out map

The Vexin offers a variety of landscapes and riding underwheel. The classical looking landscape (top) is at Villarceaux whilst the roads are quiet and often through rolling hills (middle). There are numerous track sections (bottom) some rougher than others, but all have on-road alternatives, easily decided on using the Touring Routes map.

TOTAL DISTANCE / ELEVATION: **29.5 km / 300 m ascent** | 18 mi / 984 ft ascent

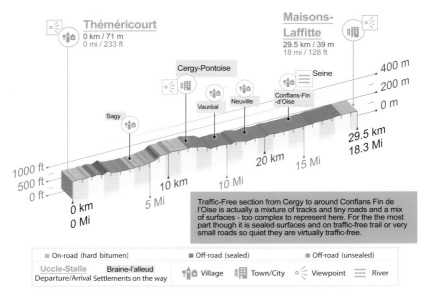

Traffic-Free section from Cergy to around Conflans Fin de l'Oise is actually a mixture of tracks and tiny roads and a mix of surfaces - too complex to represent here. For the the most part though it is sealed surfaces and on traffic-free trail or very small roads so quiet they are virtually traffic-free.

■ On-road (hard bitumen)	■ Off-road (sealed)	■ Off-road (unsealed)
Uccle-Stalle — Braine-l'alleud Departure/Arrival Settlements on the way	♦♦ Village ▦ Town/City	∘ Viewpoint ≈ River

Day 5 Ride Notes

From the Maison du Parc (north entrance) in Théméricourt follow the signs through narrow streets, turning right then left onto the D81 towards Vigny. At the town sign, turn right up a stone track beside a stone wall. If you are short of supplies you may want to continue into the town centre. Follow the track round by the stone wall, cross a road (from the town centre) and continue onto another track, which climbs up and then down again into Longuesse. The surface is bumpy in places and you may prefer to take the road, especially in wet weather. Continue on-road then join another track, which starts with a good surface but deteriorates for the central section, narrow and muddy. Again there is a convenient on-road alternative nearby. The village of Sagy is attractive with many old buildings and some recently restored or rebuilt. Turn right into the village centre with its artisan bakery (open early morning and evening). Turn left and cross the main road for Saillancourt.

On leaving the village, bear left at a roundabout up a steep hill. Continue to the edge of Courdimanche with its

watertower, where the distant cranes indicate you are leaving the "parc naturel" and entering the city. At the roundabout bear left onto the cycle track, signed to Paris for the first time. At the next junction turn left and join the road towards Cergy (new cycle tracks due on this section so exact directions may vary). Pass over two roundabouts then at traffic lights turn right, joining a bus lane for a short distance before turning left for the railway station and town centre on a contraflow cycle lane.

Turn right in front of the station and follow the ramp down to cross a busy road into the park opposite. The narrow path continues under a road bridge, winding through an attractively landscaped park and ending on a quiet road where you turn left. Continue downhill towards the Oise valley, crossing a busy road at traffic lights into the old town of Vauréal. At a T-junction of narrow streets, turn right and cross the road with the old church to your left. Now continue on a varied high level route with views across the Oise valley. There are few signs, but simply continue until you reach a major road, leading down to the bridge over the river.

You are now in Neuville-sur-Oise, where the "Beauvais loop" rejoins the main route. An improved riverside path is under construction, so you must take a temporary route until this is available. From the bridge, follow the road round to the right and turn right at the church into rue Conflans. Before the road rises to the left, take another road to the right, which turns into a rough track. Under the big road bridge and straight ahead onto a narrow bumpy track, which emerges onto a tarmac road beside the water works. Continue to the confluence of the major French rivers, the Oise and the Seine. At the railway bridge join the riverside path, where you may see large barges moored at the wharf. Pass under the road bridge and footbridge then sharp left and up the ramp to cross the Seine.

Continue straight ahead up the old road, turn left between concrete blocks then right through a narrow gap into a housing estate. Continue on the road and just before the entrance gate turn right onto a cycle track. Follow the cycle track to its end and turn left onto a crushed stone path alongside a stone wall. At the end turn right into the forest and left at the first junction. Continue on the well surfaced forest

track until you meet a wooden post at a confusing ten-way junction. Take the best surfaced track bearing right, signed Route de la Vente Frileuse. At the road turn left onto another compacted stone track. Follow this down until you emerge through an old gateway into a housing area of Maisons-Laffitte. Turn right onto the road, then left down the grand boulevard towards the magnificent château. Continue right up to the château gates, turn left then right and right again at the main road. Follow this to the roundabout on the north side of the bridge over the Seine.

Accommodation
Hôtel au Pur Sang
avenue de la Pelouse, Maisons-Laffitte
01.39.62.03.21
Hôtel IBIS Maisons-Laffitte
2 Rue de Paris, Maisons-Laffitte
01.39.12.20.20 www.ibishotel.com
Small luggage area and private car park.
Camping International de Maisons-Laffitte
1 rue Johnson 01.39.12. 21.91
www.campint.com

Bike Shops
Cycle Naturel
2 av Jean Jaurès, Sartrouville
01.30.86.01.00 www.cycle-naturel.com

The Axe Majeur

As a new town you might be tempted to keep pedalling past the Cergy area. Don't; it's home not only to a huge outdoor leisure park surrounding the ancient village of Ham but also the astonishingly grand *Axe Majeur* walkway, adorned with grand sculptures, which in good weather opens up a lovely view to the area known as *La Défense* on the outskirts of Paris and continues the grand avenue of viewpoints that crosses Paris, including the Arc de Triomphe and the Tuileries Gardens. The 3.2 km route starts at place des Colonnes Hubert Renaud at Cergy and the nearby bastide area and clock tower are also worth a look.

© Jean-Pierre Dalbéra Creative Commons

Cergy-Pontoise's *Axe Majeur* is sculpture on a massive scale

Day 6 Maisons Laffitte → Notre Dame Cathedral

TOTAL DISTANCE / ELEVATION: **44.5 km / 307 m ascent** | 27.5 mi / 1007 ft ascent

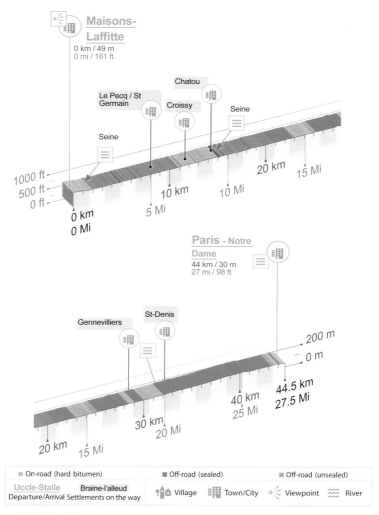

■ On-road (hard bitumen)	■ Off-road (sealed)	■ Off-road (unsealed)
Uccle-Stalle **Braine-l'alleud** Departure/Arrival Settlements on the way	🏠 Village 🏢 Town/City	○⦚ Viewpoint 〜 River

Day 6 Ride Notes

Cross the river Seine on the main bridge opposite the château and take the first right into rue de la Constituante. Turn right again then left to join the riverside road. The tarmac gives way to an uneven stone path at the edge of Sartrouville, which can be rough and muddy in places. The path improves on the approach to Le Pecq, where a new surface has been constructed through the built-up area. The majority of this improved section is alongside a quiet road, which can be comfortably used by cyclists. On leaving

the urban area, the riverside path again reverts to an uneven surface up to the first of many large riverside properties in Croissy. One of the first properties is the British School of Paris. The riverside road here is very quiet, serving only residential properties. A notable feature of the riverside route between Sartrouville and Chatou is that there are no commercial properties on the river, no shops or cafes – so make sure you are well supplied! The centre of Croissy is some distance from the river.

The riverside path/access road comes to

an end at the railway bridge in Chatou, where you will find several shops. Pass under the bridge and join the road for a short distance. A new path was under construction here in June 2012 and we guess this will become part of the cycle route before too long. The route crosses the Seine at Chatou and you need to turn left just before the bridge, up the slope and follow round to the right to join the cycle track on the south side of the bridge. Cross the river and take the zigzag ramp back down to the riverside. After a short distance on an access road, the path runs for several km to Pont de Bezons with a good compacted stone surface. There is one water crossing, a substantial footbridge over the port access channel. There is a wheeling ramp beside the steps, but if you are heavily loaded you may prefer to use the lift.

Between Pont de Bezons and Pont de Colombes the riverside path is well surfaced through a popular public park, but please note that the park closes at night. At the time of writing, the area around the Pont de Colombes was under construction, so our best advice is to look out for diversion signs. We recommend that you stay on the river side of the motorway flyover and use pedestrian crossings to access the footway beside an impressive brick building. At the end of this building leave the marked cycle track and turn left into an industrial access road. Just when you think you have taken a wrong turn, you will see a wide rough track between concrete walls. This looks uninviting, but it leads back to the riverside and a quiet road.

Turn right into a very busy road, with traffic streaming off the Pont d'Argenteuil. Make sure you are in the correct lane straight ahead for Gennevilliers. Pass over the motorway and under the railway before turning left into the port access road. This can be a busy junction and you may prefer to use the pedestrian crossing to access the cycle track in the middle of the road (not as hairy as it sounds!). The cycle track continues through the port area and you can get glimpses of the wharves on your left. The road bends gently round to the right and the cycle track comes to an end, turning into cycle lanes on the road. Follow the road round to the right, crossing over the motorway. Turn

left at the large roundabout, where we recommend the use of the pedestrian/ cycle crossings to join a two-way cycle track alongside the newly built tramway (not yet in operation).

Follow the tramway all the way down to St-Denis, crossing two branches of the river Seine. The area around St-Denis railway station is a construction site, so look out for diversion signs. The aim is to cross the railway and the canal, then turn right to follow the east bank of the Canal St-Denis. The towpath is very good where it has been renovated, with a wide smooth concrete surface. At the locks cobbles have been retained, with a narrow concrete strip for bikes. Elsewhere, the surface is bumpy with the original cobbled wharves and railway tracks. This is a great way to enter the city, sailing under busy roads and railways along the way.

At Porte de Villette you cross the road and the canal. This is another construction site and you just need to make your way across by the best available route, to join a two-way cycle track on the west side of the canal. At the canal junction, continue round to the right up to a metal lifting bridge. Turn right then immediately left to join another cycle track running parallel to the canal. At the end of this track turn left and go round the circular building. Keep right and cross over the busy road and under the elevated railway. Get into the cycle lane in the middle of the road opposite and fork left at the lights for the cycle route beside the canal. Continue alongside the canal which bends round to the left. Turn right into rue de Lancry, which has a contraflow cycle lane. Cross the busy boulevard de Magenta and turn right at rue Rene Boulanger. Great care is required at the impressive Porte St Martin where you cross the main road and follow the cycle route markings into rue Ste Apolline. Cross another main road and turn left into rue St Denis and follow into the heart of the city. The lower half of the street is pedestrianised and it can get busy, but cycling is permitted at all times despite the crowds. At rue de Rivoli turn sharp right then left to bring you to a signal crossing of the rue de Rivoli itself. Continue to the bank of the Seine, turn left then right to cross the river on Pont du Change. Continue straight ahead but don't cross the river again, turn left for your final destination – Notre Dame de Paris.

Accommodation

A place to stay with bike storage in Paris is often a problem but the following selection are usually accommodating of people and bikes.

If you are struggling to find somewhere you might consider leaving your bike at the luggage facility of Blue Marble Travel at 2, rue Dussoubs, Paris (centrally located near the Bourse / Les Halles about 1km north of the river). €5-10 daily. 01.42.36.02.34   www.bluemarble.org

Hôtel Campanile La Villette
147 avenue de Flandre 01.44.72.46.46
www.campanile-paris-19-la-villette.fr
Pricey but online discounts available. Good secure under-building car park.. Five minutes ride from the route at Bassin de la Villette.

St Christophers Inn
47, rue de Crimée 01.40.34.34.40
www.st-christophers.co.uk
Backpacker accommodation but done to a high standard - with some private rooms and bike storage allowed in rooms.

Relais Bergson
124 avenue Simon Bolivar   01.39.72.42.30
www.hotel-relais-bergson-paris.federal-hotel.com

Hôtel Picard
rue de Picardie 01.48.87.53.82
hotel.picard@wanadoo.fr
Unpretentious, reasonably priced and with overnight bike storage.

Du Bois de Boulogne
2, allée du Bord de l'Eau , Bois de Boulogne, Paris 01.45.24.30.00
www.campingparis.fr

Bike Shops

Cyclo Pouce
38 bis Quai de la Marne 01.42.41.76.98

Valmy Cycles
Quai de Valmy 01.42.09.68.16

Cycles Laurent
9 boulevard Voltaire, 01.47.00.27.47

Paris

Paris is rapidly becoming more and more cycle-friendly in a way that allows you to see its splendid river vistas and magnificent architecture, with some 400 miles (645km) of cycle paths and tracks. The best cycle lanes are separated from motor-traffic by substantial concrete kerbs. Elsewhere are 'bandes cyclables' - painted cycle lanes either on the pavement or roadside or shared use bus corridors. There are ambitious plans for 2013 to make a 1.5 mile section of main road on the south bank traffic-free.
All this means you can experience some of the world's most glamorous locations and some of its greatest museums easily on two wheels; Notre-Dame cathedral, the Louvre and the Eiffel Tower top the list in the fame rankings but there are a myriad of other delights along the route, especially around the River Seine and the canals, lined by ranks of stylish apartments and idyllic picnic spots such as the Parc de la Villette and the Tuileries.

Sumptuous river views aplenty are found on the ride through Paris

74

Leafy traffic-free cycling is possible on many of Paris's main thoroughfares - this fine cycle lane is along Boulevard de Magenta near Gare du Nord where Eurostar arrives

For mapping see separate fold-out map

Day 7	Vernon → Petit Andely

TOTAL DISTANCE / ELEVATION: **31 km / 448 m ascent** | **19 mi / 1470 ft ascent**

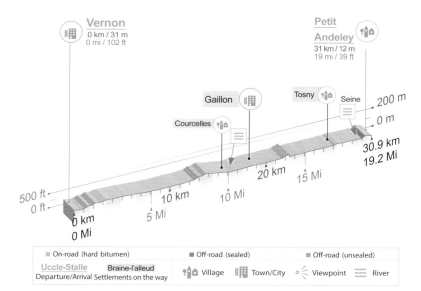

- ■ On-road (hard bitumen)
- ■ Off-road (sealed)
- ■ Off-road (unsealed)

Uccle-Stalle Departure/Arrival   **Braine-l'alleud** Settlements on the way   🏘 Village   🏢 Town/City   ⦿⊰ Viewpoint   ≈ River

Day 7 Ride Notes

Note: You may have arrived in Vernon either on the 'shortcut' avoiding Paris (see Day 4 - Bray-et-Lû to Vernon option) or by retracing the Avenue Verte cycle route from Paris to Bray-et-Lû or by taking a direct 45 minute train trip from Paris-St-Lazare to Vernon (bikes allowed on most services).

Having crossed the bridge at Vernon to the Seine's north bank, go left at the roundabout, signed Gisors and Beauvais. At the next junction bear left, signed Les Andelys

Now on the D313, follow this fast but not very busy road for nearly 7 miles, through Pressagny-l'Orgueilleux, Notre-Dame de l'Isle and Port-Mort, shortly after which go left onto the D10 for Courcelles-sur-Seine.

Coming into Courcelles follow Gaillon signs and meet the D316 to go left, again signed Gaillon. Over the river look out for a right split signed Gaillon which takes you down av Francois Mitterand passing the lycée André Malraux. At a mini-roundabout follow 'centre ville' signs which bring you to pretty Gaillon town centre. Retrace your steps outward (though heading out down rue Verdun

to avoid the one way section) then turn left onto rue de Sarstedt, signed Aubevoye centre. Through Aubevoye come to a roundabout and look for the cycle track at the edge of it. Follow it off the roundabout on the D65. The cycle lanes feed onto the minor road through La Roule (the C11). After the main street through La Roule pass under a rail bridge, bending right then left to come alongside a lovely stretch of the Seine. Just beyond Tosny village up to your left keep straight on, onto Chemin du Lac, an unsealed track, following it all the way to the main road (château Gaillard now looming on the opposite bank). Right onto the main road and across the bridge (beware fast traffic here). Over the bridge turn left then to get to Petit Andely split left (keep right here if visiting Château Gaillard or Les Andelys).

76   For mapping see separate fold-out map

Accommodation

🏨 *Hôtel le Normandie*
1 rue Grande, Le Petit Andely,
Les Andelys
02.32.54.10.52
🏨 *Manoir de Clairval*
2 rue de Seine - Val St Martin,
Le Petit Andely,
02.32.54.37.17 www.manoirdeclairval.fr
Superb location in a manor house just over
a mile along the route out of Petit Andely.

Plenty of accommodation in Les Andelys
centre, about a mile off the route.
⛺ *Camping Île de Trois Rois*
Le Petit Andely 02.32.54.23.79
Across the bridge the site is down to your
right.

Bike Shops

🚲 *GLM*
30 avenue Gén de Gaulle, Les Andelys
02.32.54.50.18

Château Gaillard

This imposing medieval castle was once the European frontier of English king
Richard I's domains in the late 12th century, and was well-placed to keep an eye on any
suspicious activity in the surrounding areas.
On a bike it's probably quickest to lock up in Petit Andely and walk up - the
convoluted road route starts up in Les Andelys itself, well off the route.

Château Gaillard (above) provides a grand finale to day seven's riding.
Day eight's riding starts by hugging the Seine just to the west of Petit Andely; you can see the
road in the picture below, taken from the magnificent panorama you visit at La Roquette.

Day 8 | Petit Andely → Pont de l'Arche

TOTAL DISTANCE / ELEVATION: **28 km / 779 m ascent** | **17.5 mi / 2555 ft ascent**

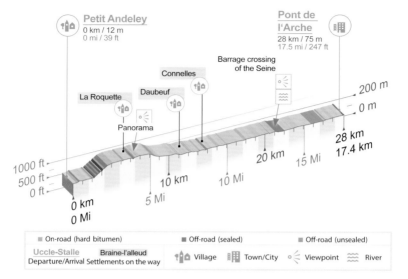

| On-road (hard bitumen) | Off-road (sealed) | Off-road (unsealed) |

Uccle-Stalle — Braine-l'alleud Departure/Arrival Settlements on the way | ⛪ Village | 🏢 Town/City | ◉ Viewpoint | ≈ River

Day 8 - Le Petit Andely to Pont de l'Arche

Having gone left at the bridge turn left (D313) into Le Petit Andely, through the town to a T-junction and left onto the D313 signed Le Val-St-Martin. Pick up signs for Le Val-St-Martin and Romilly. In Le Val-St-Martin turn right up the D126 signed Le Thuit, climbing steeply. Shortly look out for a lovely viewpoint back along the Seine towards Château Gaillard. The climb levels out and you follow the D150 at Le Thuit. Split left by the church, following signs for 'Panorama'. Bear left again, following the same sign to pass a little pond. Follow the C146 out of the village bearing left at the unmarked junction on the edge of tiny La Roquette with the small spire of its church over to your left. Split left onto the track signed for Notre Dame de Bellegarde and lock your bike at the top, as it's a five minute walk down a narrow and rocky track to this stunning viewpoint.

Retrace your steps to La Roquette and back at the unmarked junction head left to come to a crossroads, going left here signed Fretteville, onto the D150. Head straight through Fretteville keeping on the D150, signed Daubeuf. In Daubeuf

turn right over a little bridge and left onto the C7 for Connelles, just opposite a cosy little bar. Through pretty Connelles hit a T-junction and right, signed Amfreville-sous-les Monts.

After about 4 miles on this road, just through Le Val Pitant, take a tiny unsigned left, just before a road split for Pitres. This emerges by the Seine; head up to the footbridge over the locks where you might see the spectacle of huge cargo boats passing beneath your feet. The small cafe and restaurant here adds to its attraction as an interesting pit stop. There are easy ramps allowing you to cross the footbridge after which you head straight up rue du Barrage and right at the T-junction at the end. Meet a road by a campsite with a large lake opposite and turn right onto it. Follow Pont de l'Arche signs at the next roundabout then under a rail bridge and in about 200m turn right onto an unsigned unsealed track that leads through fields to emerge by a handy bar in the village of Les Damps. Turn right here to follow this lovely road by the river Eure under a main road into Pont de l'Arche. Turn left up rue Alphonse Samain into the attractive centre.

78

Accommodation

Hôtel de la Tour
41 Quai Maréchal Foch, Pont-de-L'Arche,
02.35.23.00.99

Camping l'Île Adeline
rue des Masures, Poses (site about 3 miles
east of Pont de l'Arche) 02.32.25.45.33
www.camping-ile-adeline.com

The quiet and picturesque D19 (above) preludes a chance for relaxation in Pont de l'Arche (below)

Day 9 | Pont de l'Arche → Rouen

TOTAL DISTANCE / ELEVATION: **35.5 km / 496 m ascent** | 22 mi / 1627 ft ascent

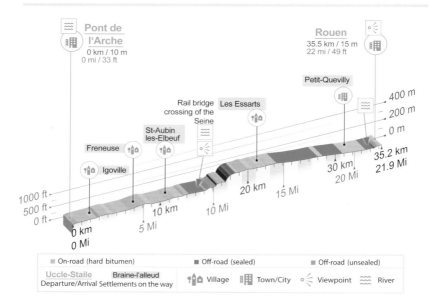

Rouen

Your approach to Rouen - after a lovely tarmac traffic-free section through forest to the south of the city - may not endear you to its suburbs. There is heavy traffic to be negotiated in a few places, though the route uses an often decent quality cycle lane for long stretches of the D938. The latter, along with the riverside area is decidedly unexciting (though the D938 gives handy access to the usual chains of budget hotels).

Rouen cathedral's magnificent facade

However the medieval centre - in fact largely a modern recreation - is a lovely area for wandering and drinking in the atmosphere. Rouen's centre is dominated by the magnificent cathedral (the crypt holding the actual heart of Richard the Lionheart) but head west up pedestrianised rue du Gros Horloge (named after the unmissable clock hanging over it) and you will arrive at the historic place du Vieux-Marché, where national heroine Joan of Arc was burnt to death by the English in 1431. Joan was a French peasant girl who ended up commanding the armies of France, going on to become France's patron saint.

The Musée des Beaux Arts has an international collection plus a couple of works by the artist most closely associated with painting Rouen, Monet (colours inspired by his works are used to light up the cathedral at night between late June and mid-September). Fans of the offbeat might want to check out the Musée de Secq Tournelles - a largely random but fascinating collection of wrought-iron items!

For mapping see separate fold-out map

Day 9 Ride Notes

Head over the Seine at Pont de l'Arche, taking care on the busy D6015 (cycle lanes on bridge). At the first roundabout head straight over, then over rail lines. At the next roundabout pick up the D79 to Igoville and follow it through quiet residential streets to a T-Junction where you go left (now on the D92). Split left to stay on the D92, passing under a motorway and into the long line of fine residences that is Freneuse.

Stay on this road with the Seine down to your left all the way to St-Aubin-lès-Elbeuf, sticking to the D92. Turn right onto the D144 in St-Aubin and follow this wide, fast road all the way over the rail lines. At the rail bridge pick up the cycle lanes and bear left onto rue de Verdun. As the road bends right (just by a little brick tunnel under the railway on your left) head up the tarmac path, keeping the railway on your left, to head over the railway bridge across the Seine. Over the railbridge pick up the D938, following signs right for Château de Robert le Diable, initially using the cycle lanes alongside this main road. At the next roundabout climb up the D64, signed Moulineaux and La Bouille, to start a steady climb through the forest. About 2km after joining the D64, the Route Forestière de Beauval crosses the road.

Head right onto its traffic-free tarmac and follow it to a crossroads, heading straight over the D132 at the next junction onto the D132A for Les Essarts. Meet the D938, bearing left on cycle lanes here to cross over a motorway. At the roundabout pick up the D13 to Les Essarts, following your nose through some light industrial units and into the village of Les Essarts. Head over the first crossroads (signed for Oissel) and out of the village go right at a major roundabout - actually you can avoid the heavy roundabout traffic as the tarmac from the previous road is still there to your right - to keep on the D13 to Oissel. Ignore the split onto the A13 and follow the D13 over this autoroute. In about half a kilometre you leave this busy and unpleasant stretch of road by picking up a forest track on the left (**easy to miss**), signed Chapeau à Trois Cornes 2.1km and Rond Point Madrillet 5.4km onto the

Route Forestière du Fond de l'Essart. At the first mini-roundabout in the forest take the left hand most option with a tarmac surface, to the left of the sign Forêt Départementale du Madrillet. Emerge at a rather nondescript road on the edge of the Rouen suburbs. Head left into Petit-Couronne and shortly come to a roundabout where you go right, onto the D938 (cycle lane on far side of dual carriageway). Pass the large silver hump of the Zenith concert hall on the left (the cycle lanes cross over the road here).

Follow the lanes for about 1.5 miles, when they run out by the football ground, just before a large roundabout. Head straight over the roundabout and into Petit-Quevilly, continuing over the junction with the lovely Jardin des Plantes over to the left and join a smooth, wide bus lane. Cross the tram lines of the huge boulevard de l'Europe and head onto rue d'Elbeuf, passing the bike shop Atelier du Cycle Rouennais in a courtyard on the right.. The pleasantest approach to the Seine is to split down the precinct to the left (rue St Sever), pushing your bike here, and remounting to go straight on at its end, across two main road junctions (cycle lanes now refound) and across Pont Boieldieu, with the cathedral spires ahead welcoming you. Follow your nose to explore the city centre at your leisure.

Accommodation

Comfort Hôtel Rouen Alba
12 place du Gaillardbois, Rouen
02.35.70.34.28
Lovely location and very helpful staff.
www.albarouen.com

Hôtel Vieux Marche (Best Western)
33 rue du Vieux Palais, Rouen
02.35.71.00.88   www.hotel-vieuxmarche.com
Pricey but with a great central location

Bike Shops

Rouen Bike
45 rue Saint-Éloi, Rouen
02.35.71.34.30   www.rouenbike.fr

Atelier du Cycle Rouennais
47 rue d'Elbeuf, Rouen
02.35.63.57.72   www.acr76.fr

Day 10   Rouen → Duclair

TOTAL DISTANCE / ELEVATION: **39 km / 304 m ascent** | **24 mi / 998 ft ascent**

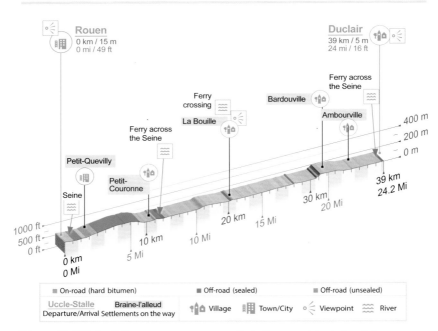

■ On-road (hard bitumen)	■ Off-road (sealed)	■ Off-road (unsealed)

Uccle-Stalle   Braine-l'alleud   🏠 Village   🏢 Town/City   ○ Viewpoint   ≈ River
Departure/Arrival Settlements on the way

Day 10 Ride Notes

Retrace your outward route from
Rouen, past the silver Zenith exhibition
centre, then at the roundabout shortly
afterwards bear right signed Petit
Couronne, onto the cycle lanes along
rue Marcel Cavalier. Bend 90 degrees
left and follow the cycle lanes under a
motorway. Out of forest surroundings
and into Petit Couronne you are now
on rue de Madrillet. Meet a roundabout
and go right, signed Centre Ville. At
the next roundabout go left onto sealed
cycle lanes through this unremarkable
suburb. Head straight over at the next
roundabout, losing the high quality off
road cycle lanes and passing under a rail
bridge. At the next junction at a more
major road head left then immediate
right onto rue Pierre Corneille. Past a
pretty park on the right head straight
over at the next junction, onto rue
Winston Churchill. (passing Musée
Pierre Corneille). Head straight over
the next junction, passing the mairie
then the church and bearing left up
to a roundabout where you go right.
Almost immediately go right signed 'bac

Petit-Couronne' (sealed cycle lanes on
the left all the way to the boat). Take
care crossing the next road junction and
railway before taking the free ferry.
Off the ferry head left on the D51 and
into Val-de-la-Haye. The Pingouin cafe
here is a favourite of local riders and
offers good value meals. The quiet D51
takes you through farmland but with a
contrasting view of the loading docks
of Rouen on the opposite side of the
river. After around 7km on this road, at
Sahurs follow signs for the boat to La
Bouille (handy supermarket and cafe off
to the right).
Head right off the ferry, to pick up the
scenic D64, wide and fast but with little
motor traffic, hugging the Seine on
your right. (Note the D265 shortcut to
the next day's ride, via Yville-sur-Seine,
to the Mesnil-sous-Jumièges ferry -
handy if you want to miss out Duclair
and head straight to historic Jumièges
abbey).
Just after tiny Beaulieu split right off
the D64 onto a near-deserted single-
track road, through apple orchards and
pasture (**easy to miss - it's right by**

a bus stop for Bardouville). There is a steep climb into Bardouville, with great views back over the Seine. Bear first right here, to pick up another spectacular road over a plateau with magnificent views of the Seine loop, to pretty Ambourville, where you jink right then left. Through rather more ordinary Berville-sur-Seine hit the D64 and go right to descend to the ferry crossing into Duclair.

Accommodation

En Bord de Seine B&B
504, rue Maurice Lefebvre, Duclair
02.35.37.88.55
There is no camping in Duclair so you may be pushed into heading on to Jumièges, adding another 13km to the day's riding:
Camping La Forêt
rue Guillame le Conquérant, Jumièges
02.35.37.93.43
Large luxury site with prices to match

The D64 beyond La Bouille (top) looks fast but carries little traffic. The single track road after Beaulieu (below) is even quieter

Day 11   Duclair → Caudebec-en-Caux

TOTAL DISTANCE / ELEVATION: **27.5 km / 516 m ascent** | 17 mi / 1693 ft ascent

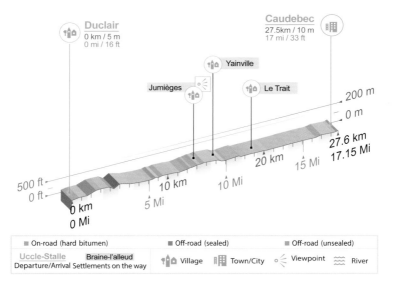

■ On-road (hard bitumen)	■ Off-road (sealed)	■ Off-road (unsealed)
Uccle-Stalle Braine-l'alleud	↑🏠 Village 🏢 Town/City	○≤ Viewpoint ≋≋ River
Departure/Arrival Settlements on the way		

Day 11 Ride Notes

Having arrived in Duclair by ferry bear left and left again, picking up the contraflow cycle lane, hugging the Seine on the D65. Note the signs for the driving route 'Route des Fruits' too. Head south for around 5 miles to Mesnil-sous-Jumièges and bear right, still on the Route des Fruits, to the magnificent abbey at Jumièges.

After about 1.5 miles on this road out of Jumièges at Yainville head left at the junction where you can see the pretty 11th century church down to the left and pass the church then a cafe on the right. The road bends left then right to meet the D20. Yet another boat crossing is down to the left here but you go right and meet the busy and fast D982 where you go left. Great care is needed as you climb on the dual carriageway here but things are easier coming into Le Trait as the road narrows and drops downhill. Around 4km after joining the D982 and having passed through Le Trait's rather unexciting commercial centre head left down rue du Maréchal Galleni (**easy to miss**), following signs for Group Scolaire G de Maupassant and shortly pass this school up to the right. Pick up rue de la

Gare and head across the next junction onto rue St Amand, with an old railway line on your left as good views of Pont de Brotonne's magnificent span over the Seine begin to appear.

At the T-junction with the D982 go left and at the roundabout by the Pont de Brotonne turn right, signed along the D37 to Pont de Brotonne and Yvetot, then take an almost immediate unsigned, switchback left which climbs then levels out to reveal spectacular views of the Pont de Brotonne that can be enjoyed from the seating area here. The road drops and you simply follow signs for Centre Ville until you arrive in Caudebec just opposite the tourist office. Enjoy a leisurely bike push on the fine river promenade here - look out for the themed crazy golf in particular! The town centre is to your right.

Accommodation

Le Cheval Blanc
place René Coty, Caudebec-en-Caux
02.35.96.21.66 Private garage
www.le-cheval-blanc.fr

Le Normandie
9, quai Guilbaud, Caudebec-En-Caux
02.35.96.25.11 www.le-normandie.fr

Camping Barre Y Va
route de Villequier, Caudebec-En-Caux
02.35.96.26.38
camping-barre-y-va.com

About 1 mile out of Caudebec on the route to Villequier.

Bike Shops

Peugeot cycle dealer in Caudebec just off the roundabout that you descend to by the tourist office.

Boats & Bridges of the Seine

Between Rouen and Le Havre the river gradually widens, bringing with it a very noticeable change in the means of crossing it. At Rouen the very jolly white and red roll-on/roll-off ferries make their appearance and the cycle route makes frequent use of them. They are for cars, bikes and pedestrians only - no HGVs are allowed which keeps the roads in the vicinity of the ferries free of these noisy cyclist-frighteners. Further downstream huge bridges replace these dinky ferries - Pont de Brotonne, Pont de Tancarville and Pont de Normandie loom larger and larger on their approaches and you get a good look at all these incredible superstructures. For the cyclist Pont de Normandie holds the most promise - you can use the cycle lanes or 'pavement push' over the bridge if you want to detour to the lovely port of Honfleur - though its a fair gradient, made even harder in crosswinds!

Both the boats and bridges are necessary as smaller, lower bridges would obstruct the very sizeable ships that travel up the Seine to Rouen - the country's fourth largest port.

Delightful ferries are part of the public transport system between Rouen and Yainville near Jumièges. They are frequent and free. This one is at Duclair.

Day 12   Caudebec-en-Caux → Lillebonne

TOTAL DISTANCE / ELEVATION: **27.5 km / 412 m ascent**   17 mi / 1352 ft ascent

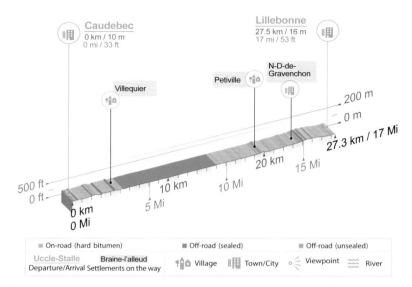

■ On-road (hard bitumen)	■ Off-road (sealed)	■ Off-road (unsealed)

Uccle-Stalle   Braine-l'alleud
Departure/Arrival Settlements on the way   †∏≙ Village   ▦ Town/City   ○≤ Viewpoint   ≈ River

Day 12 Ride Notes

As the Seine broadens towards the sea its surroundings become more industrial in character - however today's ride avoids such HGV magnets as the riverside refinery south of Notre-Dame-de-Gravenchon and heads north of the river to the charming town of Lillebonne, home to impressive Roman amphitheatre remains.

From Caudebec head west alongside the Seine, through quiet Villequier, with its Victor Hugo museum, splitting left onto a high quality traffic-free path shortly after leaving the village. This keeps you by the Seine - part of the ongoing Véloroute Val du Seine. Around 10.5km after joining the traffic-free section head away from the river and follow the road, ignoring any minor turnings off to emerge at a junction where Norville is signed to the right. Go left here and follow the road as it bridges a trunk road, before going straight on at the next roundabout. Left at the next junction, now on the D373, and meet a major crossroads at the centre of Notre-Dame-de-Gravenchon. Head straight over and through the shopping area with a wooden market shelter

building on your right. Stay on this road to leave the town and climb gradually into wooded surroundings.

Drop to a T-junction to bear right, staying on the 373, signed for Lillebonne. Over the next roundabout carry on for 'Centre Ville' to come to a T-junction opposite the pedestrian centre of Lillebonne with its magnificent amphitheatre remains and central square with more Roman relics.

Accommodation

🏨 *Au p'tit Coin*
2 avenue du Général Leclerc, Lillebonne
02.35.39.96.00
🏨 *Hôtel de France*
1 bis rue de la République, Lillebonne
02.35.38.04.88
www.hoteldefrance-lillebonne.com
🏨 *Hôtel Meublé du Cirque Romain*
4 rue Victor Hugo, Lillebonne
02.35.38.06.52

Bike Shops

🚲 *Gréverend Benoît*
26 avenue Victor Bettencourt, 76170
Lillebonne 02.35.38.02.48

Day 13	Lillebonne → Honfleur

TOTAL DISTANCE / ELEVATION: **39 km / 450 m ascent**   24 mi / 1476 ft ascent

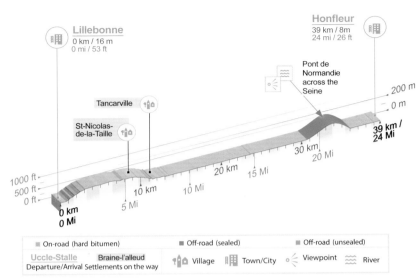

■ On-road (hard bitumen)	■ Off-road (sealed)	■ Off-road (unsealed)

Uccle-Stalle Braine-l'alleud	⛪ Village	🏢 Town/City	∘< Viewpoint	≈≈ River
Departure/Arrival Settlements on the way				

Day 13 Ride Notes

Note - the cycle lane over Pont de Normandie bridge is not for the faint-hearted. It's steep, high and subject to cross-winds. There are cycle lanes but these are next to the traffic so care is required (if in doubt dismount and push along the pavement).

Your onward route from Lillebonne climbs steadily to an upland plateau before dropping down to Tancarville and its amazing bridge. Today really is the day of the bridges - post-Tancarville some blissfully quiet countryside leads to the River Seine again at the Route de l'Estuaire, then you are on what must be one of the most stunning cycle rides in Europe, across the beautiful Pont Normandie, before a finish at Honfleur's beautiful historic waterfront. From Lillebonne follow the D473 around the edge of town before going left at a mini-roundabout onto rue du Havre. Follow this over a major road and rail crossing to pick up the D81 signed for St-Jean-de-Folleville and St-Romain-de-Colbosc.

The road climbs steadily, on and on to

clear the wooded slopes and emerge on a lovely upland plateau. Almost 5.5km out of Lillebonne turn left on the D17 signed St-Nicolas-de-la-Taille. Through St-Nicolas this lovely little road drops down to the edge of Tancarville, with a good view of the old castle perched on a rock outcrop opposite you. Turn right onto the D39, signed Tancarville-Haut and Château de Tancarville. Ignore the D39 which peels off right and follow D17^B signs to Pont de Tancarville. The broad span of the bridge heralds your arrival at the Seine and the D982, where you bear right, passing the impressively located Hôtel de la Marine.

Follow the D982 under the massive end of the Tancarville bridge. Just under the bridge turn left (easy to miss, no signs), and cross the canal and head onto a cobbled road in front of houses, bending left across another bridge. After just over 7km of gloriously quiet cycling hit a horribly busy road and go left, almost immediately turning left again, signed Route de l'Estuaire, onto a much quieter road.

Come to the northern end of the bridge (don't miss the viewing area) and follow the cycle lanes or 'pavement push' across the bridge - toll free! After the

momentous crossing the cycle lanes drop
down to the right onto a quiet road and
head away from the end of the bridge. Hit
a T-junction and go right, crossing a level-
crossing and coming into an area of light
industrial units. Follow this (boulevard
Judovice) to a T-junction and left. At the
next roundabout take the second exit
and follow the arrow straight road. This
bends 90 degrees left and passes over
a cobbled section before a magnificent
view of Honfleur's waterfront is revealed.
Bend left and head right over the port
bridge to emerge in the town proper. Turn
right onto Quai de la Quarantine to find
yourself at Honfleur's beautiful waterfront.

Accommodation

🏨 *Belvédère*
36 route Emile Renouf, Honfleur
02.31.89.08.13
www.hotel-belvedere-honfleur.com

🏨 *Hôtel Monet*
Charrière du Puits, Honfleur
02.31.89.00.90
www.hotel-monet-honfleur.com

⛺ *Camping du Phare*
boulevard Charles V, Honfleur
02.31.24.22.12 www.campings-plage.fr

© Francois Roche Creative Commons

The elegant outline of the Pont de Normandie. There are cycle lanes across it and cyclists go free
- though it's equivalent to cycling up a sizeable hill! It is built to withstand 200 mph winds.

Honfleur

The best preserved of the Calvados ports with a series of interlinking port basins backed by fine old buildings, just inviting you to wander around. It's undeniably touristy but you still get a bit of a feel for what 18th century Honfleur might have been simply because there are so many well-preserved buildings. To pick just one fascinating example, the church of St Catherine was built entirely of wood by local ships' carpenters after the Hundred Years War to thank God for the departure of the English! If you visit the nearby Musée Eugène Boudin (mentor of impressionist painter Monet) you'll also get access to the detached Belfry of Saint Catherine's church. The museum honouring composer Erik Satie is also worth mentioning - suffice to say many of the interactive exhibits reflect his avant-garde and eccentric traits. Côte de Grace, a short walk from Honfleur's centre, gives fine views over the Seine estuary.

© LoboStudio Hamburg Creative Commons

The old harbourside buildings at Honfleur, above and below, are much photographed and for good reason

© Christine and Hagen Graf Creative Commons

Day 14   Honfleur → Le Havre

TOTAL DISTANCE / ELEVATION: **41 km / 132 m ascent**   **25 mi / 433 ft ascent**

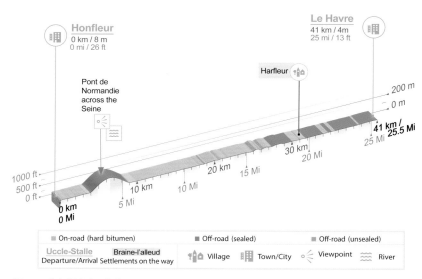

On-road (hard bitumen)	Off-road (sealed)	Off-road (unsealed)

Uccle-Stalle Braine-l'alleud				
Departure/Arrival Settlements on the way	⁺⛪ Village	⊞ Town/City	⊙≤ Viewpoint	≈ River

Day 14 Ride Notes

The initial 17.5 km of the day is simply a matter of retracing your steps back over the Pont de Normandie and to the end of the route de l'Estuaire. Turn right here and follow this heavily trafficked road over the A131 autoroute and then take a left slip signed Gonfreville l'Orcher and immediate left again to pick up the D982 along the cliff base, also known as route des Falaises. Pass under a factory conveyor belt over the road and past the edge of Sandouville. Simply stay on this road until about 6.5km after joining it you pass under a couple of flyovers and climb over a busier slip road to a roundabout, heading straight over for Gonfreville l'Orcher and Le Havre. Shortly after the roundabout pick up a fine new tarmac cyclepath paralleling the road (now avenue Marcel le Mignot). Your surroundings become decidedly more urban from hereon in, to Le Havre. The cycle lanes end, but you carry on following signs for Harfleur and Le Havre, still on the D982.
Now on the route d'Oudalle follow it to a busy road junction where Harfleur's attractive old centre and church are up to your right; the church spire is a handy landmark to aim for if you want a look around the centre or want to attempt the northern entry into Le Havre along the Véloroute de la Pointe de Caux. This is a high quality, largely traffic-free tarmac path linking the northern and eastern suburbs of Le Havre and linking the existing Véloroute du Littoral with the forthcoming Véloroute du Val de Seine. Whilst it is a superb and relaxing ride through green surroundings such as the lovely Parc de Rouelles, its western end is suffering from disruption due to the construction of a new tramway, due to open by the end of 2012. When this is complete it will hopefully mean a trouble-free ride, using minor roads through Bléville and dropping down via Les Jardins Suspendus (an old military installation converted to a park and botanical centre), at Sainte Addresse, from where you can zig-zag down on more small roads to the lovely beachfront promenade and head along cycle lanes towards Le Havre's centre. The best course of action if you want to try this route is to enquire at Harfleur's tourist information office if the tramway project is finished and if they have an up to date map of the Véloroute.

Otherwise your onward route lies ahead, still on the D982 (now avenue de la Résistance) which very shortly crosses the river Lézarde. Immediately over the bridge turn left on rue de Courtine and next left on quai des Canaques. This quiet riverside route eventually becomes totally traffic free and passes under a couple of major flyovers before meeting the Le Havre-Tancarville canal. Bend round and follow the excellent tarmac surface to emerge at a roundabout. Here pick up the pavement cycle lanes along boulevard Jules Durand on your left, once again in retail park land. The cycle lanes falter briefly as you approach a roundabout but soon return as you head straight over, still on boulevard Jules Durand. They are lost for a longer section after going straight on at the next roundabout but a cycle lane soon appears on your right. Climbing over railway and road you lose the lanes again before picking them up on the left of Jules Durand.

Across a major crossroads the lanes swap sides as you come onto boulevard Amiral Mouchez, continuing over another junction before hitting a major roundabout. Go second right here,

up rue Marceau using the pavement cycle lanes. At the third roundabout go left onto quai Frissard, alongside the attractive Bassin Vauban. Head across the water on the pontoon style bridge. Carefully head across busy quai Colbert and onto cours Lafayette, before long picking up the excellent cycle lanes straight ahead on boulevard de Strasbourg (tram works here should be finished by the end of 2012). This leads to the fine place de l'Hôtel de Ville. Head straight over onto avenue Foch and follow the cycle lanes here to the sea and journey's end.

Accommodation
Les Gens de Mer
44 rue Voltaire, Le Havre
02.35.41.35.32 www.lesgensdemer.fr
Hôtel Le Séjour Fleuri
71 rue Emile Zola, Le Havre
02.35.41.33.81   www.hotelsejourfleuri.fr
Basic rooms at a decent price

Bike Shops
Cyclocéane
93 quai Southampton, Le Havre
2 35 42 23 13
Bouticycle
1 rue Paris, Le Havre 02 35 42 24 57

Le Havre

As with Rouen, your approach to the city may seem unpromising, as you pass through the outskirts of some of its 2,500 acres of docks (assuming the much more attractive Véloroute de la Pointe de Caux is still disrupted at its western end); however, the cycle lane network is remarkably good for what is industrial hinterland.

The centre, though, is a revelation; the main architect of it, Auguste Perret, believed 'concrete is beautiful' and whilst there may be too much of it on show for some tastes, Le Havre is certainly a place like no other, the area around the Bassin du Commerce in particular (pictured below) having an airy and very futuristic feel to it. The town hall square and church also help in creating the town's unique architectural mix. There is also a fine art gallery and a museum documenting old Le Havre.

The wholesale 1940's attempt at a futuristic city was largely a product of WWII when Le Havre was the most heavily damaged European port and suffered 4,000 deaths and nearly 10,000 buildings destroyed. There are fine panoramas from Forte de Sainte-Adresse.

Though much of Le Havre was destroyed in WWII and susequently rebuilt in concrete, the town centre features some bold, attractive buildings; the gleaming white building is the Oscar Niemeyer Cultural Centre, or 'the yoghurt pot', whilst behind is the tower of the church of Saint-Joseph.

Boulogne to Lille

Route Info

Boulogne to Lille

This five day ride begins in the port of Boulogne-sur-Mer and takes you over the border to Ypres in Belgium. Along the way you'll enjoy your very own tour of Flanders along good quality, quiet roads with plenty of opportunity to sample French (and increasingly Belgian influenced) life. The flat, open landscape is occasionally interrupted by a handful of short, sharpish climbs whose reward comes in the form of splendid views across the Flanders countryside. Traffic-free riding along the Ypres and Deûle canals takes you back into France after a hop over the border into Belgium. Cosmopolitan and attractive Lille provides plenty of diversions and fine opportunities for eating and drinking at journey's end.

Grade EASY / MEDIUM

Start / Finish Boulogne / Lille

Route Length 210km / 131 miles
168km / 104 miles excluding bocage loop

Length of Suggested Days
21-63.5km / 13-39.5 miles OR
21-43km / 13-27 miles without the 'bocage' cycle route loop

Route Surface & Signing
13.5% off-road
Mainly quiet roads. First follow North Sea Cycle Route LF1 signs (in reverse) before leaving them at Watten. At Loker in Belgium follow the LF6 to Ypres (opposite, top).

Access to Boulogne

Daily Dover-Calais crossings, 2hrs
www.dfdsseaways.co.uk
www.poferries.com

Eurotunnel services from Folkestone to Calais. It's necessary to e-mail 14 days in advance to sales.support@eurotunnel.com
From Calais there are regular trains to Boulogne www.voyages-sncf.com
or you could cycle the D940 Calais to Boulogne - around 40km or 25 miles of a hilly coastal road

i Offices
Boulogne, Pont Marguet, riverside on Boulevard Diderot   03.21.10.88.10
www.tourisme-boulognesurmer.com
Le Wast By the turn-off for Colembert
Watten 2, rue de Dunkerque
03.21.88.27.78   OTWATTEN@aol.com
Cassel Main square 03.28.40.52.55
Lille Palais Rihour, Place Rihour
From France 0891 56 2004
From UK 00 33 359 579 400
www.lilletourisme.com

Don't Miss

Cassel's Views
Hills are rare in Flanders and so Cassel would be notable anyway for the fine views it gives over the surrounding countryside. The fact that some of the best views are from the cafes and restaurants of the fine main square is the icing on the cake.

WWI Remembered at Ypres
Also known as Ieper in Flemish, this small town in western Belgium is most associated with the various First World War battles and the huge loss of life they caused. This is now commemorated in the remarkable Menin Gate to the east of town, where local buglers from the fire service sound the last post every evening at 8pm - and have done so since 1927. The ceremony is not a tourist attraction but a way to show appreciation for those Commonwealth troops who laid down their lives. The cycle route between Ypres and Lille is dotted with WWI war cemeteries.

The 'Hell of the North'
For the cycling enthusiast no tour of Flanders is complete without a visit to Roubaix, the finish point for the most infamous slog of the cycle racing calendar: This one day 'Hell of the North' sends riders juddering over the cobbles for large, bone-shaking sections of its 250km. The field emerges into the downbeat, characterful Roubaix velodrome. Roubaix itself is a suburb of Lille, 15km from the city centre. The velodrome lies south-east of Roubaix centre, in Lannoy. The ride from Lille to Roubaix via the velodrome can be done largely on an excellent cycle path parallel to the tram lines between the two cities or along the Roubaix canal (see pg 199).

For mapping see separate fold-out map

The LF6 is well-signed very shortly after entering Belgium

Lille is a fine city, all too often known only as a Eurostar rail transfer point. Here is the Chamber of Commerce, just one of many beautiful buildings.

Day 1 **Boulogne → Le Wast and the Bocage bike route**

TOTAL DISTANCE / ELEVATION: **22 km / 245 m ascent** | 13.5 mi / 805ft ascent
WITH BOCAGE ROUTE CIRCULAR OPTION: **63.5 km / 811 m ascent** | 39.5 mi / 2661ft

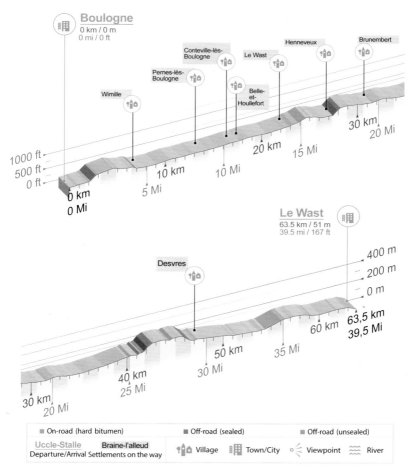

On-road (hard bitumen)	Off-road (sealed)	Off-road (unsealed)

Uccle-Stalle Braine-l'alleud
Departure/Arrival Settlements on the way   Village   Town/City   Viewpoint   River

Boulogne-sur-Mer

Despite the fact the ferry service from the UK was discontinued some time ago,
Boulogne still has plenty going for it. The medieval, walled centre upstages the rest
of the town and there are several reasonable hotels in the lower reaches of the Ville
Basse quarter, close to the tourist office and the River Liane, portside. And as soon as
you exit Boulogne, passing the spectacular column-top statue of Napoleon, you'll find
yourself in lovely, green rolling countryside with coastal views.

Day 1 Ride Notes

This is a short first day but you could miss out the bocage cycle loop and combine days 1 and 2 to make a total of 62km / 38.5 miles.

If you arrive at the Channel Tunnel terminal near Calais you have three options:

1. Coast road to Boulogne: From the terminal pick up signs into Coquelles before coming to a roundabout where you take the D243ᴱ to Sangatte. After about 4km hit the D940 and go left, following this road for some 30km to come into Boulogne.

2. Train to Boulogne: Head into Coquelles and follow the road through it into Calais to pick up signs for the train station.

3. Shortcut along the Canal to Watten (start of Day 3): From near Calais train station head down rue Paul Bert and just over the bridge Pont Mollien head right to follow canalside roads and towpaths all the way to Watten.

From Boulogne find Boulogne-Tintelleries train station and you then have two options:

1. Quiet option, avoiding town centre: From in front of the central Boulogne-Tintelleries station head right to boulevard de Clocheville and right onto it. Follow this for about 850m, under the railway and uphill, to turn right onto rue Louis Duflos then bear right and uphill at the next junction onto rue de la Colonne. At the crossroads with Chemin Vert turn right onto it, then heading over a roundabout onto rue Napoleaon.

2. Via medieval town centre with busy traffic: From in front of the station head left onto rue de Belleterre and straight over the next junction onto pl de Picardie. At the end of here head left, onto rue Félix Adam and climb very briefly until you see the old town walls over to the right. Once you've explored its charms pick up avenue Charles de Gaulle to the north east of the old town. In just over 1km head left, signed Wimereux, onto rue d'Aiglon. Head right at the next roundabout onto rue Napoleon.

Rue Napoleon leaves Boulogne by the 'Colonne de la Grand Armée' with Napoleon standing atop it and immediately you are on a glorious road through green rolling countryside. Shortly after crossing the D96 bear right at a split. Head over the next minor crossroads and at the T-junction with the D237 go left. Coming to the outskirts of Wimille ignore the D237 splitting off right (by Cycles Marius) and continue on to the split in front of the church, bearing right onto the D233. The road offers a steady, village by village introduction to French Flanders, with many boulangerie opportunities along the way and some excellent topiary to keep you entertained. Look out too for the green North Sea Cycle Route signs on the other side of the road, which all point in the opposite direction back to the coast.

Simply follow D233 signs through quiet countryside, through Pittefaux, Pernes and Conteville, all the way to Belle-et-Houllefort and bear right onto the D238. Still in the village turn left onto the D252 following it to Le Wast.

If today's ride was too short you could dump your gear in le Wast and follow this 32km round trip tour of local villages, starting and ending in Le Wast itself. The route is well signposted and detailed at the beginning of the LF1 cycle route turn off to Colembert.

Accommodation

🏨 *Hôtel de Londres*
22 place de france, Boulogne
03.21.31.35.63 contact@hoteldelondres.net
(Close to the river and the port, a small, reasonably priced establishment).

🏨 *Boulogne Youth Hostel*
Place Rouget de Lisle, Boulogne
03.21.99.15.30 www.fuaj.org

🏨 *Château des Tourelles*
8 rue principale, Le Wast
03.21.33.34.78 contact@hotel-le-wast.com
Grand, yet relatively reasonably priced and very friendly, with its own restaurant and bike friendly bike storage; 100m out of the village on the left of the Desvres road.

Bike Shops

🚲 *Cycles Berquez*
5 place des Cafucins, Boulogne-sur-Mer, 03.21.31.34.41 www.cyclesberquez.fr
(300m from the tourist office, at the 'river end' of Grande Rue de la Lampe)

Day 2 Le Wast → Watten

TOTAL DISTANCE / ELEVATION: **40 km / 411 m ascent** | **25 mi / 1350ft ascent**

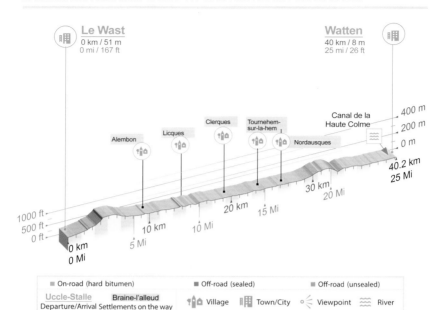

On-road (hard bitumen)	Off-road (sealed)	Off-road (unsealed)

Uccle-Stalle	**Braine-l'alleud**	🏘 Village	🏢 Town/City	⊙ Viewpoint	〰 River
Departure/Arrival	Settlements on the way				

Day 2 Ride Notes

This is a quiet meander through agricultural heartlands. As with yesterday the route starts with a rousing climb but mostly you'll pedal through gently undulating wide open spaces, with ducks and chickens providing much of the road traffic.

Exit Le Wast on the quiet road that climbs gradually up to Colembert after 2km, (ignoring the green véloroute sign suggesting a right turn 1km out of Le Wast). Things get steeper on the far side of Colembert as you ride up through the forest and then descend pleasantly into Alembon.

Here head left then take the next right at the church. The road to Licques is a winding one indeed, through Sanghen and past several farmyards with wandering livestock. Ignore a left on the edge of Sanghen then go left on the D191 into Licques. This final section has some traffic to keep you alert. Licques is a metropolis compared to what has gone before. There are restaurants, camping, a supermarket, a cattle market and a bike shop. At the foot of the hill in the town centre, turn left at the T-junction (Baron

Motoculture is on your left), then right at the next roundabout, taking the D217 towards Tournehem (the supermarket is on your right). The next section is long, straight, fast and slightly downhill, with the river to your right and occasional green La Chapelle St. Louis cycle signs to spur you on. Ride straight on through Clerques (Klerken – Flemish spelling) and take a right at the elevated roundabout into Tournehem, which sprawls across the river. Hop the river, going left under the stone archway and out onto the D218.

Hastily making your way past the rather tacky Bal Parc, ride onward on another fast, straight section of road until you come to the busy N43, which you should cross over. The small road across the N43 bends round to the left and down to the church in Nordausques. Here, turn right onto rue de la Panne, then at the next roundabout take the exit which is at '10 o'clock' on the roundabout, heading for la Panne. Now climb up on the solitary, winding road as it bends to the left and offers you panoramic views of la Panne. At the next T-junction go right and head up into the forest. The undulating

D219 takes you to Le Mont, from where a left turn onto the D207 will drop you down into Watten. This final 2km is slightly busier than the previous, more rural sections, but it takes you past Watten train station, over the river and into the centre of town.

Accommodation

 *La Ferme Cadart* Holque 03.21.95.07.42 3km north of Watten town and along the canal at Holque. Well sign-posted with bright red mini-billboards. Very comfortable and reasonably cheap chalets, as well as a characterful restaurant and garage for bike storage.

L'Auberge Flamande 2 Grand Place, Watten 03.21.88.56.16 Smart, intriguing and slightly camp restaurant/chambre d'hôte with its own cabaret club; in the centre of town.

Wattendamhuys B&B 24, rue de Dunkerque, Watten 03.21.88.95.39

Bike Shops

Baron-Motoculture Cycles 33 place H&C Collette, Licques, 03.21.35.01.98 (en route between Le Wast and Watten)

MBK Cycles Grand Place, Watten (across the road from the tourist office)

Watten

Watten stands on the canal that has first listing in your handy alphabetical directory of inland waterways: the Aa. For centuries Watten has been squabbled over by various warring factions and has, at various times, been Flemish and French, which it has remained since the 17th century. At 172 metres Watten offers some grand views of the surrounding landscape, especially from the worthy vantage points of the Abbey Tower and Windmill at the highest points of the town. Here you can also learn about the role of Watten's monastic traditions in saving it from destruction during its volatile military past. Nowadays Watten is a thriving town, taking full advantage of its excellent rail, road and waterway links. It also has some refreshingly quirky accommodation options.

Hilltop view from Watten

Day 3   Watten → Cassel

TOTAL DISTANCE / ELEVATION: **21 km / 305 m ascent** | 13 mi / 1002ft ascent

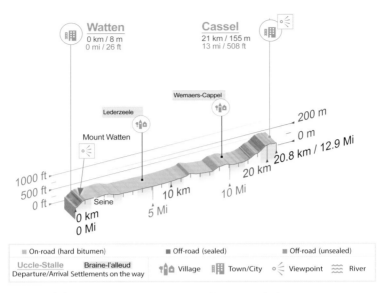

| On-road (hard bitumen) | Off-road (sealed) | Off-road (unsealed) |

Uccle-Stalle **Braine-l'alleud**
Departure/Arrival Settlements on the way | Village | Town/City | Viewpoint | River

Day 3 Ride Notes

Today two steep climbs are interrupted by a long, straight glide through wide open spaces. There are few twists and turns here, so minimal thought is required.

From Watten's Grand (though actually quite small) Place follow the North Sea Cycle Route signs out of town, signed for Cassel and Wulverdinghe. The steep 2km climb out of Watten pays you back handsomely with a fine view of the town astride the canal. Although the North Sea route beckons you left at the top of the hill, the more direct D26 going straight on is a perfectly pleasant, fast ride. The elevated, quietish road projects you through (or near) a series of increasingly Flemish sounding villages of Lederzeele, Noordpeene and Wemaers-Cappel before the undulations begin and Mont Cassel appears dramatically on the horizon. The steep climb to Cassel will take your breath away and the town itself is one of the highlights of the region.

Accommodation

Hôtel Restaurant Le Foch
41 Grand Place, Cassel
03.28.42.47.73   www.hotel-foch.net
Camping Val De Cassel
Contour de l'Église, Zuytpeene
06.28.04.41.67
Just off your route into Cassel, some 4km to the west

Cassel

In many ways more Flemish than French (despite the grand hilltop views in an area known for its flatness), Cassel's central square, the Grand Place, is lined with magnificent mansions and from here small cobbled streets lead outwards to ramparts. Some of the best views of all are to be had from the public gardens, where you'll also find the Kasteel Meulen, a wooden windmill once typical of the area. The bars and restaurants on the southern side of the square offer a mixture of French and Flemish cuisine and great views.

The language divide expressed in road signs at the French-Belgian border en route to Ypres (see day 4)

Day 4	Cassel → Ypres

TOTAL DISTANCE / ELEVATION: **43 km / 327m ascent** | 27 mi / 1073ft ascent

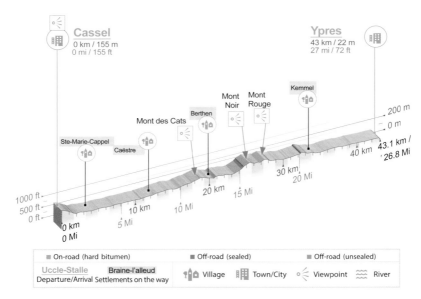

■ On-road (hard bitumen)	■ Off-road (sealed)	■ Off-road (unsealed)

Uccle-Stalle	Braine-l'alleud				
Departure/Arrival	Settlements on the way	↑⌂ Village	▦ Town/City	○≷ Viewpoint	≋ River

Day 4 Ride Notes

This is an eventful ride with plenty
of twists and turns. With two serious
climbs and two that aren't so serious,
plus a glimpse of 'border tourism', as
well as an introduction to Belgium itself,
there's plenty to keep you occupied.
Begin your descent from Cassel on the
D933 from the cobbled centre (signed
Steenvoorde) and out of town to the
south.
Less than a kilometre out from Cassel
centre turn right across from the
supermarket ('Shopi'), signposted for
Oxelaëre then shortly on this twisting
descent look out for a left to Ste-Marie-
Cappel. At the next junction bear right
onto the D53 into Ste-Marie-Cappel.
Turn left by the church, then split right
and right again to exit on route de
Borre.
Follow this road for about 4.5km,
crossing over the busy D916. Turn
right at the next junction, left at the
next t-junction and right at the next
crossroads. At the D161 go left and
follow this busier road into Caëstre.
In Caëstre bear left up rue de la
Libération and at the church turn
right (D933 to Flêtre), then first left

onto a (thankfully) quiet road, signed
'Batiflander', next to the bar on the
corner. Now you're back on more
agreeable lanes, the climbing begins.
Ride up past the sign for Le Mont des
Cats until you reach the crest of the
hill. The road descends with the busy
A25 reverberating to your left. At
the t-junction go left under the A25,
following the sign to Poperinge. Now
you find yourself doubling back with the
A25 thundering away once more on your
left. Climb up on the quieter route for
another 2km before turning right onto
Yperstraet. Go left at the next junction,
left again at the next T-junction, briefly
joining the busier D18, before taking the
next right turn and, with Mont de Cats
receding to your left, quietly climbing
once again. At the top of the first of
the day's challenging climbs take a first
left past the summit and ride down into
Berthen. Here, cross over the D10 onto
chemin de l'Hazewinde,to begin the
second climb of the day, up to Mont
Noir.
The ascent starts in earnest at the next
major junction (opposite the brick
edifice with 1883 patterned into the side)
where a left turn sends you along the

D318, with some traffic to accompany your climb. A 2km pull takes you to the brink of Belgium. Ignore all left turns going up the hill and over the top, where the descent takes you to the border (no passport required).

Hurtle past the sign for 'France' and the first chocolate shop on Belgian soil. The border has become an inexplicable tourist attraction in its own right, so take care not to skittle any trippers. Stay on the D318 (N372 in Belgium), following signs for Ieper (Ypres in French) which climbs the much less taxing Mont Rouge, before turning right onto the N375 for a brief busy spell before entering Loker, your first proper Belgian village. Belgium brings with it plenty of green LF6 signage, which points all the way to Ieper. From Loker turn left on the quiet (if a little potholed) LF6 route. At the next crossroads go right to stay on Kemmelbergweg and keep on this for a long, fast section all the way to Lokerstraet, which is a left turn taking you into the (currently or recently being re-built) Kemmel village on a quiet lane with encouraging LF6 signs along the way. In Kemmel centre bend left past the village green area and with the excellent deli-cum-bakery directly in front of you, go left at the t-junction,

then first right on Nieuwstraet, gently down the hill to the next t-junction. Go right here. Sticking doggedly with the LF6, cross over a main road and keep straight on until you pop seamlessly into the town of Ieper along Dikkebusseweg. This takes you across canal and railway to meet the busy N37. Head diagonally right to cross here, and follow LF6 signing past the moat of the old fortifications before heading left onto Montstraat then right onto Boterstraat to the lovely central square.

Accommodation

Hôtel Ambrosia
D'Hondtstraat 54, Ypres
057.366.366 www.hotel-foch.net

Hortensia B&B
Rijselsestraat 196, Ypres
0479.31.99.22 www.bbhortensia.be

Jeugdstadion
Bolwerkstraat 1, Ypres
057.21.72.82 www.jeugdstadion.be

Bike Shops

Defever
Gildentraat 2, Ypres
057.21.32.44

Noyelle Sport
Goesdamstraat 23, Ypres
057.20.13.97

Some of the features on this ride are decidedly Flemish rather than French, for instance the windmill at Boeschepe, just north of Mont des Cats. There is also an 'estaminet' (inset), a rather archaic French word roughly meaning a pub. This one, *Le Vierpot* (www.estaminetdevierpot.com), has a fantastic selection of beers, drinks and snacks.

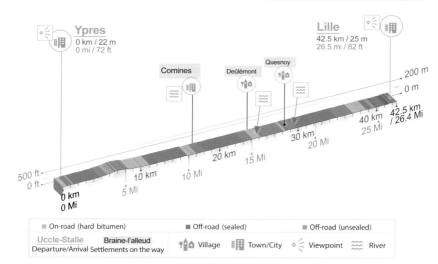

Day 5 Ride Notes

From the clock tower of Ypres' massive Cloth Hall (Lakenhall) head down Neermarkt, then second left (Patersstraat) and continue straight on down De Montstraat. Just past O.L. Vrouwstraat on the left go right onto the small alley called Vestingroute. Continue on the path to the old ramparts. Leaving the ramparts keep heading left to cross the parking area, hitting the main road, Oudstrijderslaan (N37b). Jink over the pedestrian crossing to pick up Dikkebusseweg (N375), following "Dikkebus" signs.

A few hundred metres further on cross the canal bridge (the disused Ypres canal) immediately taking the small cycle track on the left down the side of the canal (Bijlanderpad). The canal itself goes all the way to Comines though there isn't a continuous cycle track.

After around 3 km the track crosses the N336 Rijselseweg and 10m later swaps canal banks. Further on is the tiny Spoilbank Cemetery where the track crosses Vaartstraat. Don't continue along the canal here but take the earth track down to the right which zig-zags across the fields; in around 500m this tiny track meets Bernikkewallestraat, a tarmac-surfaced pathway, which you bear left onto.

After another few hundred metres you'll find Oak Dump Cemetery on the right. Just after this cross a golf course (dismounting advisable). At a 90 degree right turn take the small track on the left towards Palingbeek forest.

After a short, quick descent you are once again at the Ypres canal. Head right onto the 'pavée' surface until Komenseweg. Here go left then right onto Kasteelhoekstraat. After about 250m just under the rail bridge go right, towards Houthem. After 1.3 km fork right onto Korterwildstraat and in a further kilometre or so, at the first sign of houses, go right onto rue du Corbeau.

Arriving at the canal again pass over what remains of it here and immediate left onto a good quality cycle track. Follow it for 2.8 km to Comines. A little before Comines the track finishes at a park and crosses the N515 to pick up the far bank of the canal.

Meet the river Lys after 2km, where the cycle track meets the "Route des Écluses". Cross the road bridge 500m to your left, over the Lys, landing you in Comines. Continue straight on and at the traffic lights go right (rue de la République) and then the fifth right (rue Bonaparte) to rejoin the cycle track on the left, alongside the river. This leads to

Deûlémont; before the village you will see a blue barge on the bank. Just after the barge pick up the cycle track on the right - don't go into the village.

The track then ends at Les Écluses village (impasse des Prairies). Head down the Impasse and right onto rue des 3 Frères Fretin then joining Rue Virginie Ghesquières to the yellow and grey metal bridge. Across this head left onto the riverside track again.

3.5km further on hit a road bridge: go under it then up and right across the river and rejoin the river towpath. Follow the mini-railway which accompanies the cycle track ; beware not to snag your tyres in the tracks!

At the port of Wambrechies pass under the road bridge, following the cycleway and rails still. After passing under the huge motorway bridge (Rocade Nord-Ouest), you'll notice the industrial remains of old Lille; there's an info board about it. A little further on the track narrows and starts to climb towards a road bridge (la rue du Pont de l'Abbaye). 50m before it turn left, meeting the road and head right to the traffic lights. Head straight on at the lights, on the roadside cycle track towards Lille.

In 1.2km go right onto rue Roger Salengro, and just before the river bridge turn left then pick up the small street

of rue de Constantine) that descends back to the river. In 200m you'll find the riverside cycleway again on your right. Head up onto the next road bridge and take the cycle lane along the avenue "Façade de l'Esplanade", following it for a kilometre into Lille centre. Crossing boulevard de la Liberté, turn left then third left onto rue Nationale bringing you to the main square with its impressive belltower.

Accommodation

Lille Youth Hostel
12, rue Malpart, Lille
0.3.20.57.08.94 www.hihostels.com

Hôtel Flandre Angleterre
13 place de la Gare, Lille
03.20.06.04.12
www.hotel-flandreangleterre-lille.com
Bike storage in garage 200m from hotel -
needs booking in advance.

Camping les Ramiers
1 chemin des Ramiers, Bondues
03.20.23.13.42 9km north of Lille

Bike Shops

Cycles Lecolier
64 rue Léon Gambetta, Lille
03.20.54.83.39 www.cycles-leger.com

VillaVélo
24 place Louise de Bettignies, Lille
03.20.74.17.58 www.villavelo.com

The Ypres canal (above left) is not only disused but totally overgrown in places. The former towpath now makes an excellent traffic-free trail through Flanders countryside dotted with war cemeteries. In Ypres itself (above right) you'll find fine Flemish architecture.

Paris to Champagne Country

Route Info

Paris to Champagne Country
To the east of Paris, along the canal de l'Ourcq cycle path, beyond the commercialism of EuroDisney, through suburbia and into the Marne Valley, this is a wonderful ride amongst gentle hills and water features to the gateway of the Champagne region. From place de la République, the canal de l'Ourcq makes for a fascinating escape route out of Paris, through leafy Parisian suburbs and onto the meander of the Marne River.

This six day route plots an indirect course from Paris to Épernay. You'll leave Paris along tarmac riverside paths and quiet roads, climb above the valley on often deserted roads and have time to view sites of artistic and religious inspiration.

As a finale you will find yourself firmly in Champagne country at Épernay, an ideal place both visually and alcoholically, for relaxing at journey's end. If you can tear yourself away there are plentiful trains back to Paris.

Grade MEDIUM

Start / Finish
Paris (Gare du Nord) / Épernay

Route Length
6 day linear route with loop spurs
250km / 155 miles
Days 2 and 3 are easily combined to make it 5 days if consecutive days of 15 and 16 miles are just too easy.

Length of Suggested Days
24-55km / 15-34 miles
If days 2 and 3 are combined, day ride length varies from 43.5-55km / 27-34 miles

Route Surface & Signing
15% off-road
Some good quality riverside paths, but mainly quiet roads. Routes in Paris itself are signed (see photos below for more detail) but beyond the city centre limits you are on unsigned canal towpath and minor roads.

Access to Paris
Just over two hours from London St. Pancras by Eurostar, direct to the route start at Gare du Nord in Paris. **www.eurostar.com**

i Offices
Paris Gare du Nord, 08.92.68.30.00
www.parisinfo.com open 8am-6pm daily
Meaux 1, Place Doumer, Meaux, 01.64.33.02.26
www.tourisme-paysdemeaux.fr
La Ferté-sous-Jouarre
Espace public des Pelletiers
34, rue des Pelletiers 01.60.01.87.99
tourisme@la-ferte-sous-jouarre.fr
Jouarre rue de la Tour 01.60.22.64.54
www.tourism-jouarre.com
Château-Thierry 11, rue Vallée
03.23.83.51.14 www.otsiChâteau-thierry.com
Épernay 7, Avenue de Champagne
03.26.53.33.00 www.ot-epernay.fr

Many signs in and around Paris centre are self-explanatory, as above. However, there are also nine numbered and colour-coded routes linking some of the most important destinations, usually shown on smaller signs (above right); this route initially follows purple route 9 which goes to the Cité des Sciences (Science Museum). Once on the country roads of the Marne Valley you will rely on the usual D-road signs (Right).

For mapping see separate fold-out map

The shiny sphere known as the Géode marks your exit from Paris's central area and your passage under the Périphérique ring road into the suburbs.

Don't Miss

Parc de la Villette & the Big Shiny Ball

This big shiny ball across the water, visible (to say the least) as you pedal through the Parc de la Villette on the outskirts of Paris, is called the Géode. Inside, films are projected onto the ceiling, illustrating the wide diversity of scientific projects featured in the Cité des Sciences et de l'Industrie. Since opening in 1986 the museum has become the biggest of its kind in Europe, with interactive exhibitions on the human body, photography and aviation.

WWI detailed

Opened in 2011 at a cost of 28 million Euros, the museum of the First World War, just north-east of Meaux centre is everything you might expect - complete with planes, tanks and uniforms. Yet it also details the less well-documented aspects, typified by the likes of the mobile pigeon artefacts; some 300,000 birds were used in the war and were the most reliable form of communication.

The heart of the museum is the 50,000 objects accumulated by Jean-Pierre Verney, over 40 years, even including prosthetic limbs and smoking paraphernalia!

A dramatist's retreat: Beckett's House

2km from Ussy is the house to which Samuel Beckett retreated to write in the latter phase of his life. From the 1950s he used its wonderful valley views to inspire his work. Or at least he did until his desire for privacy prompted him to build a wall round it. To see the house take a quiet detour from Ussy village en route to La Ferté-sous-Jouarre. Turn left immediately after the village church and follow the road gently uphill past the cemetery (1km on your left), across the busy D3 road, up rue Samuel Beckett. The great man's house is the first one on the left. Enjoy the dramatic silence.

Painting the valley: Hayden's footsteps

The Ourcq valley landscapes around La Ferté-sous-Jouarre and Ussy-sur-Marne were inspirational for the Polish émigré artist Henri Hayden (1883-1970). A circular route through Avernes, Lizy and Ussy takes you through many of the scenes which are reflected in the work he produced in the latter part of his career, when he made regular journeys from his Paris home. For those wishing to follow the footsteps of Hayden, La Ferté tourist office offers route maps and guides to his impressionistic paintings of Averne and Ussy landscapes.

Day 1 Paris → Meaux

TOTAL DISTANCE / ELEVATION: **52 km / 281 m ascent** | **32 mi / 920 ft ascent**

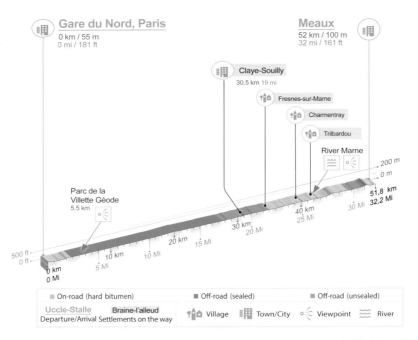

Gare du Nord, Paris
0 km / 55 m
0 mi / 181 ft

Meaux
52 km / 100 m
32 mi / 161 ft

Claye-Souilly
30,5 km 19 mi

Fresnes-sur-Marne

Charmentray

Trilbardou

River Marne
200 m
0 m

51,8 km
32,2 Mi

Parc de la
Villette Géode
5.5 km

40 km
25 Mi

30 Mi

30 km
20 Mi

20 km
15 Mi

10 km
10 Mi

5 Mi

500 ft
0 ft

0 km
0 Mi

| On-road (hard bitumen) | Off-road (sealed) | Off-road (unsealed) |

Uccle-Stalle   Braine-l'alleud
Departure/Arrival Settlements on the way

Village   Town/City   Viewpoint   River

The Canal St Martin is on your route out of Paris and is a hugely popular sunny weekend hangout for Parisians and visitors alike.

Day 1 Ride Notes

Today is a superb escape from the big city, westward via the canals St. Martin and l'Ourcq, through parks and forests, as well as graffitied and floral Parisian suburbs, then out onto the banks of the Marne River. Note beyond the city limits the canalside lacks a ready supply of cafes and bakeries. Since you'll be leaving Paris by canal towpath along the St. Martin it makes sense to arrive by Eurostar at the nearby Gare du Nord. Out of the station ride straight ahead for 100m and then pick up the safe roadside cycle path, left down the hill on the other side of boulevard Magenta, all the way down to place de la Republique, then down rue Léon Jouhaux to emerge at the Canal St. Martin. Head north-west along the canal-side quai de Jemmappes, picking up the number '9' cycle signs to place Stalingrad. Navigate your way over the traffic confusion of the place de la Bataille de Stalingrad to pick up the canalside path on the far side. Stay with this excellent waterside path, separated from the road, past the quirky and helpful Cycle-Pouce shop on quai de la Marne on the canal de l'Ourcq. The northern Parisian setting for this section is futuristic and expansive, with galleries and fairgrounds left and right. In the parc de la Villette an enormous reflective metallic sphere across the water (which only adds to the unreality of the place) signals the Science and Industry Museum.

Stay on the canal cycle track and follow green cycle signs to Bobigny. At the school of dance the path crosses the canal but continues alongside it. Out west through the suburbs of Bobigny the tarmac surface helps you gather speed. Glide between the tracks of the TGV on your left and the waters of the canal on your right, with joggers and cyclists your only company. Beyond the peaceful parc départemental de la Bergère, florally decorated canal footbridges signify the higher income brackets of the outer suburbs of Bondy, Aulnay and Sevran (with its own impressive park). Underwheel conditions remain smooth and level irrespective of the affluence of the surroundings. From the forest at Villeparisis the path emerges into the light and hops over the canal once again and at Claye-Souilly the tarmac runs out. The canal-side path continues on gravel, favouring touring tyres and mountain bikes, though still of reasonably good quality.

At Fresnes-sur-Marne it's time to take to the road. Quit the canal and join the road signed for Precy-sur-Marne, following signs for the leisure route known as Circuit de la Marne. Just before you enter Precy a sign going left indicates Moulin de la Marne. Follow this and leave the village outskirts to cross the canal and bend right towards Trilbardou on the fast, quiet road. Stay on the D54a through Charmentray. At Trilbardou run alongside the river then take the left turn, signed to Vignely and Esbly, following these signs to pick up the D27 out of the village.

As the D27 enters Vignely on a right hand bend take a left turn (unsigned) towards Meaux - a short section of traffic-free trail accompanies the road initially!

Follow Villenoy signs over a couple of roundabouts and above a trunk road to follow the D5, as it gets busier and faster. Very shortly split right, signed Villenoy centre, and head down rue de Lagny to the Canal de l'Ourq and left onto the towpath (signs say no cycling but it's a widely used unofficial route and avoids the horribly busy traffic into Meaux!).

Follow the towpath for just under 3km until exiting right at a small bridge, where tarmac leads to the main D330. Carefully negotiate busy roads into the centre (you may well wish to pavement push this next little section); go right then immediate left, following Centre Ville signs and at the next main intersection look straight across to the little stone bridge under the railway - head under here onto rue St Rémy, to bring you to the magnificent cathedral and the town centre.

Accommodation

For Paris accommodation see pg 74

🏨 *Hôtel Le Richemont*
Quai de la Grande Ile, Meaux 01.60.25.12.10
www.hotel-lerichemont.com

Bike Shops

🚲 *Cycles Richard*
8 Cours Raoult, Meaux 01.64.34.07.57

Day 2 | Meaux → La Ferté-sous-Jouarre

TOTAL DISTANCE / ELEVATION: **24km / 270 m ascent** | **15 mi / 886 ft ascent**

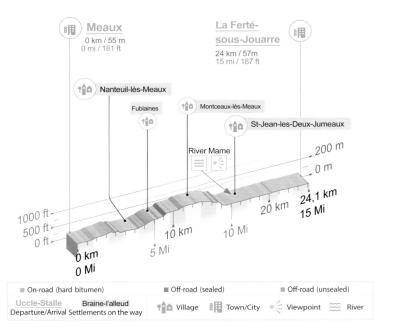

- On-road (hard bitumen)   - Off-road (sealed)   - Off-road (unsealed)

| Uccle-Stalle | Braine-l'alleud | | | | | | |
| Departure/Arrival | Settlements on the way | 🏠 Village | 🏢 Town/City | ○ Viewpoint | ≈ River | | |

Day 2 Ride Notes

This is a short ride, which can be combined with the next day's loop to Nanteuil (see Day 3) if you're looking for something longer. You'll wiggle up into the gentle hills and back down to the valley, avoiding the traffic and seeing the Marne valley from various perspectives. The brevity of the route allows time for a look at the house of Samuel Beckett and a wander round the lively town of La Ferté, where they say Beckett used to do his shopping.

Head south out of Meaux by crossing the Marne over Pont Jean Bureau picking up the brief cycle lanes along rue François de Tessan (N36 / D360), and in just under a kilometre after the bridge cross a smaller bridge and head left onto a much quieter road, chemin bas de Meaux.

Bear left twice in succession before heading right and uphill into Fublaines. Head straight across a crossroads then left onto rue des Brinches, following the D17 out of the village. In Brinches hit the D33 and go left, then very shortly right, signed to Montceaux-lès-Meaux. Hit the D19 and head left into Montceaux.

From the village of Montceaux leave the main D19 (rue de Lizy), turning right onto the smaller rue de St. Jean (across from the restaurant), bearing left at the split on the edge of the village, downhill towards Les-Deux-Jumeaux. From Les-Deaux-Jumeaux descend steeply to St.-Jean-les-deux-Jumeaux, crossing over the busy D603 and the river Marne, to go right signed Changis-sur-Marne. In Changis bear right onto the D3e (signed Lizy and Jaignes), then right at a small roundabout signed Ussy.

Head straight through Ussy, passing the church on the left, following the D3 to La Ferté-sous-Jouarre.

Accommodation

Polish Catholic Mission (La Mission Polonaise)
31 rue d'Hugny, La Ferté-sous-Jouarre
01.60.22.03.76.
An oasis of calm, with very comfortable
rooms at a ridiculously good price with
a locked courtyard for bike storage and
a lovely ornamental garden. You'll find
it 300m north of the railway station.

Bike Shops

Christophe Chinot
11, avenue Franklin Roosevelt
La Ferté-sous-Jouarre 01.60.22.15.60
christophe.chinot@wanadoo.fr

The quiet Marne at La Ferté-sous-Jouarre

Day 3   La Ferté-sous-Jouarre → Nanteuil-sur-Marne loop

TOTAL DISTANCE / ELEVATION: **25.5 km / 422 m ascent**   16 mi / 1384 ft ascent

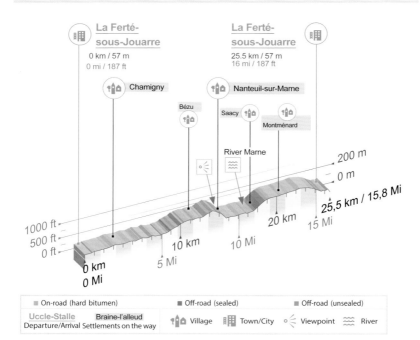

■ On-road (hard bitumen)	■ Off-road (sealed)	■ Off-road (unsealed)

Uccle-Stalle Braine-l'alleud		
Departure/Arrival Settlements on the way	⛺ Village 🏢 Town/City	○ Viewpoint 〰 River

Day 3 Ride Notes

This ride makes an ideal supplement to the route from Day 2, or a short, scenic ride in its own right. From the bridge over the Marne (near the tourist office) leave La Ferté on the D80, passing through Chamigny and on to Ste-Aulde. Here pick up the D16 for a wonderful climb through the vineyards, to the village of Bézu. At the main village roundabout take a right, signed to Villier St. Denis, then first right again signed Nanteuil-sur-Marne, for the final ascent, before dropping down into Nanteuil-sur-Marne. The leftward view during this descent is panoramic, revealing Nanteuil, Ste-Aulde and Saacy in all their miniscule glory.

From Nanteuil begin the return leg to La Ferté by heading west beside the river on your left, on the D402 (signed Méry and La Ferté) for around 2km before turning left over the bridge onto a smaller road, signed for Saacy (which, though less picturesque, is more functional than Nanteuil if you're looking for shops and services). At the roundabout in Saacy village follow the sign (going right) to Montménard, then take the first left turn onto an even smaller road, signed up to Montepeine. Climb steeply for 3km, past Camping de Saacy-sur-Marne (see below), until you see the right turn for Montménard on this wonderful quiet road, with deer in the vicinity. Plunge down from Montménard, back into downtown La Ferté-sous-Jouarre.

Accommodation

Auberge du Lion d'Or
Nanteuil-sur-Marne, 01.60.23.62.21 (closed Wednesday and Sunday). An out of town option with a good restaurant, in the much quieter village of Nanteuil

Camping de Saacy-sur-Marne
Saacy-sur-Marne   01.60.23.75.81
Atop a steep hill just outside Saacy.

110

Day 4   La Ferté-sous-Jouarre → Lizy loop

TOTAL DISTANCE / ELEVATION: **50 km / 761 m ascent** | **31 mi / 2496 ft ascent**

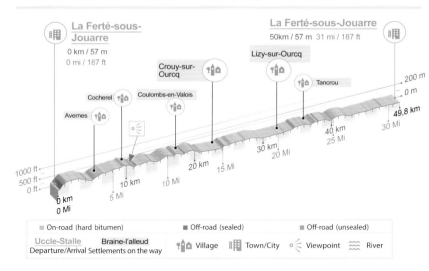

- On-road (hard bitumen)   - Off-road (sealed)   - Off-road (unsealed)

| Uccle-Stalle | Braine-l'alleud | 🏠 Village | 🏢 Town/City | ᵒ⤢ Viewpoint | ≈ River |
| Departure/Arrival Settlements on the way | | | | | |

Day 4 Ride Notes

A little further today, though the rewards are considerable. You'll ride up hill and down dale on an often deserted circular trip from village to village, with the splendid Ourcq valley in your sights for much of the way.

From La Ferté railway station, take the D603 (signed for Château-Thierry) for 150m. Turn left up the steep hill towards Le Limon, then right to Favières before joining the D73 going left towards Cocherel. It's a solitary ride now with just a few horses dotted around disinterestedly, downhill most of the way to Avernes, of which there is precious little. Stick with the D73 to Cocherel, crossing the busy E50 en route. At the T junction in Cocherel go right, follow D73 signs to Lizy, bearing right again at the next junction. Go over the D401 and sail down into Chaton, with more wonderful valley views. From Chaton head right, freewheel to Vendrest and on to Coulombs-en-Valois on the D17. This last 2km takes a main road, though not a busy section. You're soon off it too, taking a left, small road, signed to Certigny and Crotigny. Post Certigny go left at the T-junction onto rue de l'Amandière, then left again onto the D23. The descent into Crouy-sur-

Ourcq is thrilling, past perhaps the most misused stately home known to humanity, where paint-balling is available (at time of writing).

If you're not fussed about exploring the village of Crouy-sur-Ourcq take a left towards Fussy and follow the long, straight D102, where the Ourcq valley reveals itself splendidly to your right. Head through Ocquerre and descend into Lizy, going left at a small roundabout up avenue de la Gare, and following it past the railway station over to the right and over the rail bridge to take the D17 to Mary-sur-Marne on a relatively urbanised section (there are retail sheds); or so it seems after what has gone before.

Coming into Mary-sur-Marne take an (**easy to miss**) left turn for Tancrou (route de Tancrou), which is tranquility itself once again. Continue straight on at Tancrou until you reach a T-junction at the end of rue de Vivier. Go right here, then first left to Jaignes. From here the D53 will take you towards Changis, but before you get there follow the left-bearing SNCF sign down to the railway station, then go sharp left from the roundabout into Ussy, which is familiar from Day 2. Follow the same route back into La Ferté.

Day 5   La Ferté-sous-Jouarre → Château-Thierry

TOTAL DISTANCE / ELEVATION: **43.5 km / 496 m ascent**   27 mi / 1627 ft ascent

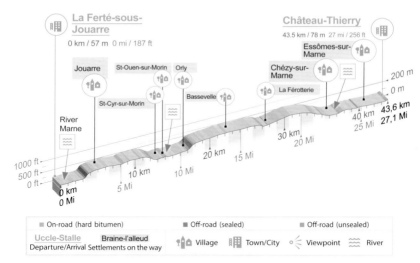

■ On-road (hard bitumen)   ■ Off-road (sealed)   ■ Off-road (unsealed)

Uccle-Stalle   Braine-l'alleud   🏰 Village   🏢 Town/City   ○ Viewpoint   ≋ River
Departure/Arrival Settlements on the way

La Ferté-sous-Jouarre

A tranqil looking river Marne at La Ferté-sous-Jouarre.

La Ferté straddles the river Marne and is bustling enough to provide all you need for a brief or elongated stop-over, without being besieged by tourists. Access to several really excellent circular rides out of the valley couldn't be better, with gentle hills, artistic landmarks to look out for and views across the valley. The tourist office is well-informed about local rides, offering maps and suggested routes, as well as reasonably priced and excellent suggestions for accommodation in and around the town. On the south bank of the river there is a war memorial commemorating the lives of 3000 British soldiers who died in WWI.

Jouarre

For its size the lofty town of Jouarre certainly punches above its weight in terms of tourism. The short, stiff climb is rewarded with a chance to look round 7th century crypts and abbey. The 18th century convent is still occupied by Benedictine nuns, who by all accounts maintain an enviable fruit and vegetable garden. The crypts beneath the Romanesque Abbey hold several sarcophagi encased burials of note, some dating back to the 7th century. There's also a Brie museum, next to the crypts, with artefacts, information and demonstrations of traditional crafts from the region (not just cheese).

Church door, Jouarre

Day 5 Ride Notes

This is a varied, often sumptuously silent ride with several high points (literally and metaphorically speaking). Long stretches are spent in barely any traffic at all, with valley, forest and river landscapes to marvel at. There's also chance to visit the popular monastery at Jouarre, whose ambience contrasts with the mundane ending of the ride itself - the last few kilometres showcase the retail parks of Château-Thierry.

From the tourist office take the pretty riverside gravel path to Pont Europe, the larger of the two bridges over the Marne. At the roundabout take the main (though not especially busy) D204 (signed for Rebais) to Courcelles. From here take a right and climb steeply up the quiet, winding road to Jouarre where the popular abbey and monastery are perched. From the heights of Jouarre follow the quiet D114, heading right on the rue de Vrou before entering Romeny. Continue to the crossroads, turn right to join the D204 for 500m, then left onto the D37, signed for St. Cyr-sur-Morin, into which you now descend pretty swiftly. The road here is still fairly quiet but watch out for a few potholes as you drop into St-Cyr. By the museum at the foot of the hill turn right onto the D31 towards St-Ouen sur-Morin. St-Cyr and St-Ouen are joined at the hip by the ornate River Morin, which you will cross between the two villages. Press on to Orly on an undulating road which ploughs a lone furrow through the river valley's expanse. Take the 4th turn off on the left in Orly, signed to Boitron, Petit Villiers and Bassevelle. Now it gets really quiet. Climbing through the forest, with only the sounds of creaking timber to distract, the riding is sublime. Follow signs for Petit Villiers

and emerge from the trees onto the D55, where you head left and onwards to Bassevelle which lies across the D407. Take the high road, resisting the temptation to go leftwards and downwards (that will come), through Petit Bassevelle and Bassevelle, crossing the D222 and freewheeling down to La Fèrotterie. Turn right here, the first left again, signed for Chérost. At the D15 finally take the leftward plunge to reacquaint yourself with the Marne at Chézy. The descent is sluggish at first but soon gathers speed. From the D15 follow the D151 filter out of Chézy, hopping the river to Azy. The closing stages of the ride into Château-Thierry follow the anticlimactic D969. Retail sheds lined up in unison do not paint the town in its best light. Yet Château-Thierry itself, once you're in, is a more than functional stop-over, like so many others that are decorated by the Marne River.

Accommodation

Hôtel Les Fabliaux
3, avenue de Château-Thierry, Brasles, 03.23.83.23.14   www.les-fabliaux.com
A welcoming little hotel by the river, within walking distance of the main square and bike shop.

Bike Shops

Sport Passion
47, avenue de Château-Thierry, Brasles 03.23.69.45.97 (on the same road as Hôtel Les Fabliaux a few blocks further out of town).

Château-Thierry

The town itself is know for an eponymous battle in the dying months of WWI, in which French and American forces surprised German encampments behind their own lines. The battle is memorialised a few kilometres west. The best view of the town is from the top of the 13th century battlements, which you can climb (on foot) using the steps by the Hôtel De Ville, which is also home to the tourist office and the art deco Théâtre Jean Cocteau cinema and theatre, with a refreshing mix of mainstream and art-house.

Day 6 | Château-Thierry → Épernay

TOTAL DISTANCE / ELEVATION: **55 km / 638 m ascent** | 34 mi / 2067 ft ascent

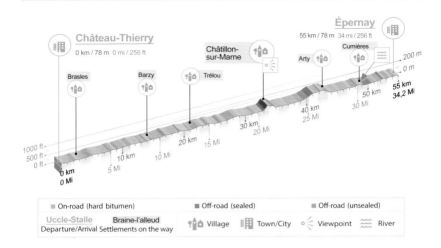

- ■ On-road (hard bitumen)
- ■ Off-road (sealed)
- ■ Off-road (unsealed)

Uccle-Stalle   Braine-l'alleud
Departure/Arrival Settlements on the way   🏠 Village   🏢 Town/City   ∘ Viewpoint   〜 River

The final approach to Épernay features one of the very few cycle paths in the Marne valley, between Cumières and Mardeuil.

114

Day 6 Ride Notes

As the previous day ended, so this one begins; inauspiciously. Yet today's ride has plenty to offer, notably the striking fortress village of Châtillon and an introduction to the Champagne region. Start by riding the D3 east out of Château-Thierry with the River Marne for company (more than just an acquaintance by now) on your right, out of Brasles and through Gland. After five days of peace and quiet this first stretch will seem a little busy, so take care. Respite comes at Jaulgonne when you bear right onto the quieter D320 towards Barzy-sur-Marne. At Trélou go right at the T-junction, signed for Vincelles, then fork right 1km out of Trélou, again towards Vincelles. This much quieter road picks its way through the vineyards of Vincelles, Verneuil and Vandières. The champagne producer's signage starts in earnest here. Expect your spirits to elevate along with the route itself. Straight ahead is an apparitional view of the hilltop village of Châtillon - well worth a leftwards detour. The climb up to Châtillon is tough (cruel, even), but brief. The rewards though are panoramic. From the village you can share the view with the statue of its most famous son, the Gregorian reformer Urban II (1042-99), who scans the valley majestically 24/7. The wonderfully preserved church of Notre-Dame might catch your eye after a well-earned lunch stop. Leave the village by careering (carefully) down the D23 spiral to the roundabout by the WWI memorial, then follow the D1 turn-off to Reuil and Damery (not Épernay).

Back in the basement of the valley you're shadowing the Marne's meander once again, at least for a spell. Stay on the D1, ignoring invitations to head for Épernay on the D601. On the D1 from Reuil to Tincourt climb away from the river. A worthwhile detour to preserve the height you've earned and stay on quieter roads takes you up to Venteuil and Arty, which has a splendid roadside fountain and unmanned book exchange. From Arty fork right down the hill to Damery and the D1. At Cumières go right, signed to Épernay, cross the Marne and pick up the cycle path to Mardeuil, bearing right. When the cycle path runs out continue over the rail bridge and go left onto the D401 rue Victor Hugo for the final stretch into Épernay. At the roundabout on the edge of Épernay centre head straight across onto place Léon Bourgeois and immediate left up Cour Montilleul. This backstreet will bring you out by the grand Notre-Dame church, the town centre being just the south-west of here and the main champagne houses to the east, on avenue de Champagne. Trains back to Paris Gare de l'Est are frequent.

Accommodation

🛏 *Hôtel Villa St Pierre*
1 rue Jeanne d'Arc, Épernay
03.26.54.40.80 www.villasaintpierre.fr
Reasonably priced and near the centre.
⛺ *Camping Municipal, Épernay*
allée des Cumières 03.26.55.32.14
www.epernay.fr   Some riverside pitches and snackbar on site.

Bike Shops

🚲 *Sport Passion* 47, avenue de Château-Thierry, Brasles 03.23.69.45.97 (on the same road as Hôtel Les Fabliaux, a little further out of town).

Épernay

Firmly in Champagne country and a more manageable and attractive centre for exploring all aspects of the bubbly stuff than the larger and more famous Reims to the north. Its most famous street is the avenue de Champagne - 'the most drinkable street in the world' according to Churchill, who certainly liked a tipple. Even if you are teetotal the town is still a very attractive place to stroll.

For champagne connoisseurs, or just the curious, there are numerous tours of the many 'houses', from famed names like Moët et Chandon to smaller concerns such as Leclerc-Briant.

River Rhine & The Vosges

Route Info

River Rhine & The Vosges

Though this area of north-east France is not that visited by UK tourists it is very popular with German visitors - especially the sumptuous hill country of the Vosges. These are certainly steep hills but this route wanders along the foothills taking in great views but avoiding the steepest gradients. The route actually starts in Switzerland at Basel - the heart of this very cosmopolitan and attractive city is Swiss but there are also large chunks of it in France and Germany. The route passes through Germany and into France almost immediately without a border control in sight!

Although pancake flat at the start, after Colmar you head into and along the edge of the once volcanic Vosges mountains for the hardest climbing of all the routes featured here.

Access to Basel

SNCF Direct high speed services from Paris to Basel take about three and a half to four hours, plus services via Strasbourg and Mulhouse. Also services from major cities in Switzerland and Germany.
www.voyages-sncf.com

Grade MEDIUM / HARD

Start / Finish

Basel (Bâle) / Strasbourg

Route length

238km / 148 miles
Also plenty of short-cut options on day 2 to make the route shorter still.

Length of Suggested Days

32-81km / 20-50.5 miles - though note you can cut down on the longest day (day 2) as there are plenty of shortcut options to Colmar

i Offices

Basel Aeschenvorstadt 36
061 268 68 68 www.basel.com
Neuf-Brisach 6 place d'Armes
03.89.72.56.66
www.tourisme-paysdebrisach.com
Colmar 32 Cours Sainte-Anne
03.89.20.68.92 www.ot-colmar.fr
Munster 1 rue du Couvent
03.89.77.31.80 www.valleemunster.eu
Riquewihr 2 rue de la 1ère armée
03.89.73.23.23 www.ribeauville-riquewihr.com
Ribeauville 1 Grand Rue
03.89.73.23.23 www.ribeauville-riquewihr.com
Sélestat boulevard Leclerc
03.88.58.87.20/26 www.selestat-tourisme.com
Barr place de l'Hôtel de ville
03.88.08.66.65 www.pays-de-barr.com
Obernai place du Beffroi
03.88.95.64.13 www.obernai.fr
Molsheim 19 place de l'Hôtel de ville
03.88.38.11.61 www.ot-molsheim-mutzig.com
Strasbourg 17 place de la cathédrale
03.88.52.28.28 www.otstrasbourg.fr

Route Surface & Signing

Around 50% off-road depending on route options taken. Initially you follow the Rhine cycle route - officially signed as route 6. Initially you'll see Swiss national route signing in red (below left), which soon changes once in France (below middle). There are a plethora of local circular routes too - for example the numbers in the middle photo below relate to these. After the first day to Neuf-Brisach signing usually takes the form of a white cyclist on a blue background pointing you to the next village along, as below right.

The circuit of the Fecht valley (day 2) uses Voie Vertes signing - VV21 and VV212 - usually on access restricted roads with virtually no traffic as above left. Finally, approaching Strasbourg you'll pick up the multi-coloured signs (above right).

116

Don't Miss

Basel's Riverside Beauty

Undoubtedly the River Rhine makes the city - despite its host of cultural attractions and museums. It has a fine old bridge that colourful trams rattle across, the MittlereRheinbrücke, remarkable cable-guided ferries that use the current to push themselves across the river (bikes can go on them for a small fee) and well-used public swimming areas along its edges (including a lovely sunning and bathing platform on the southern bank in the St Alban area). And to top it all riverside cycle routes let you drink it all in.

A Fortress Town - Neuf-Brisach

This is a planned late 17th century defensive town, built after France lost the nearby town of Breisach to the great European Habsburg dynasty. This is most obvious when you walk around the massive defensive walls that surround it. Lovely spacious central square and church.

Castles and Wines - the Vosges

Wine is everywhere in the lovely rounded volcanic outlines of the Vosges mountains. The most famous quality wines are made from Gewürztraminer and Riesling grapes and roadside tastings in caveaux are all along the route.

Less accessible but very noticeable are the hilltop castles dotted along your way. If you take day 2's high level option you'll pass close to five of the very, very many that testify how Alsace has been at the heart of European conflict in centuries past. Of these Hohlandsbourg is the most touristy - but also the most impressive by quite a way.

Not Just Another Cathedral

Even those with no natural inclination to visit cathedrals will probably admit on seeing it, that Strasbourg cathedral is something special.

From the outside it's the immensely tall yet slim spire that is astonishing whilst inside the Pilier des Anges statues and the ancient astrological clock are wondrous.

One of Basel's four cable ferries that cross the Rhine. They are in daily service except for flood periods and are 'reactive' - they use no motor power at all; the operator harnesses the flow of the river to push them across.

Day 1   Basel → Neuf-Brisach

TOTAL DISTANCE / ELEVATION: **63 km / 392 m ascent** | 39 mi / **1286ft ascent**

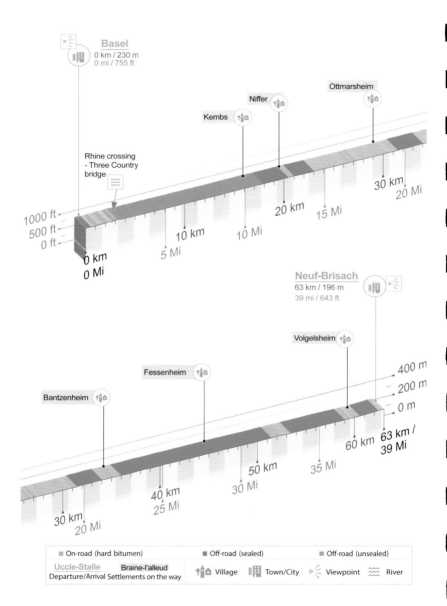

Basel
0 km / 230 m
0 mi / 755 ft

Niffer

Ottmarsheim

Kembs

Rhine crossing
- Three Country
bridge

1000 ft
500 ft
0 ft

30 km
20 Mi

20 km
15 Mi

10 km
10 Mi

0 km
0 Mi

5 Mi

Neuf-Brisach
63 km / 196 m
39 mi / 643 ft

Volgelsheim

Fessenheim

400 m
200 m
0 m

Bantzenheim

60 km   63 km /
39 Mi

50 km
30 Mi   35 Mi

40 km
25 Mi

30 km
20 Mi

On-road (hard bitumen)   Off-road (sealed)   Off-road (unsealed)

Uccle-Stalle   Braine-l'alleud   🏘 Village   🏢 Town/City   ◦⟨ Viewpoint   ≋ River
Departure/Arrival Settlements on the way

For mapping see separate fold-out map

Day 1 Ride Notes

Basel's reputation as a cycle-friendly city is well-founded and its cycle lane network promises an easy exit from its historic heart.

The route north of Basel is easily found on the eastern side of the central bridge by Basel's old centre, the MittlereRheinbrücke. Almost immediately over the bridge pick up the red cycle signage for Freiburg / Rheinfelden/Riehen then immediate right again down the passage under buildings (Wild Ma-Gässli) to arrive at the Rhine. Go right to follow the lovely riverside route, finally bearing away from the river alongside a rail line, as the road changes from Unterer Rheinweg to Altrhein Weg. This bends 90 degrees right, shortly coming to a bridge which you head left over, across the River Wiese, now approaching Three Countries Corner , where Switzerland, Germany and France meet.

Head up Dorfstrasse, still following the EuroVelo 6 route signs. Past the white church bend right on Weilerweg and left at the main road to climb over a railway and harbour entrance.

Pass through German customs and very shortly take **the easy to miss** first left down Am Rheinpark (by the Rheincenter shopping centre) which leads to a magnificent foot and cycle bridge.

Now in France, the compact centre of Huningue lies ahead of you but the route bears left, sticking by the Rhine to arrive at the mouth of the Huningue Canal.

It's now simply a matter of following the unsealed canalside path north all the way to Kembs.

Here you cross the lovely little drawbridge at Kembs, shortly after which it becomes a tarmac track that leads to a roundabout, heading right on the path, under the D468 up to the Bief de Niffer (canal reach). Cross over the canal and ignore the bridge over to your left. Head over the large lock to your right, leaving EuroVelo 6 here, and right then left, following signs to Chalampe and Niffer. Past the mairie and church in Niffer turn right on a left-hand bend onto a lovely agricultural road.

This comes into Petit-Landau where you bear right into the village, then left down rue des Fleurs. This very quiet country road comes into Hombourg

where you bear left and follow the signs on a convoluted route through a housing estate (rues des Landes, rue des Pins, rue du Chêne) before turning right onto rue d'Ottmarsheim and along another whisper quiet country road.

Coming into Ottmarsheim the road uses a tunnel under the A36 then heads over the D108 onto Rue de Hombourg before meeting the D468. There is a signed cycle route through the centre on your right but this is complex - easiest to stick to the D468 then pick up the roadside cycle lane on your exit. Stay on the D468, crossing the D39 and through Bantzenheim village to pick up the excellent cycletracks out of it. Now simply follow the road through a string of neat though unremarkable villages that give lovely views of the distant Black Forest in Germany on the far side of the Rhine.

Through Rumersheim stay on the D468 (ignoring cycle route signs to Mulhouse) and on to Blodelsheim. At Fessenheim head left up the D3bis, signed Hirtzfelden and Hensisheim, and very shortly go right onto a superbly surfaced cycle track, picking up signs for Neuf-Brisach and Heiteren, the cycle track merging back alongside the D468 to come into Heiteren.

Here you turn right immediately before the church and in about 1km left, onto the traffic-free cycle route. Follow this for just over 4.5km where you cross a road on the edge of Algolsheim, continuing on the cycle track to a junction with the D60 and right (ignore the immediate right where the cycle track emerges) and head into Vogelgrun. Take the first left in this village, signed rue des Cignes and left again onto rue des Blés, to pick up the cycle track on your left under the main D415. Left on meeting the road, following it into Volgelsheim, where you meet the main crossroads. Though the cycle route is signed straight across onto rue de la Fôret Noire, this is very circuitous - a much quicker way into Neuf-Brisach is to go left here onto rue de la Paix, then first right onto rue Neuf-Brisach. Pick up the cycle lane on the right and follow it all the way to cross a mini-roundabout and canal, turning right on the D468 to bring you through the city walls into the remarkable town of Neuf-Brisach.

Accommodation

Basel Backpack Hostel
Dornacherstrasse 192, Basel
061.333.00.37 www.baselbackpack.ch
Single, double, 4-bed and dorm rooms
at comparatively reasonable rates.

Hôtel Rochat Petersgraben 23, Basel
061.261.81.40 www.hotelrochat.ch
Stylish hotel near the centre.

Basel Youth Hostel
St. Alban-Kirchrain 10, Basel
061.272.05.72 www.youthhostel.ch/en
Pricey for the usual youth hostel
facilities, but better value for groups.

Easyhotel Riehenring 109, Basel
0900.327.927 www.easyhotel.com
Rather claustrophobic rooms but good
value.

Hôtel Aux 2 Roses
11 rue de Strasbourg, Neuf-Brisach
03.89.72.56.03 www.alsace2roses.com

Camping Au Petit Port
8 allée des Marronniers, Huningue
03.89.70.01.71
http://campinghuningue.free.fr/
Cosy little site, only real disadvantage
being some km from Basel centre, but
nearby Huningue has most services.

Bike Shops

Cenci Bikes 51 Clarastrasse Basel
061.681.88.08 www.cenci-bikes.ch
Wenger 143 Gartenstrasse Basel
061.283.80.80
2 Roues 54 rue du Maréchal Foch
Village-Neuf, Huningue 03.89.69.16.04

The MittlereRheinbrücke is a stylish and colourful start to your route out of Basel .

The Rhine cycle route shows signs of serious traffic-free investment in this bridge at Basel -
official title Three Country Bridge, located where Switzerland, Germany and France meet.

Basel

As well as its undoubted riverside charms (see Don't Miss description) Basel also boasts a fine old town dominated by its hilltop Münster (the cloisters being particularly atmospheric) surrounded by medieval streets and leafy courtyards. The main squares are Barfüsserplatz, where you'll find a fine history museum documenting the town's past and Marktplatz, with colourful fruit and veg stalls often found in front of the equally colourful town hall (Rathaus).

Other attractions include the trundling, bell-ringing trams that lend a decidedly eastern-european atmosphere to much of the city, the quiet area around the 13th century gateway St Alban Tor (near the youth hostel) and the museum Tinguely celebrating one of Switzerland's most loved modern artists - in large part because of the sense of humour displayed in his moving sculptures.

The Rhine in Basel centre is a real hive of activity; not only are there traffic-free cycle routes along its edges but swimming areas and traditional ferries. Fine buildings add to the unique spectacle.

Day 2   Neuf-Brisach → Colmar Low Level Route

TOTAL DISTANCE / ELEVATION (SEE OTHER MILEAGE OPTIONS OPPOSITE:
75 km / 811 m ascent   46.5 mi / 2661ft ascent

Traffic-Free Sections: Note from now on this route uses a number of virtually traffic-free routes marked as green. These are roads often open only to residents (sauf riverains) or agricultrual vehicles (sauf engins agricoles), but despite no entry signs bicycles are allowed on the particular roads chosen here as they are official bike routes. You might also see 'sauf ayant droits' or 'sauf usagers autorisés' next to no entry signs meaning 'except those with rights of way / authorised'. Again, if the bike route goes down here cycling will be officially allowed.

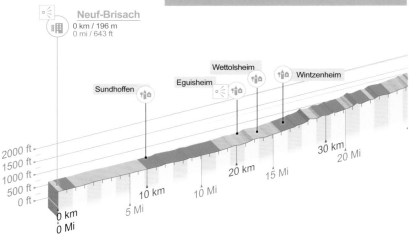

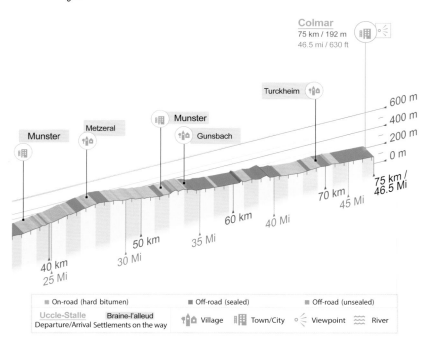

■ On-road (hard bitumen)	■ Off-road (sealed)	■ Off-road (unsealed)
Uccle-Stalle Braine-l'alleud Departure/Arrival Settlements on the way	🏘 Village 🏢 Town/City	⦿ Viewpoint ≋ River

For mapping see separate fold-out map

Day 2 Ride Notes

Distance: 75.5 km / 47 miles with other options as follows:
High level route 81km / 50.5 miles
Neuf-Brisach - Colmar 18.5km / 11.5 miles
Neuf-Brisach - Metzeral and train return to Colmar 45km / 28 miles
Neuf-Brisach to Munster 39km / 24 miles
From Neuf-Brisach's lovely large central square head up rue de Colmar (D29) and out through the fortifications. Very soon look for a right, signed as a bike route to Wolfgantzen and Colmar, which takes you past a cemetery on the left to come alongside a railway on the right. Through Wolfgantzen you pick up signs for Appenwihr, along the D1 and in Appenwihr take the D13 to Sundhoffen. Cross the river and head along the main street. On the far edge of the village turn left up Rue des Alpes then first right, onto a tiny agricultural road. This heads through a forest section which eventually passes under a trunk road to hit a busy main road. Turn right across the River Thur then immediate left over a railway line, onto a small tarmac road ('sauf engins agricoles'). Keep left at the first split staying by the river. You now have **two options:**
An Early Finish in Colmar Centre Take the next right, staying on the tarmac of rue Allmend-Weg, bearing left onto chemin Lauchwerb. Follow this, bearing left at several splits, to parallel the River Lauch to your left, to come into Colmar on the cycle track along Rue Serpentine. Meet Avenue Georges Clemenceau and jink right then left onto the cycle lanes of route de Bâle. Head onto rue Turenne and back over the Lauch to find the Grand Rue on your right, leading to the heart of the city.
(To access the Fecht Valley from Colmar follow the above route in reverse).
Around the Fecht valley via Munster
Ignore right turns, keeping the river on your left, following the Herrlisheim sign as the surface becomes unsealed. Through woods the track emerges at an unsigned crossroads (small metal bridge on your left). Turn right onto tarmac, and follow this agricultural road in a straight line to climb over the railway. Just descending over the railway turn right and meet the D14 and head left to pass under the D83. Head straight over the small roundabout signed Eguisheim. Coming into Eguisheim you have a couple of options:

1. Low level route

Before you hit Eguisheim centre there is a right onto rue du Riesling (though don't miss the unmissable village centre). Turn right onto rue de Colmar, which soon splits left onto a quieter road which leads through vineyards into Wettolsheim. Here turn left at a T-junction and follow the road through the village and right onto rue du Château into the centre, bending right past the church. Head left onto rue Kleb to leave Wettolsheim and almost immediately enter Wintzenheim. In Wintzenheim take a left up rue des Trois Châteaux (cycle signage for Turckheim), then a right to stay on rue des Trois Châteaux to meet the main D417. Head left here through the village centre, picking up the excellent cycle lane to exit at the far side to continue on to a roundabout. Bear left at the roundabout, along a dead end road into the h   amlet of St Giles (now picking up VV21 signs). The high level route emerges on the left but you carry on to pick up VV21 signs for Mittlach and Munster.
Route continues overleaf after High Level route description.

2. High level route.

Coming into Eguisheim centre turn left

Munster is fine old town whose name is synonymous with the local cheese - sold here at the market in front of the main church

Day 2 Neuf-Brisach → Colmar High Level Route

TOTAL DISTANCE / ELEVATION: **81 km / 1390 m ascent** | **50.5 mi / 4560ft ascent**

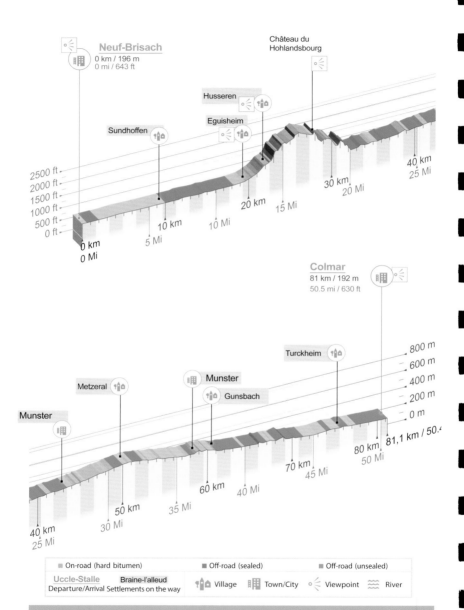

On-road (hard bitumen)   ■ Off-road (sealed)   ■ Off-road (unsealed)

Uccle-Stalle   Braine-l'alleud   †🏠 Village   🏢 Town/City   ○ᶜ Viewpoint   ≋ River
Departure/Arrival Settlements on the way

Traffic-Free Sections: Note from now on this route uses a number of virtually traffic-free routes marked as green. These are often open only to residents (sauf riverains) or agricrual vehicles (sauf engins agricoles), but despite no entry signs bicycles are allowed on the particular roads chosen here as they are official bike routes. You might also see 'sauf ayant droits' or 'sauf usagers autorisés' next to no entry signs meaning 'except those with rights of way / authorised'. Again, if the bike route goes down here it will be officially allowed.

up rue du Muscat, signed for Husseren-les-Châteaux. At the D14 turn left, signed Husseren, and climb steadily for just over a mile into Husseren itself. Here follow signs for route des Cinq Châteaux and follow them out of the village into the woods of the Vosges proper, now climbing more steeply. It's now simply a matter of following this road - climbing and climbing through the trees - first passing les Trois Châteaux before passing a small, old 'lagoon', the Étang Herzog, now dropping down before a left fork that takes you up to the unmissable Château du Hohlandsbourg, a massive hilltop fortification (the biggest in Alsace) which has fantastic views from its walls. A major renovation programme saw the castle due to reopen in spring 2012. Head back to the 'main' road through the mountains and, now firmly on the descent, you pass signs to Château Pflixbourg. Sadly this is now a crumbling ruin, despite the shored up central tower, and entry to the site is forbidden on safety grounds.

The road descends to finally meet the route up the Fecht valley at St Giles, and you turn left onto it.

High level and low level routes now having merged, you come alongside the railway then climb away from it into the hamlet of d'Aspach, following V21 signs there to climb to a lovely viewpoint / picnic area over the valley and descending again alongside the railway.

Pass Wihr-au-Val station and meet the road to jink left and right keeping on the VV21 (the VV212 heads up the road to Wihr-au-Val). After passing through the northern end of Soultzbach another very scenic traffic-free section leads to Griesbach, following signage on small village roads to exit on yet another 'sauf ayant droit' (access only) track.

Enter the edge of Munster. The attractive town centre is down the walkway and through the tiny archway under the railway on your right, following rue du Pont to the D10, from where the town centre is at about ten o'clock.

To continue on to Metzeral ignore the turning off to Munster and carry

on the cycle route, turning right over the River Fecht and left just before the school, following the well-signed route onto allée du Chêne and to tiny Luttenbach. Head left back over the Fecht by Camping Amis de la Nature, following signs for Breitenbach. Here the route threads its way through the tiny centre, past the mairie, then alongside the Fecht river to the right before crossing it to come alongside the railway on the right and past Mulbach station. Jink right then left over the railway to join a lovely traffic-free section, decorated by painted bikes. Heading into Metzeral you meet the road - the VV21 is signed straight across and continues up to the head of the valley at tiny Mittlach, but our route just heads down the road to the left to Metzeral's small but attractive centre. You can cycle back to Munster from here or take a train.

The return from Munster to Colmar heads through Munster's lovely Albert Schweitzer park on a cycle lane that comes alongside the D417. Bear left onto the D10 and follow it into Gunsbach, where you'll find the Albert Schweitzer museum (and the less cerebral Maison du Fromage). By the mairie head down rue de la Gare, heading left onto the VV212 for beautiful riverside ride alongside the River Fecht. Simply follow the well-signed route, past Camping Beau Rivage, to rejoin your outward route to Wintzenheim by heading right onto the D43 then right and left across the main D417 and across the railway to pick up VV21.

Having followed your outward route back to Wintzenheim follow the road through the village centre and at the far edge turn left, following cycle signs to Turckheim, onto rue des Trois Épis and almost immediately left at a mini-roundabout. Head across a bridge over the main D417 and follow the road through the vineyards and into a housing estate at Turckheim. Follow the cycle lane through the suburbs to emerge near the centre, crossing a railway and then the river Fecht to meet the D10. The sumptuous town centre lies through a tower gateway ahead and to your left, whilst the onward route means heading right onto the D10 but almost immediately splitting off right, - through a small picnic area - and onto rue du Marechal de Lattre de Tassigny, with the Fecht now paralleling your route, down to your right. Bear right onto rue du Muguet and coming into Ingersheim pass a road bridge and look for a traffic-free bridge on the right - cross it and drop down onto the riverside path, the Fecht now on your left.

The tarmac cycle track peters out at the next road bridge; head back up to the road and pick up the D1bis at the junction here, signed Colmar and Wintzenheim. At the next roundabout take a second right down a more heavily trafficked road, the D11^{II}.

At the next roundabout pick up the well-hidden cycle lanes - their convoluted path takes you straight over here, onto the D418 and into Logelbach. Just follow this through the suburbs, under the railway and into Colmar on the route d'Ingersheim, heading to the pedestrianised heart of the city on rue des Unterlinden.

Accommodation

Hôtel-Bar des Vosges
58 Grand' Rue, Munster
03. 89.77.31.41 www.hotelbardesvosges.fr/
Decently priced Logis style accommodation.

Au Val St Grégoire
5, rue Saint Grégoire , Munster
03.89.77.36.22 www.hotel-munster.com

L'Hôtel Turenne
10 route de Bâle, Colmar
03.89.21.58.58 www.turenne.com
Secure bike parking for a small extra charge. Pricey but sumptuous and very convenient hotel .

Most budget options in Colmar are found in the area north-east of the train station and all offer a similar package for a similar price. They are well signed and include the Colbert (www.hotel-colbert.net) and well-known chains such as Kyriad and Etap.

Camping de Lill
1 allée du Camping, Horbourg Wihr
03.89.41.15.94 www.campingdelill.com
Around 2.8km east of Colmar centre

Bike Shops

Cycles Hausherr
65 rue Clemenceau (near the church)
Wintzenheim 03.89.27.14.54

Cycle Hop
5 rue de la République, Munster
06.07.16.56.35

Cycles Geiswiller
6 boulevard Champs de Mars, Colmar
03.89.41.30.59

La Cyclothèque
31 route d'Ingersheim, Colmar
03.89.79.14.18

The tour around the Fecht valley takes in some magnificent restricted access roads - virtually traffic-free in fact - like this one at Mulbach whimsically decorated with painted bikes

Many Vosges villages, including those in the Fecht valley are a riot of colour - as here at Turckheim

Munster and the Fecht Valley

Whilst Munster is an attractive town in its own right, it is its location near some of the Vosges's highest peaks, and the links to the local network of bike paths along the valley that really make it a great base for cyclists. You can drink in the magnificent hills from the ease of the valley bottom whilst tootling along quiet roads and traffic-free cycle routes.

Munster itself is centred around the market place in front of the church from where it's a short hop over the River Fecht to some magnificent cycling south of the river. If you are short on time or just want to rest your legs there are good train services with spacious bike storage areas running along the valley and back to Colmar.

| Day 3 | Colmar → Sélestat |

TOTAL DISTANCE / ELEVATION: **33 km / 341 m ascent** | **20 mi / 1119ft ascent**

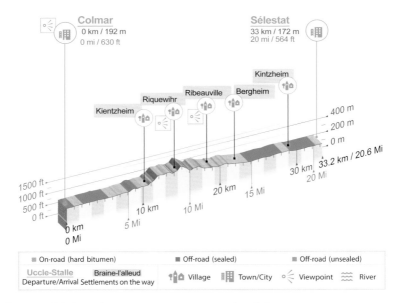

■ On-road (hard bitumen)	■ Off-road (sealed)	■ Off-road (unsealed)

Uccle-Stalle   Braine-l'alleud   🏘 Village   🏢 Town/City   ◦ Viewpoint   ≋ River
Departure/Arrival Settlements on the way

Day 3 Ride Notes

From the north-west edge of Colmar city centre pick up cycle lanes along the D418, route d'Ingersheim. Pass under the rail bridge and take the first right onto rue de la Bagatelle and next left onto rue de Vignes. Follow this to a T-junction and head right, onto rue de la Mittelharth. Follow this as it exits Colmar under the ring road. Bear left at the next split, which shortly leads past Café de la Harth. Follow signs for Centre de Loisirs (leisure centre) to come to a forest section and at the next T-junction go right and past the leisure centre on your left. Go left at next crossroads, signed as an 'Itinéraire Cyclable' to Sigolsheim and Bennwihr. Bend left over the river, and climb gently to the D10 and right onto it.

Head over the next roundabout, onto the D1bis, signed Bennwihr, then almost immediately turn left onto the agricultural road through the vineyards, signed as a cycle route to Sigolsheim. Follow the road through Sigolsheim and onto pretty Kientzheim. Arriving via the rue des Remparts the village centre is down to the left whilst right, by a crucifix, a road climbs into the vine covered hills. The route follows the latter, climbing to a split by another crucifix and picnic area, where

you bear left.

Follow the 'main' road, ignoring minor turnings, as you skirt the Vosges and crest a hill to drop down into Riquewihr. The route bears left at a T-junction and left again to skirt the small but often very busy village centre down to the right, bearing left out of town opposite the village entrance tower down to your right. Follow the signed minor roads to come into Hunawhir along rue de Riquewihr, where you jink right and left (again easy to miss), to head out of the village on rue Roger Kuhlman. This road wends its way through more delightful vineyards and past castle-topped peaks to descend into Ribeauville along rue des Vignobles. Head across the first main crossroads after entering the suburbs and swing right, signed Centre Ville. Descend on rue de la Marne and rue Klobb to emerge by the entrance tower to the medieval Haute Ville up to your left (tourist info and onward cycle route are down to the right).

Heading down the shop-laden main street swing left at its end, picking up the D1bis, signs confirming you are bound for Bergheim as you leave Ribeauville behind. Follow this road all the way to Bergheim, bending left by the signs to Thannenkirch and going right at the next small

128

roundabout into Bergheim centre, under the main tower gateway. Follow the cobbles down the pretty main street then out of town, shortly after the war memorial on the left split left, following cycle route signs for Kintzheim. Right on the edge of the village take a minor left turn onto an agricultural road ('engins agricoles') signed as a cycle route to Kintzheim.

You now follow the signed route along these extremely quiet backroads, crossing the D6 and D1bis in quick succession. Up to your left rises the imposing form and massive tourist draw of the fortress of Haut Koenigsbourg. Pass the little cycle shelter.

The signage changes hereabouts to a cyclist on a multi-coloured background. Continue to follow Kintzheim signs, entering the suburbs on rue de la Légion and heading over the D159 onto rue des Romains by the cemetery. Well-hidden signs here give you a choice - straight on to Châtenois and Villé or right to Sélestat and Elzach. Take the right onto allé de Stadtpfad and across a minor crossroads onto a superb cycle lane.

Now on the run in to Sélestat, the cycle lane runs alongside the D159 and passes over the A35 trunk road on a bridge, then straight across a couple of major roundabouts and left signed 'Centre Hospitalier', to follow route de Kintzheim towards Sélestat's centre. Look out for a

traffic-free cycle track (**easy to miss**) on your right through a small car park area that will take you over the rail tracks (look for the unusual brick tower in the distance over to your right to know you're in the right area - it's the spot just before the rue des Vosges on the right). Head left onto rue St. Léonard and left onto the main road at its end. Swing right onto the busy thoroughfare of avenue de la Liberté and straight on, onto the quieter rue de Quatrième Zouaves. Sélestat's centre is just to the left here.

Accommodation
Hôtel Majuscule
9 route de Sainte-Marie-Aux-Mines, Sélestat 03.88.92.92.88
www.hotelmajuscule.fr
Auberge des Allies
39 rue des Chevaliers, Sélestat
03.88.92.09.34   www.logishotels.com
Camping Les Cigognes
rue de la Première Division Française Libre, Sélestat, 03.88.92.03.98

Bike Shops
Jean-Phillippe Binder
82 Grand Rue, Ribeauville
03.89.73.65.87
Boespflug
5 rue Ste Barbe, Sélestat
03.88.92.05.14

Half-timbered buildings and vineyards are the picture postcard backdrop to this tour once you get north of Colmar - here seen at Hunawihr, between Riquewihr and Ribeauville

Colmar

Hugely historic and massively popular with visitors, Colmar is packed with ancient half-timbered houses and fine squares which all invite aimless and hugely enjoyable wandering and cafe hopping. There are plenty of specific points of interest too, top of most tourists list being the Unterlinden art museum and *the* picture that most of those queueing outside are no doubt eager to see, the Isenheim altarpiece. Also look out for the cathedral (Collégiale St-Martin), the Dominican church, Maison Pfister and the old customs house or Koïfhus. Really though the delight of Colmar is the sheer multitude of ancient buildings all linked by narrow alleys opening out into countless small squares. You'll inevitably find yourself strolling down and across the picturesque tourist magnet of Grand' Rue but there are plenty of quieter nooks and crannies too. The River Lauch cuts through the heart of the old town and is at the centre of the area known as La Petite Venise - Little Venice. This is also very much worth a look, boasting colourful ancient fishermen's dwellings on quai de la Poissonerie.

Boat trips are available on the River Lauch through the Petite Venise area of Colmar

For mapping see separate fold-out map

Wine Route Villages and Towns

Having reached the Vosges west of Colmar a multitude of villages nestle up to the eastern side of these exceptionally verdant mountains, all vying with each other for the most astounding floral displays on their buildings and the number of chances to taste the local wines they can offer the visitor. Here's a quick run down of village highlights for along the bike route. (Note there is a driving route called Route des Vins, or Wine Route - don't confuse this with your bike route and start following its signs, as it tends to use faster, busier roads. The bike route uses some blissfully quiet roads and tracks):

Eguisheim Wonderful little centre dominated by a statue of Pope Leo IX, the most important medieval German pope, who was born here. You'll also find more floral displays than you've ever seen in one place.

Turckheim Another very pretty village very firmly on the tourist trail, but fascinating nonetheless. Most well-known for its three doors, the Munster Door, Door of the Brand and the Door of France. The Night Watchman, a traditionally dressed Turckheim resident, cloaked in black and carrying a halberd and lamp makes the rounds at 10pm each night from May to October. As he strolls the protected city, he sings a number of Alsatian favorites.

Riquewihr Walled village with wonderfully preserved medieval houses and a château housing a postal museum - probably the busiest of all the wine route villages

Hunawihr 14th century walled church and a nearby wildlife centre for storks and otters amongst other things

Ribeauville Wonderful main street looking straight up to a ruined hilltop castle

Colourful and ancient villages in fantastic settings, such as Ribeauville (top) are linked by many virtually traffic-free wine-growers' roads such as that near Bergheim (bottom)

Day 4	Sélestat → Obernai

TOTAL DISTANCE / ELEVATION: **32 km / 455 m ascent** | **20 mi / 1493ft ascent**

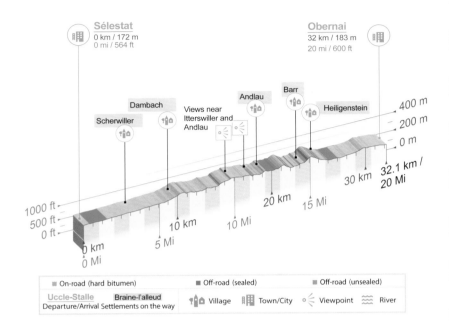

Day 4 Ride Notes

From Sélestat's centre head west down avenue de la Liberté and across a large traffic-intersection onto avenue Général de Gaulle, crossing the railway lines. Filter right at the first main junction onto rue de la Lohmuehle, heading to the second roundabout and left, almost immediately splitting right onto vieux chemin de Scherwiller to head into the countryside vineyards.

Follow this road for around 3km, all the way into Scherwiller and to a T-junction and left. The lovely village centre is left down rue de la Mairie, but the main cycle route continues on the main road before heading off next left, signed for the D35 for Châtenois, then turning first right up rue de Dieffenthal. Follow for just under 2.5km (it becomes residents and cyclists only part way up), where you turn left onto the D35, following this wider, busier road for another couple of kilometres, through the outskirts of Dambach-la-Ville and swinging left, staying on the D35, at a junction with the D210, signed

Blienschwiller. This brings you under the town gates, the centre being down to your left. The main route continues on the D35, exiting under the town gates, following the road all the way to Blienschwiller.

In Blienschwiller follow signs for Nothalten and Barr. Turn left having passed through Blienschwiller centre, on the edge of the village, signed Nothalten and Barr. Follow the D35 through Nothalten and Ittersviller (left at the T-junction here), climbing through increasingly spectacular scenery, following D35 signs for Andlau at the junction after Ittersviller and picking up the D253 signed for Andlau on the left shortly afterwards. As you pass the D603 on the right glorious views open up over Andlau in the valley below. Descending steeply into Andlau centre follow signs for Mittelbergheim, leaving on the D62. Turn left about 900 metres out of Andlau (there are in fact two lefts next to each other - you want the second), to climb on a very minor road through vineyards, heading right at the first split. Follow this delectably quiet road, ignoring minor turnings off, all the way to

Mittelbergheim.

In Mittelbergheim head across a minor crossroads and descend to the D362 and left, away from the village. Follow the 362 all the way to Barr and at the first main crossroads head straight across, signed 'Centre Ville.'

In the cobbled heart of Barr bear left then right, to come onto Rue Taufflieb, swinging right then left to emerge in a lovely square by the Hôtel de Ville and tourist office. Head on the main road past here and at a split bear left on the D35, signed Heiligenstein.

In Heiligenstein take a right turn onto a minor road signed Bourgheim (rue Ehret Wantz). Descend to a level crossing and just before the crossing turn left onto a tiny tarmac track, parallel to the railway on your right. Follow this restricted access road to emerge near Goxwiller, picking up D709 signs for Bernardswiller. Here meet the D109 and turn right on it, heading to a roundabout where you head straight across signed 'Obernai Centre'. Now just follow signs for the centre, where you'll find a fantastic collection of ancient buildings.

Accommodation

Hôtel St Odile
9 rue du Marché, Obernai
03.88.95.48.88 www.hotelsainteodile.com

La Diligence
23 place du Marché, Obernai
03.88.95.55.69 www.hotel-diligence.com

Camping Municipal
1 rue de Berlin, Obernai 03.88.95.38.48

Statue celebrating wine above Andlau

A cracking viewpoint above Andlau. The variety of signing along this route can be a bit bewildering; now coming into the northern Vosges mountains you are following the multi-coloured cycle signage seen here. See page 116 for full signage details.

Day 5   Obernai → Strasbourg

TOTAL DISTANCE / ELEVATION: **35 km / 159 m ascent** | 22 mi / 522ft ascent

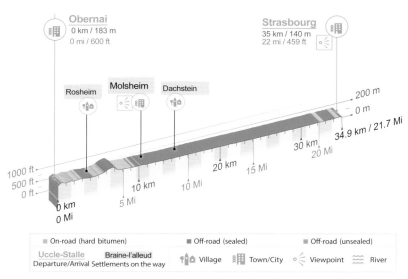

Obernai
0 km / 183 m
0 mi / 600 ft

Strasbourg
35 km / 140 m
22 mi / 459 ft

Rosheim

Molsheim

Dachstein

200 m
0 m

34.9 km / 21.7 Mi
30 km
20 Mi
20 km
15 Mi
10 km
10 Mi
5 Mi
0 km
0 Mi

1000 ft
500 ft
0 ft

■ On-road (hard bitumen)   ■ Off-road (sealed)   ■ Off-road (unsealed)
Uccle-Stalle   Braine-l'alleud   ♦♦ Village   ▦ Town/City   ∘ Viewpoint   ≋ River
Departure/Arrival Settlements on the way

Day 5 Ride Notes

From the centre of Obernai head on the road down the left hand side of the cathedral (as you face the front) and take the first right signed A35 and Molsheim.

Take the next left up rue de la Montagne (not extreme left up rue de la Paix). At the first split ignore the left signed sentier Viticole and drop back down into countryside, keeping right at the first split.

Ignore smaller turnings off to right and left and follow the road into Bischoffsheim. At the junction at the end of rue des Cerisiers turn right onto rue Monseigneur Frey and follow it to a crossroads. Head straight across here (town centre up to your left) onto rue du Mont des Frères. Follow the road to its end on the edge of the village where it turns into a cycle track.. Follow the cycle track to the D207 and hop across, turning left onto the accompanying cycle track.

On the edge of Rosheim turn left onto route de Bischoffsheim (signed Boersch and Mont St-Odile) then second right - still called route de Bischoffsheim, to meet the D35. Turn left here, into the village centre, under the town gate tower.

Head right up rue Braun which lies opposite the tourist information office. Follow rue Braun as it bends right then left to pass under another town gate tower to a roundabout. Head straight over signed Rosenwiller on the D435. Almost immediately this peels off left, but you carry straight on, climbing into the countryside as the road becomes a restricted access one. Follow it to descend over a major road and into the suburbs of Dorlisheim. Turn right onto rue Ettore Bugatti, following to a mini-roundabout there taking the third right onto the cycle lane along rue des Remparts. Look out for cycle lanes which take you left and across another road, onto rue Luther. Follow Luther as it bends left and merges with another road from the right, to come to a church. Follow cycle signs on the right here, onto av Général de Gaulle and follow it all the way over a tiny bridge across the River Schiffbach. Follow the tarmac track that comes alongside a railway line on your left and turn left over the line at the next road junction, continuing on over the bridge, using the pavement cycle lane to come onto rue Henri Meck. Turn right onto rue Sainte-Odile and just past the Coop store on the left pick up the cycle track by the river to your left. Follow the river on this track, passing under the D2422 (to divert to the town centre head left up the D2422, av de la Gare, and then right through the town gate tower on to rue de Strasbourg which takes you to the lovely main square).

Meet rue Charles Mistler. Turn right,
heading across rue des Sports and out
of Molsheim, passing the campsite and
swimming pool on the left.
Cross a bridge and swing left, following
the tarmac path before bearing right
to emerge at a road roundabout. Take
the exit for Furdenheim, Dachstein and
Ergersheim (D93), picking up the excellent
roadside cycle track. Stay on it across the
next roundabout, onto the D30,
simply staying on this road all the way to
the canal de la Bruche just on the southern
edge of Ergersheim, passing Dachstein on
the way.
Turn right onto the signed tarmac path
(Molsheim - Offenburg) alongside the
canal on its southern side. This lovely path
passes through some beautiful countryside.
Follow it for around 17km to swap banks
and head away from the canal, to come
alongside the river Ill. Head under the
main route de Schirmeck (D392). Don't
cross the river on the traffic-free bridge,
but stay on the northern bank, to join quai
du Brulig. Look out for the cycle path
that splits off right to take you under a
main road and then under the huge A35
autoroute. Soon after that a cycle path
splits off right, which you follow under a
rail bridge. At the next road bridge, pont
Louis Pasteur, find your way up and over
it to join a path along the opposite river
bank, with the river now on your left.

Stick by the river all the way to the Ponts
Couverts. The heart of Strasbourg now
lies ahead of you, over these beautiful
'covered bridges'.

Accommodation
Hôtel Patricia
1a rue du Puits, Strasbourg
03.88.32.14.60 www.hotelpatricia.fr
Hôtel Couvent des Franciscain
18 rue du Faubourg de Pierre, Strasbourg
03.88.32.93.93 www.hotel-franciscain.net
Hostel Deux Rives
rue des Cavaliers, Strasbourg
03.88.45.54.20
www.fuaj.org
Auberge René Cassin
9 rue de l'Auberge de Jeunesse,
Strasbourg
03.88.30.26.46
Camping Montagne Vert
2 rue Robert Forrer, Strasbourg
03.86.37.95.83 www.aquadis-loisirs.com

Bike Shops
Accro Bike
22 rue Fbg de Pierre, Strasbourg
03.88.21.43.43 www.accrobike.fr
Cycles Blondin
5 rue Brigade Alsace Lorraine, Strasbourg
03.88.36.22.15

Molsheim's elaborately decorated central square is an ideal stopping off point

Strasbourg

Strasbourg's magnificent cathedral is detailed in the don't miss section, but like Basel at the start of the route, this is an extremely civilised and relaxing city in which just to wander and enjoy the surroundings and the many diversions. The cosmopolitan atmosphere of this self-styled 'crossroads of Europe' is reinforced by the variety of languages you are likely to hear on the streets, from the local Alsatian (a kind of German dialect - though very different from standard German - which is often mingled in with French, depending on the conversation) to a variety of European languages brought here as it's the seat of several European Union institutions including the Council and Parliament.

The centre is enclosed in a watery and very picturesque oval formed by the River Ill and its canalised northern spur which both make for some lovely waterside walks, especially to the south of the centre around the area of half-timbered houses known as La Petite France. In particular the area has the unusual so-called covered bridges and a dam, all built as part of the city's ancient fortifications, but today providing a postcard photographer's prize view.

The canal de la Bruche (top) allows a wonderfully quiet countryside approach to the big city of Strasbourg (below), whose gleaming European parliament and Court of Human Rights lie a short bike or tram ride from the centre (bikes allowed on trams)

For mapping see separate fold-out map

Most of the museums lie just south of the cathedral but there is perhaps most pleasure to be had from wandering the streets and discovering the local shops, cafes and restaurants. If you need refuelling at journey's end the local Alsatian cookery, often based around smoked and salted pork, is abundant and most certainly filling. To keep away from the tourist traps around the cathedral try a 'winstub' on rue du Fauborg Saverne. Or, if you have plenty of energy left for cycling, Strasbourg has a pretty good network of often segregated cycle lanes - especially useful for exploring more far flung attractions such as the clean, futuristic looking area around the European Parliament and Court of Human Rights and the lovely nearby parc de l'Orangerie or the pont de l'Europe over the Rhine to the town of Kehl in Germany.

Just one corner of Strasbourg cathedral's entrance is enough to dominate this picture; it also shows that bikes mingle easily with pedestrians in traffic-free areas

Northern Burgundy

Route Info

Northern Burgundy

This gentle 6 day amble along canals and quiet roads combines the ever so French vineyards of Burgundy with cosmopolitan Dijon and Auxerre. The first 3 days track a traffic-free towpath along the Canal de Bourgogne before arching west, mainly on minor roads, through the vineyards of Chablis and on towards Auxerre, where you complete the trip on the Canal du Nivernais (considered one of the most beautiful canals in France) down to Clamecy where you can catch a train back to Dijon.

Grade EASY

Start / finish   Dijon / Clamecy

Route length   303km / 188 miles

Length of Suggested Days

32-68 km / 20-42 miles
Some long days with significant climbing - however much of it is on the very steady inclines of canal towpath

Route Surface & Signing

52-57 % off-road
Generally well-signed, well-surfaced canal towpath to Montbard - a cinch to follow anyway once you have found your way out of Dijon. Just north of Montbard the surface deteriorates just a little then uses mainly quiet minor roads before a final unsigned 9km stretch of rather potholed towpath to Auxerre. From Auxerre to Clamecy the majority of the riding is on sealed, smooth surfaces.

Access to Dijon

Regular trains to Dijon from Paris Gare de Lyon (1hr45)
From journey's end at Clamecy there are a small number of 3 hour trains via Laroche Migennes back to Dijon and quite a number of longer connections.

i Offices

Dijon Place Darcy 08.92.70.05.58
www.dijon-tourisme.com
Pouilly-en-Auxois   Le Colombier
03.80.90.74.24 www.pouilly-auxois.com
Montbard   Place Henri Vincenot,
03.80.92.53.81, www.ot-montbard.fr
Helpful tourist office by the Gare SNCF
Chablis
1, rue du Maréchal de Lattre de Tassigny,
03.86.42.80.80   www.chablis.net
Auxerre 2, quai de la République
03.86.52.06.19   www.ot-auxerre.fr
Clamecy 7-9 rue du Grand Marché
03.86.27.02.51 www.nievre-tourisme.com

www.burgundy-by-bike.com
Superbly compendious source of web info for 600km or so of official bike route

Ideal cycling conditions on the Burgundy Canal

For mapping see separate fold-out map

Don't Miss

Dijon's Green Spaces

Besides sight-seeing and cycling, Dijon is an excellent place for having a rest and watching the world go by. Several very green lungs adorn the city. There's the Port du Canal, where day 1 of the ride begins at the very south east corner of the city. Other excellent places to prevaricate prior to setting off include the Jardin l'Arquebuse (by Gare SNCF) and Square Darcy (by the tourist office).

The Vault of Pouilly

Just north of Pouilly the Canal de Bourgogne goes underground. The 333m tunnel, known as the vault, dates back to the 1820s and its 32 ventilation shafts can be seen from the cycle path that runs by its side. As you peer down into the abyss spare a thought for the 200 construction workers who died for the cause. Pouilly tourist office organizes boat trips through the vault and promises a commentary complete with 'historical anecdotes'.

Fontenay Abbey

This 11km return side trip on minor roads from Montbard pays back the effort many times over. A Cistercian monastery founded in 1118, Fontenay became a world heritage site in 1981, owing to its Roman architecture and former status as a paper mill during the French Revolution. Its lush grounds and forest footpaths are a treat to stroll round and the abbey itself is open all year round. www.abbayedefontenay.com

Chardonnay Grapes

The 20 or so wine producing villages in the Chablis region owe their unique character to the special qualities of the Chardonnay grape, whose defining taste accrues from a high concentration of fossilized oyster shells in the limestone soil. To taste the difference the oysters really make without shelling out too much, go the extra miles to one of the vineyard outlets south of the town, downriver.

Dijon

Warnings from the tourist office that there are few cycle lanes in Dijon do not deter a healthy proportion of cyclists from taking to the intricate street layout of this attractive city. Dijon is a joy to wander around, both smart and surprising and actually small enough to explore on foot. There is a vibrant atmosphere around the old centre, which has the feel of being designed without cars in mind.

Many of the abundant ancient buildings are a riot of colourful roof tiles. The sightseeing heart of the city is the Ducal Palace and the shopping heart the place de la Libération.

Dijon's historic centre has some magnificent public buildings, such as the Ducal Palace

Day 1   Dijon → Pouilly-en-Auxois

TOTAL DISTANCE / ELEVATION: **58 km / 529 m ascent** | 36 mi / 1735 ft ascent

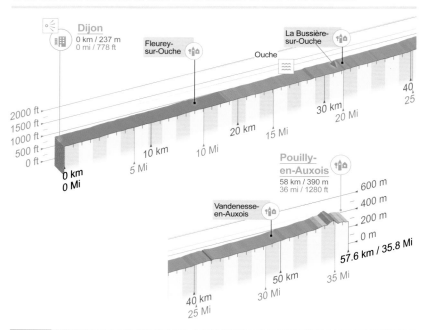

Day 1   Dijon → Pouilly-en-Auxois via Châteauneuf

TOTAL DISTANCE / ELEVATION: **55 km / 681 m ascent** | 34 mi / 2234 ft ascent

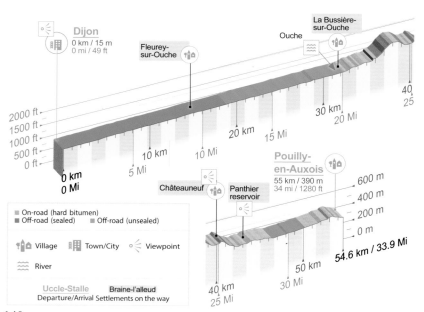

- On-road (hard bitumen)
- Off-road (sealed)   ■ Off-road (unsealed)

🏠 Village   🏢 Town/City   ◦≶ Viewpoint

≈≈ River

Uccle-Stalle   **Braine-l'alleud**
Departure/Arrival Settlements on the way

Day 1   Ride Notes

Leaving the comforts of Dijon may be a bit of a wrench but the beginning of the ride is easy to negotiate. At the south-west tip of the city, 2km south of the Gare SNCF, the waterside cycle path at the pont du Canal heads west towards Lac Kir. The canal de Bourgogne cycle route begins in earnest in the lakeside scenic public park. The going is good on a confidence giving concrete surface, enabling you to look around and clock the range of activities on offer; water-sports, tennis, trim trail, bike hire [Location vélos Lac Kir 06.32.35.22.16]. As the cycle path runs away from Dijon you're never far from supplies as you pass by a sequence of canal side villages. At Pont-de-Pany after 15km the concrete downshifts to good quality track - still suitable for touring tyres.

If you are looking for an alternative to riding the canal all the way to Pouilly, a good option is to delay your breakaway until La Bussière-sur-Ouche. Here, peel away right from the canal and climb steeply on the quiet, winding road up to the picture postcard hill town of Châteauneuf, above the forest of Bouhey. This detour cuts a few kilometres from the day's journey, though the climb ensures there is little time saved. For variety though, it's very worthwhile. Leaving Châteauneuf (which has café and hotel opportunities), the green cycle signs plunge you down towards the Réservoir de Panthier. At the foot of the hill take go left on the D977B to Vandenesse-en-Auxois and then immediate right over the bridge up to Réservoir de Panthier and its pleasant campsite. About 700m after leaving lovely views over the reservoir take an unsigned road that joins acutely from your left. Follow this all the way to a T-junction on the edge of Vandenesse-en-Auxois and go left to the D977^B to turn right back to the canal. Rejoin

the towpath on your right.
Ride on as far as Pouilly-en-Auxois, undaunted by the short and rather noisy signed detour (the canal itself heads underground), taking you underneath the reverberating A38 and into Pouilly.

Accommodation

Le Thurot
4-6 passage Thurot, Dijon
03.80.43.57.46, www.hotel-thurot.com
Five minutes ride, going left, from the Gare SNCF. There's a secure barrier for locking bikes to in the pleasant courtyard.

Hôtel le Sauvage
64 rue Monge, Dijon
03.80.41.31.21 www.hotellesauvage.fr
Beautiful half-timbered building, decent rooms and secure garage parking for your bike.

Hôtel-Restaurant de la Poste
place de la Libération, Pouilly-en-Auxois
03.80.90.86.44 (garage for cycle storage)
www.hoteldelapostepouilly.fr

Camping du Lac Kir Dijon
03.80.43.54.72 www.camping-dijon.com
Near the canal on the route exiting Dijon.

Le Lac de Panthier
Réservoir de Panthier
2km north of Vandenesse-en-Auxois and directly on the Châteauneuf option
03.80.49.21.94 ww.lac-de-panthier.com

Bike Shops

Cycles Dutrion
29 rue Pasteur, Dijon, 03.80.66.54.50
www.cycles-dutrion.com

Pouilly Evasion
avenue du Général de Gaulle,
Pouilly-en-Auxois
03.80.90.86.39

The Burgundy Canal

The 200km long Canal de Bourgogne links north and east Burgundy, joining towns, villages and the magnificent city of Dijon. Along with the Nivernais, it's viewed by many French people as one of the country's most picturesque canals and incredibly it's been in development since the early 17th century. However, it wasn't until 1822 that the last stretch was completed, allowing boats to travel right across the country from the Seine to the Rhône. The first day's riding finishes at the compact little town of Pouilly-en-Auxois, which sits astride the Burgundy canal at the highest point of the highest canal in France - nearly 400m. It has everything you need for a stop-over, with the considerable bonus (after 58kms in the saddle) that alls amenities are within a stone's throw of each other - and of the canal. These include a bike shop, banks, tourist information, restaurants and a tasty outdoor market. At the canal museum here - Cap Canal - there is the option to get on a boat through the 300m plus long canal tunnel to the north of town (see Don't Miss section) and continue the ride further on.

Day 2	Pouilly-en-Auxois → Semur-en-Auxois

TOTAL DISTANCE / ELEVATION: **42 km / 212 m ascent** | 26 mi / 695 ft ascent

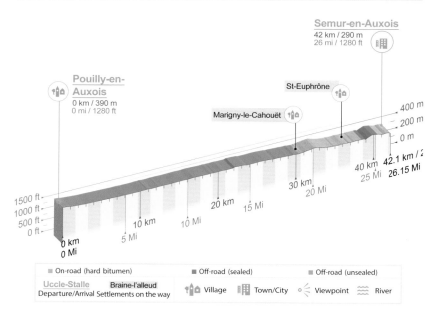

Semur-en-Auxois
42 km / 290 m
26 mi / 1280 ft

Pouilly-en-Auxois
0 km / 390 m
0 mi / 1280 ft

St-Euphrône

Marigny-le-Cahouët

400 m
200 m
0 m

40 km   42.1 km /
25 Mi   26.15 Mi

30 km
20 Mi

20 km   15 Mi

10 km   10 Mi

1500 ft
1000 ft
500 ft
0 ft

0 km
0 Mi

5 Mi

■ On-road (hard bitumen)	■ Off-road (sealed)	■ Off-road (unsealed)
Uccle-Stalle Braine-l'alleud Departure/Arrival Settlements on the way	★↑👁 Village ▓▓ Town/City ○< Viewpoint	≈≈ River

Day 2 Ride Notes

Today's ride hugs the canal and allows you to enjoy glorious countryside for much of the way and gradient-wise the locks are stacked firmly in your favour. The going on the waterside track is once again good, with plenty of village stops. Once past Braux at 25km the locks come thick and fast and the ride becomes a staccato descent down a huge flight of them. Though a little gravelly in the early stages the surface is generally well-kept and improves as you move north.

Around 30km after leaving Pouilly meet a small bridge on the edge of Marigny-le-Cahouët and head left over it. Almost straight away turn left onto the D10^C, signed Semur. Follow this road for some 7.5km, passing through St-Euphrône, to come to the D907 and head straight across onto the D103^B.

Follow this road to a T-junction and right, picking up the excellent tarmac cycle track on the far side of the road. Follow this all the way until it joins the road and at the next roundabout head left, signed 'Centre Ville'. Bend left and climb steadily on this road for about 250m then head right, following small green and white cycle route signs, onto rue de Lattre de Tassigny and left onto the D954, a handsome cobbled street. At the end of here you'll find yourself at the tourist office on your left. The ancient town centre of Semur is just through the arched entrance next to it.

Accommodation

🏨 *Hôtel du Commerce*
19, rue de la Liberté, Semur-en-Auxois
03.80.96.64.40 www.hotel-du-commerce.fr
🏨 *Hôtel des Cymaises*
7 rue du Renaudot, Semur-en-Auxois
03.80.97.21.44 www.hotelcymaises.com
🏕 *Lac de Pont* Pont-et-Massene
03.80.97.01.26 www.camping-lacdepont.fr
3km south of Semur but just off your route in to the town.

© Sylviane Moss Creative Commons

The river Armançon at Semur-en-Auxois

Semur-en-Auxois

One of those French towns veritably dripping with history and beauty - and so a
big tourist draw. It has a great natural setting on a rocky outcrop and a huge array of
ancient buildings. Its centrepiece is the handsome thirteenth century church of Notre-
Dame but there is also a castle and ample opportunity for wandering through streets
lined with some opulent architecture.

Day 3   Semur-en-Auxois → Montbard

TOTAL DISTANCE / ELEVATION: **41 km / 393 m ascent** | **25.5 mi / 1289 ft ascent**

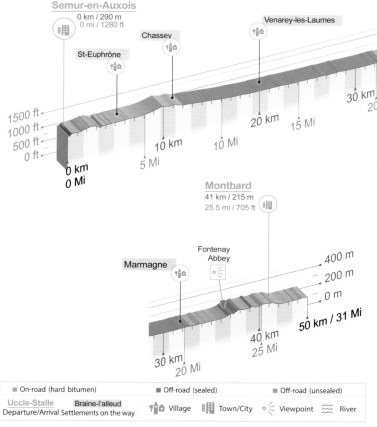

■ On-road (hard bitumen)   ■ Off-road (sealed)   ■ Off-road (unsealed)

Uccle-Stalle	Braine-l'alleud						
Departure/Arrival	Settlements on the way	🏠 Village	🏢 Town/City	○ Viewpoint	≋ River

Day 3 Ride Notes

Though roughly the same length as yesterday's ride today requires much less thought and effort. No need for maps - just retrace your route out of Semur to the towpath and turn northwards to hug the canal and enjoy the countryside. Gradient-wise the locks are stacked firmly in your favour again. Despite rolling hills and village temptations there's a real danger that you'll find yourself hurtling towards Montbard like a runaway stairlift, averaging 25kmh. Though a little gravelly in the early stages the surface is generally well-kept and improves as you move north. As you pull into Montbard you're even honoured with a final stretch of concrete.

The only navigational test comes with the signed detour to Fontenay Abbey. Leave the canal at Nogent-Le-Petit, heading north on the D119 across the river Brenne. Bear left at a right hand bend and after paralleling the railway to your right swing right under it and meet the D905 in Marmagne. Go left then right by the church onto the D32, following it all the way to Fontenay Abbey.
Retrace your steps all the way back and under the rail bridge where you go right. Follow this track and bear right back under the railway, onto rue Lamartine, to meet the D905 in Montbard. Turn left here and next major left to cross back over the river. The town centre is a short hop to your right.

Accommodation

Hôtel de l'Ecu
7, rue Auguste Carré, Montbard
03.80.92.53.81
www.hotelecu-montbard.fr
Free internet access, garage bike space

Hôtel de la Gare
10 av. Foch , Montbard   03.80.92.02.12
www.hotel-de-la-gare-montbard.com/
Reasonably priced option

Camping Municipal
rue Michel Servet, Montbard
03.80.92.69.50
www.ville-montbard.fr/camping.html

Montbard & Fontenay Abbey

Montbard is no bustling metropolis but it is large enough to be an urban shock to the system after long stretches of towpath. Many people use Montbard as a base when visiting Fontenay Abbey, 11km return ride to the east. Besides this and other historical attractions the town offers plenty for lovers of wine, walking and the arts. In particular search out the Phénix Cinema - even if you are not an art-house cinema fan you might well appreciate the fading Art Deco facade or the cosy bar and outside tables.
The slopes of its centre will also come as some surprise after the canal's terrain, but a stroll along the banks of the river La Brenne or through the Park Buffon are a nice warm up for 68km in the saddle on the following section.

The towpath heading towards Montbard couldn't be much easier - a nice freewheeling surface and lush surroundings (above). Founded in the 12th century, Fontenay Abbey (below) is one of the oldest Cistercian abbeys in existence and is only a detour of a few miles north of the canal near Montbard.

© Sylviane Moss Creative Commons

Day 4 **Montbard → Chablis**

TOTAL DISTANCE / ELEVATION: **68 km / 671 m ascent** | **42 mi / 2201 ft ascent**

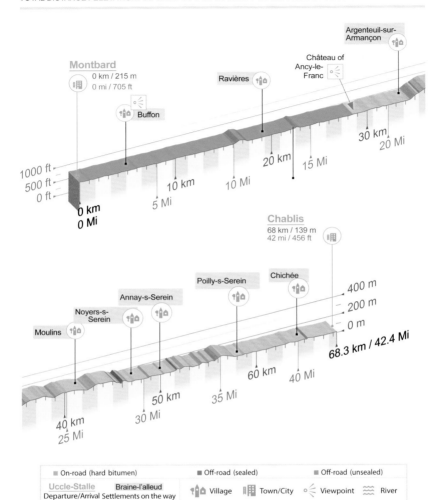

■ On-road (hard bitumen)	■ Off-road (sealed)	■ Off-road (unsealed)

Uccle-Stalle	**Braine-l'alleud**	🏘 Village	🏢 Town/City	∘⊰ Viewpoint	〰 River
Departure/Arrival	Settlements on the way				

Ancy-le-Franc and Chablis

A short detour off the canal, just as you leave it, the Château at Ancy-le-Franc is certainly worth at least a brief stop-off. A fine 16th century renaissance building - said to be the finest in France outside of Fontainebleu.

Noyers-sur-Serein has been described as a stunningly unspoilt medieval town and features half-timbered houses, some with remarkable carvings, all set in a loop in the river. It's most definitely worth the two mile there and back trip up the D86.

Deep in Chardonnay country and surrounded by plains of vines, Chablis is a smallish town that's awash with water as well as wine. Public transport is a little thin on the ground though (good job you've got your bike then). The River Serein runs through the town and there are well established wine tasting walks which meander beside (and perhaps sometimes into) the river, taking in commercial vineyards en route. These are promoted by the local tourist office if you have the time and the taste for it. Wines and other local produce are available at the Sunday market.

Day 4   Ride Notes

Back on the canal de Bourgogne heading north-west, the gradient is favourable. However after the Grande Forge at Buffon at 6km the surface deteriorates a little for the first time since Dijon, though not seriously. Ride on past Cry-sur-Armançon, using the names on the lock houses to establish your location (assuming that there are no greenway signs on this section of the path, as was the case at the time of writing). At Cusy bid the by now rather uneven path along the canal farewell. Turn left on the D905 for 200m, then right onto the D109 and head up to Argenteuil-sur-Armançon. Despite the 2km climb the road is quiet and the surface blissfully even. Continue up to Moulins-en-Tonnerrois, signed left in Argenteuil. At the D86 go right, signed Yrouerre and Tonnerre (though Noyers is worth a detour up to the left - see opposite), 2km further on leaving onto the D45 signed Annay-sur-Serein, continuing on peaceful, undulating roads. At Perrigny pick up the D200 for the short hop to Annay and there look out for the attractive Touring-Club de France sign (pictured opposite) and turn left onto the rue de Chablis. Follow to the D45 and turn left (Môlay village is just to your right).

From here it's a gentle run following D45 signs, across the D944, as you enter serious vineyard country. Chemilly and Chichée herald your approach to Chablis. Coming into Chablis following your nose will bring you to the centre.

Accommodation

🏨 *Hôtel de la Poste*
24 rue Auxerroise, Chablis
03.86.42.11.94 www.hotel-poste-chablis.com

🏨 *Relais de la Belle Étoile*
4, rue des Moulins, Chablis
03.86.18.96.08   www.chablis-france.fr
Very comfortable rooms as you would expect from the Logis chain. Secure garage space for bikes and buffet breakfast

⛺ *Camping Municipal*
route des Sept Miraux, Chablis
03.86.42.44.39 A few minutes from the centre

In Annay, ready to descend the Serein valley

© Peter Curbishley Creative Commons

The quiet river Serein runs through Chablis

Day 5 | Chablis → Auxerre

TOTAL DISTANCE / ELEVATION: **32 km / 402 m ascent** | 20 mi / 1319 ft ascent

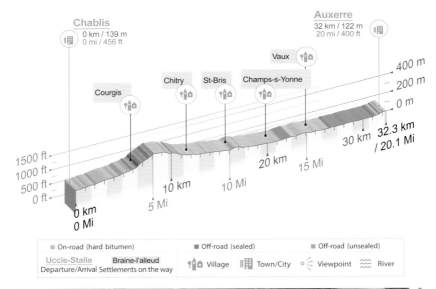

On-road (hard bitumen)	Off-road (sealed)	Off-road (unsealed)

Uccle-Stalle | Braine-l'alleud | ⬤ Village | 🏢 Town/City | ◦⟨ Viewpoint | ≈ River
Departure/Arrival Settlements on the way

© Chelmsfordblue Creative Commons

Auxerre's town centre attractions include the Tour d'Horloge

Day 5   Ride Notes

Get your climbing in early is the motto for today, with a steep wake up call from Chablis to Courgis. From rue Auxerroise in Chablis centre head west and pick up D62 signs to Courgis, which becomes the D462 at a roundabout on the outskirts. Meet the D62 again, heading right for Courgis. Vineyards now abound as you climb through Courgis to pick up D62 signs for Chitry and the views become intoxicating.

After passing under the A6 autoroute a well-earned descent lands you in attractive Chitry, staying on the D62 through the village of St. Bris (heading across the D956) and crossing over the D606 and a railway into Champs-sur-Yonne centre where you pass the mairie and then left down the ungrand Grand' Rue. Follow until meeting a junction with a little bridge on your right and head over it. Head right onto the D606 to Avalon and just across the Pont de Vaux bridge briefly join the tarmac canal path on the right before being dumped back on the road.

Stay on the road through Vaux and rejoin the canal path at Écluse D'Augy 79. Follow the canal du Nivernais for the remaining 6km to Auxerre, past the home of Auxerre F.C. and the new outdoor velodrome, whose track is 333m. Unlike the smooth concrete surface of the velodrome these last few kilometres are full of holes, so hold on tight for the final half hour. The path runs all the way down to the quai de la Republic, improving in quality towards the end, where you'll find the Maison du Tourisme by the Yonne river. The town centre is easily (if steeply) accessed by heading up rue Lebeuf by the tourist office.

Accommodation

🛏 *Le Seignelay*
2 rue du Pont, Auxerre
03.86.52.03.48   www.leseignelay.com
Secure parking and free Wi-Fi

⛺ *Camping municipal d'Auxerre*
8, route de Vaux 03.86.52.11.15
camping.mairie@auxerre.com

Bike Shop

🚲 *Cycles Guenin*
5 rue Brazza, Auxerre
03.86.51.28.06 www.cycles-guenin.fr

Auxerre

A hill town of narrow lanes and open squares and an interesting riverside area with fine views, especially around Pont Paul Bert. The cathedral here is unfinished, and the abbey church of St Germain is also worth a look, especially for its ancient crypt. Other pleasant areas include the spot around the town hall (Hôtel de Ville) and the place des Cordeliers and the nearby Tour d'Horloge city gateway.

© Nelson Minar Creative Commons

Auxerre's splendid waterfront

Day 6 | Auxerre → Clamecy

TOTAL DISTANCE / ELEVATION: **62 km / 487 m ascent** | 38.5 mi / 1598 ft ascent

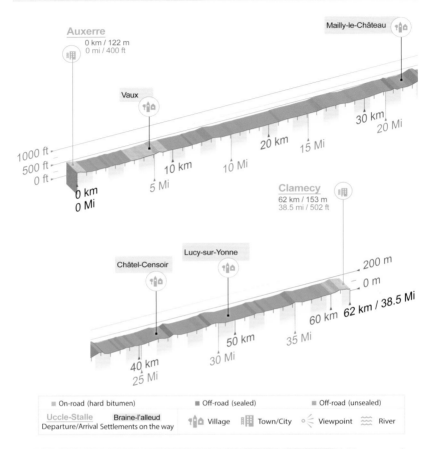

Legend:

▪ On-road (hard bitumen)	▪ Off-road (sealed)	▪ Off-road (unsealed)

Uccle-Stalle **Braine-l'alleud**
Departure/Arrival   Settlements on the way   🏘 Village   🏢 Town/City   ○⟨ Viewpoint   〰 River

Many towns along the Nivernais Canal give excellent views over the canal and river, as here at Mailly-le-Château

© AEngineer Creative Commons

Day 6 Ride Notes

Retrace your route alongside the Yonne to Champs-sur-Yonne and continue alongside the river, passing Pont de Vaux bridge on the left. The excellent quality path follows the canalised Yonne south of Vincelles to the bridge at the attractive town of Cravant. At the railway bridge just south of Cravant swap sides to the eastern bank.

Shortly past the bridge at Mailly-la-Ville you are in 'rochers' country - limestone blocks much frequented by climbers and even the occasional peregrine falcon.

Continue on the towpath, past Châtel-Censoir, to the bridge at Lucy-sur-Yonne where you pick up the D211 along the western side of the canal, jinking right then left over the N151 to rejoin the canal towpath. Follow the towpath for another 5.75km or so where the signed route leaves the towpath and follows the D144 under a railway and over the N151 into Clamecy, jinking right and left over rue Jean Jaurés into the medieval centre.

Accommodation

Auberge de la Chapelle
5 place Bethleem, Clamecy
03.86.27.11.55 www.auberge-la-chapelle.com
Camping de Pont Picot
On the southern edge of town on route des Chevroches 03.86.27.05.97

Villages and towns of the Avallonnais

Heading south of Champs-sur-Yonne there are a string of attractive villages and towns on or near the Canal du Nivernais; the fortified village of Mailly-le-Château, panoramic views at Châtel-Censoir, pretty little Lucy-sur-Yonne and your day's end at Clamecy. Clamecy was known for its riverside community of 'flotteurs' - workers who made up logs floated downstream to here into huge rafts to be floated on to Paris.

Taking in the tranquility of the Nivernais Canal

Brittany

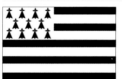

1	Route number (see following pages)
----	Railway
■■■■	Greenway - sealed (Voie Verte)
═══	Greenway - unsealed (Voie Verte)
────	Signed road route (Véloroute)

Note: unnumbered véloroutes are very short sections

There are over 800 kilometres of greenway and véloroute in Brittany. Much of this developing network is on former rail lines, towpaths and forest roads. When it is completed, it will cover some 2,000 kilometres, half on traffic-free trails. Eight long distance routes will (and in part already do) crisscross Brittany; many of the routes described here will become part of one of these longer routes. For more detail see pg 173 and www.randobreizh.com Nantes and the surrounding area is actually in the modern Pays-de-la-Loire area but both historically and culturally it is still firmly part of Brittany. It's also the southern end of the Nantes-Brest canal ride and so is included here.

Culture, Food & History

The pleasures of Breton food and drink are many. Calfodfpotfe is a pork and vegetable hotpot. Cotriade is a fish stew and Far Breton is a kind of custard pie often containing prunes or other variants. There is little wine production to speak of but locally produced cider, still or sparkling is popular and there is a pear cider. The Pommeau of Brittany is a blend of Breton cider brandy and fresh apple juice aged in oak casks. Lambic is a Breton cider brandy aged four years and La Fine Bretagne is one aged for ten, twelve or more years. Breton beers include Cervoise Lancelot, a light amber beer and Telenn Du, a soft, dark beer. Coreff de Morlaix and Blanche Hermine are also well known.

The Breton language (Brezhoneg) is most likely to be heard used by older people in rural areas of the west of Brittany and is much in evidence in place names. Out of a population in Brittany of around four million, there are thought to be around a quarter of a million fluent Breton speakers but the number is fast declining, despite efforts being made to promote use of the language. There's a network of schools using Breton, a little Breton language TV and radio and some municipalities have a policy of bilingualism. There is a number of Breton language magazines. In eastern Brittany, Gallo (more akin to French) is sometimes spoken alongside Breton and French.

A widely known feature of Brittany is its prehistoric standing stones. There are thousands of them, menhirs (a single stone) and dolmens (at least two uprights with a stone on top), and if you're going to be out and about in the countryside by bike, you're likely to chance upon them from time to time. The best known ones are at Carnac in Morbihan, an area generally rich in these monuments.

Organised Holidays

There are probably a dozen or more companies offering a range of organised cycling holidays, some accompanied, others self-guided. Some are large companies offering destinations across the globe, others small specialist companies. Breton Bikes is an English-speaking firm based in Brittany offering a range of camping, hotel-based and gîte-based tours, mainly ones organised for you to travel independently but some accompanied ones available too. Brittany Borders Cycling include in their offerings a 'Coastal Classique' self-guided tour around Saint-Malo and the Ille-et-Rance canal. Sentiers Maritimes offer a range of cycle holidays in Brittany.

Access to Brittany

Travel to Brittany from the UK is easy. If you choose rail Eurostar carries bicycles and there are good high speed services to Brittany from Paris (Nantes and Rennes for example are only a couple of hours or so) and most trains will carry bikes. Both the UK connected ferry ports connect into the rail system - there are regular bike carrying trains out of Saint-Malo but only a few out of Roscoff. Ferries go from Plymouth to Roscoff and from Portsmouth and Weymouth to Saint Malo with a summer service also from Poole to Saint-Malo. Many UK airports have flights to Rennes and there are a number to Nantes. Quimper, Lorient and Dinard can be reached by air but normally with a change. Cycle carriage by air can range from difficult to not possible.

i More Info

www.randobreizh.org An excellent outdoor activity site with tons of cycling maps and info.
www.brittanytourism.com has a large cycling section
Brittany's Greenways published by Red Dog Books 2010 is very detailed and useful. Various French titles to cycling in Brittany.

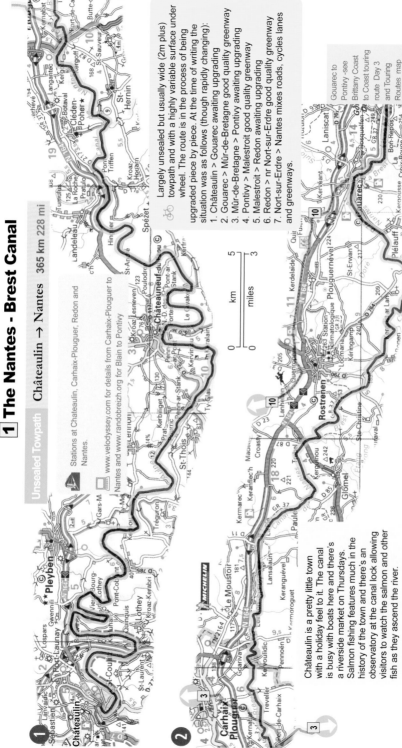

1 The Nantes - Brest Canal

Unsealed Towpath   Châteaulin → Nantes   365 km 228 mi

Stations at Châteaulin, Carhaix-Plouguer, Redon and Nantes.

www.velodyssey.com for details from Carhaix-Plouguer to Nantes and www.randobreizh.org for Blain to Pontivy

Largely unsealed but usually wide (2m plus) towpath and with a highly variable surface under wheel. The route is in the process of being upgraded piece by piece. At the time of writing the situation was as follows (though rapidly changing):

1. Châteaulin > Gouarec awaiting upgrading
2. Gouarec > Mûr-de-Bretagne good quality greenway
3. Mûr-de-Bretagne > Pontivy awaiting upgrading
4. Pontivy > Malestroit good quality greenway
5. Malestroit > Redon awaiting upgrading
6. Redon > nr Nort-sur-Erdre good quality greenway
7. Nort-sur-Erdre > Nantes mixes roads, cycles lanes and greenways.

Gouarec to Pontivy -see Brittany Coast to Coast touring route Day 3 and Touring Routes map

Châteaulin is a pretty little town with a holiday feel to it. The canal is busy with boats here and there's a riverside market on Thursdays. Salmon fishing features much in the history of the town and there's an observatory at the canal lock allowing visitors to watch the salmon and other fish as they ascend the river.

154   Greenway - unsealed   Greenway - sealed   Signed road route

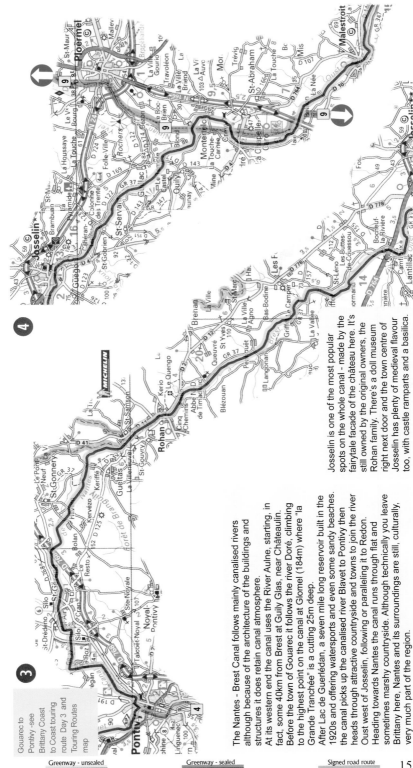

The Nantes - Brest Canal follows mainly canalised rivers although because of the architecture of the buildings and structures it does retain canal atmosphere.

At its western end the canal uses the River Aulne, starting, in fact, some 40km from Brest at Guily Glas, near Châteaulin. Before the town of Gouarec it follows the river Doré, climbing to the highest point on the canal at Glomel (184m) where "la Grande Tranchée" is a cutting 25m deep.

After Lac de Guerlédan, a seven mile long reservoir built in the 1920s and offering watersports and even some sandy beaches, the canal picks up the canalised river Blavet to Pontivy then heads through attractive countryside and towns to join the river Oust west of Josselin, following or paralleling it to Redon. Heading towards Nantes the canal runs through flat and sometimes marshy countryside. Although technically you leave Brittany here, Nantes and its surroundings are still, culturally, very much part of the region.

Josselin is one of the most popular spots on the whole canal - made by the fairytale facade of the château here. It's still owned by the original owners, the Rohan family. There's a doll museum right next door and the town centre of Josselin has plenty of medieval flavour too, with castle ramparts and a basilica.

Gouarec to Pontivy - see Brittany Coast to Coast touring route Day 3 and Touring Routes map

Greenway - unsealed   Greenway - sealed   Signed road route

155

Redon is a small town but a major transport hub. It's on the rail lines between Nantes and Rennes and Paris and Quimper. As a port it's these days very much a leisure concern, not the major commerce interchange it was when access from the sea and its place at the intersection of the Nantes-Brest canal and the Vilaine up to Rennes were so advantageous. Entertainments on offer include a waterways museum, a swimming pool with diving pool and various events at different times of the year.

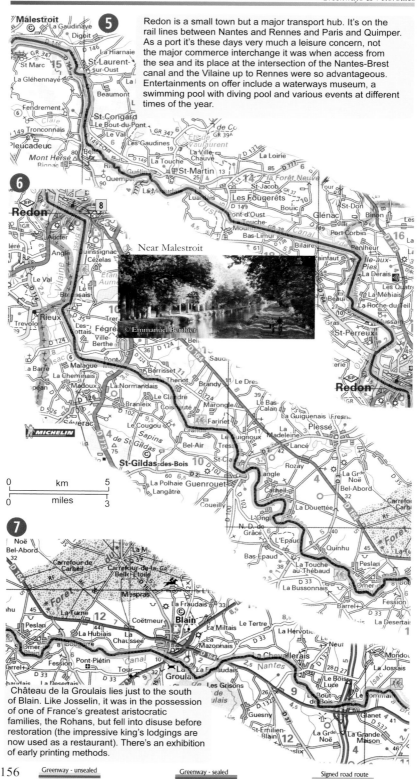

Near Malestroit
© Emmanuel Berthier

Château de la Groulais lies just to the south of Blain. Like Josselin, it was in the possession of one of France's greatest aristocratic families, the Rohans, but fell into disuse before restoration (the impressive king's lodgings are now used as a restaurant). There's an exhibition of early printing methods.

Greenway - unsealed   Greenway - sealed   Signed road route

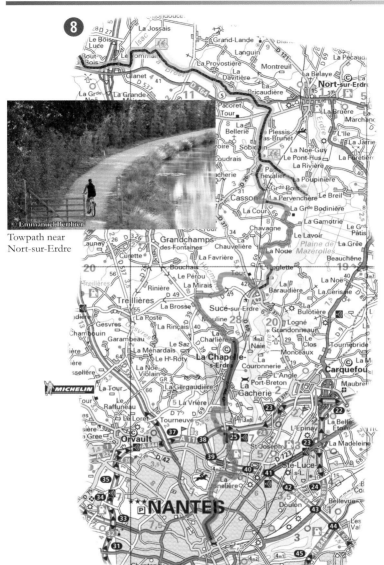

Towpath near
Nort-sur-Erdre

Although not a tourist centre, Nantes is a rewarding and easy place to spend a few days at the start or end of your journey. Pristine parks and fine neo-classical buildings are complemented by a huge choice of cafes and restaurants and a modern tram system that makes travel across France's seventh largest city a cinch. Worth a look are the gothic cathedral and surrounding old town, the nineteenth century 'new town' to the west and the Jardin des Plantes - one of the finest botanical gardens in France.

And if you happen to see a giant clockwork elephant wandering by the waterside at Île de Nantes and wonder why, it's just one of the amazing creations at the Machines de l'Île.

Check out the giant clockwork creations at Les Machines de l'Île, such as this elephant.

2 Voies Vertes around Quimper

Unsealed Railpath	Quimper (Ty Planche) → Douarnanez	16 km 10 mi
Unsealed Railpath	Quimper (Pluguffan) → Pont l'Abbé	11 km 7.5 mi

Quimper. Bicycle-carrying TGVs arrive in Quimper every couple of hours or so from Paris Montparnasse.

www.voiesvertes.com

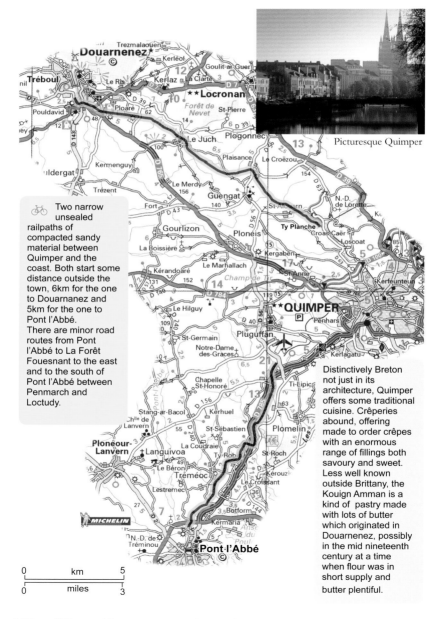

Picturesque Quimper

🚲 Two narrow unsealed railpaths of compacted sandy material between Quimper and the coast. Both start some distance outside the town, 6km for the one to Douarnanez and 5km for the one to Pont l'Abbé.
There are minor road routes from Pont l'Abbé to La Forêt Fouesnant to the east and to the south of Pont l'Abbé between Penmarch and Loctudy.

Distinctively Breton not just in its architecture, Quimper offers some traditional cuisine. Crêperies abound, offering made to order crêpes with an enormous range of fillings both savoury and sweet. Less well known outside Brittany, the Kouign Amman is a kind of pastry made with lots of butter which originated in Douarnenez, possibly in the mid nineteenth century at a time when flour was in short supply and butter plentiful.

3 Voie Verte from Morlaix to Rosporden

Unsealed railpath **Morlaix → Rosporden** 100km 62.5mi

 Morlaix, Carhaix-Plouguer, Rosporden

💻 www.randobreizh.com

Morlaix to Carhaix-Plouguer - see Brittany Coast to Coast touring route Day 1 and Touring Routes map

🚲 Lengthy sections of this railpath run across wooded slopes on a generally reasonable surface (hybrid bike recommended), with the occasional rutted, softer section and a road link through Carhaix-Plouguer. The Gourin-Rosporden section was better surfaced than the part further north at the time of writing.

Morlaix is a pleasant and busy little town set under a huge nineteenth century railway viaduct on the Paris-Brest line. One of its attractions is the large weekly Saturday market which has stalls brimming with local produce from the rich Breton countryside and surrounding seas. Saltmarsh lamb, artichokes, langoustines and exotica such as Tart'Alg, a kind of seaweed spread, are amongst the huge range of temptations on offer.

This route runs along the southern slopes of the Monts d'Arrée from Morlaix to Carhaix - Plouguer and then across the Black Mountains to Rosporden. It is the major part of Brittany Voie Verte No. 7, a regional coast to coast greenway across the peninsula which will ultimately link Roscoff and Concarneau.

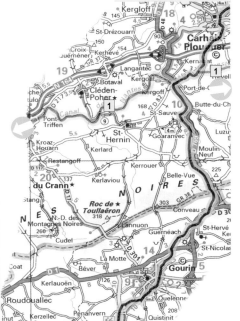

Route near Scaer

© Emmanuel Berthier

Greenway - unsealed   Greenway - sealed   Signed road route   159

4 The Voie Verte du Blavet and around Lorient

Unsealed & sealed towpath	Pontivy → Hennebont 62km 39 mi
Unsealed railpath	Quéven → Pont-Scorff 6km 4 mi
Unsealed path	Guidel-Plages → Kerroc'h 9km 5.5 mi

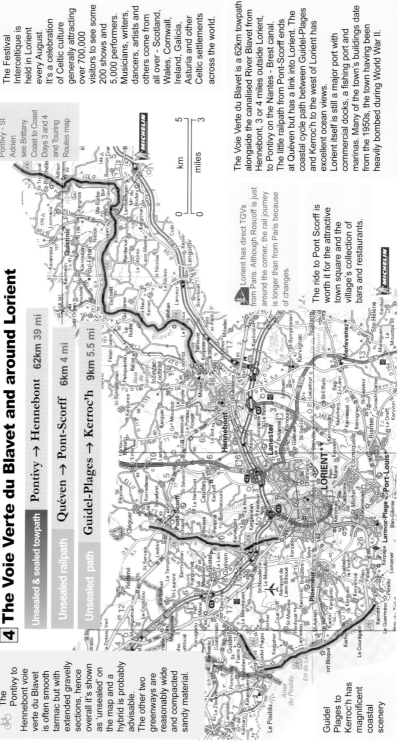

The Festival Interceltique is held in Lorient every August. It's a celebration of Celtic culture generally attracting over 700,000 visitors to see some 200 shows and 5,000 performers. Musicians, writers, dancers, artists and others come from all over - Scotland, Wales, Cornwall, Ireland, Galicia, Asturia and other Celtic settlements across the world.

Pontivy - St Adrien see Brittany Coast to Coast Days 3 and 4 and Touring Routes map

The Voie Verte du Blavet is a 62km towpath alongside the canalised River Blavet from Hennebont, 3 or 4 miles outside Lorient, to Pontivy on the Nantes - Brest canal. The little railpath from Pont-Scorff ends at Quéven but has a link into Lorient. The coastal cycle path between Guidel-Plages and Kerroc'h to the west of Lorient has excellent ocean views.
Lorient itself is still a major port with commercial docks, a fishing port and marinas. Many of the town's buildings date from the 1950s, the town having been heavily bombed during World War II.

Lorient has direct TGVs from Paris. Although Roscoff is just around the corner, the rail journey is longer than from Paris because of changes.

The ride to Pont Scorff is worth it for the attractive town square and the village's collection of bars and restaurants.

The Pontivy to Hennebont voie verte du Blavet is often smooth tarmac but with extended gravelly sections, hence overall it's shown as 'unsealed' on the map and a hybrid is probably advisable.
The other two greenways are reasonably wide and compacted and sandy material.

Guidel Plages to Kerroc'h has magnificent coastal scenery

Greenway - unsealed   Greenway - sealed   Signed road route

5 Presqu'île de Rhuys and the Vannes Voie Verte

Minor roads and tracks	Saint-Armel → Port Navalo	25 km 15.5 mi
Unsealed railpath	Vannes → Gulf of Morbihan	7 km 4 mi

The off-road sections are generally wide, well-compacted tracks.

Direct bicycle carrying trains from Paris and a good service from Rennes as well. Services from St-Malo and Roscoff require changes.

The voie verte at Vannes runs along the water's edge round the south side of the town from place Gambetta to chemin de Bernus. It leaves Vannes along the busy quaysides, passes the aquarium and the departure point for cruises around the Gulf of Morbihan before going through a less developed area with great sea and sky views and ending up at the Ile de Conleau on the edge of the Gulf of Morbihan. Automated cycle hire is available in Vannes.

Vannes is an unusual blend - part port town, part medieval heart and a thriving tourist centre in its role as a gateway to the Gulf of Morbihan.

The Gulf itself is dotted with islands, some private, a couple with a permanent population and many with megalithic remains disappearing beneath the water. Undoubtedly the most famous is Gavrinis.

The coastal route around Brittany is emerging bit by bit. One of the best developed sections is the signed network of the Presqu'île de Rhuys, some 70km, allowing you to cross from east to west, between Port-Navalo and St-Armel, with spurs out to St-Gildas-de-Rhuys and Le Tour-du-Parc. Around 70% of the network is on quiet backroads and 30% on unsealed greenways, including railpaths and forest tracks.

Greenway - unsealed   Greenway - sealed   Signed road route   161

6 Vélocéan Nord Loire, Brière Marshes & Beyond

Unsealed railpath & roads   Férel → Kerséguin   28 km 17.5 mi

Sealed and unsealed paths & minor roads

Piriac sur Mer → St-Nazaire   46 km 29 mi

Stations at La Baule and Saint-Nazaire. Trains include bicycle-carrying TGVs from Paris.

www.randobreizh.com www.penestin.com (cycle paths in the area between Tréhiguier and Kerséguin for the Férel to Kerséguin route).

Vélocéan is a developing coastal route running from Piriac in the north to Bourgneuf-en-Retz in the south. This northern part of the route is a mixture of roads and paths with a voie verte most of the way between Guérande and La Baule.

Piriac is a seaside resort and fishing town, Guérande a medieval fortified town and La Baule a renowned seaside town with beautiful sandy beaches. Saint-Nazaire is one of the main ports of France.

Other attractions along the route or nearby include the rugged coastline between Piriac and La Turballe featuring coves, cliffs, nice beaches and sandy creeks. The huge salt marshes near Guérande and La Baule offer refuge to much birdlife and feature highly photogenic saltpans producing fine sea salt. The D99 and D92 would make a nice return loop from Piriac back towards Guérande, though you have to mix in with a fair bit of traffic. Even quieter though are the two tiny tarmac roads heading south of the D92 and known as Route des Marais.

Piriac harbour

The Férel to Kerséguin coastal route with a rocky shoreline and little access roads down to beaches at the bottom of the ochre-coloured cliffs will become part of the future long distance coastal route.

It's only in the past few years that the *Parc Naturel Régional de Brière* has begun to open up to tourists and the burgeoning path network is one of a range of diversions-punt hire and watching exotic birdlife are just two others. There is a véloroute from St-Lyphard to Férel. www.parc-naturel-briere.fr has lots more detail.

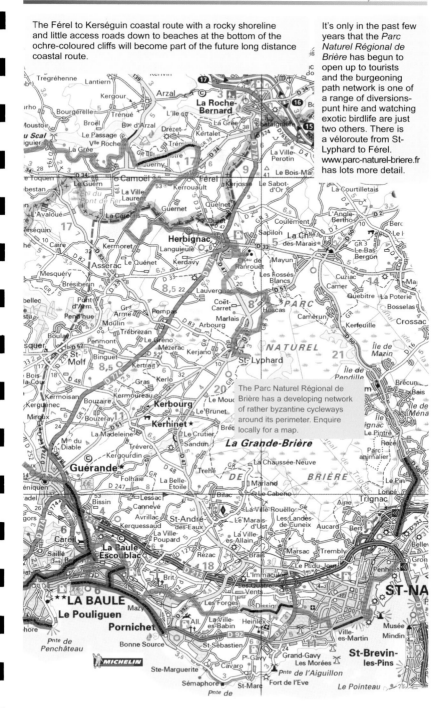

The Parc Naturel Régional de Brière has a developing network of rather byzantine cycleways around its perimeter. Enquire locally for a map.

7 Dinan to Rennes along the Ille et Rance canal

Unsealed towpath | Dinan → Rennes | 78 km | 48.5 mi

Dinan station has access from Roscoff, Cherbourg and Paris but all involve one or two changes. It's the only station for the first fifty kilometres of the route but then a number of stations between Montreuil-sur-Ille and Rennes give good rail/cycling options. Rennes has a regular supply of bike-carrying TGVs from Paris.

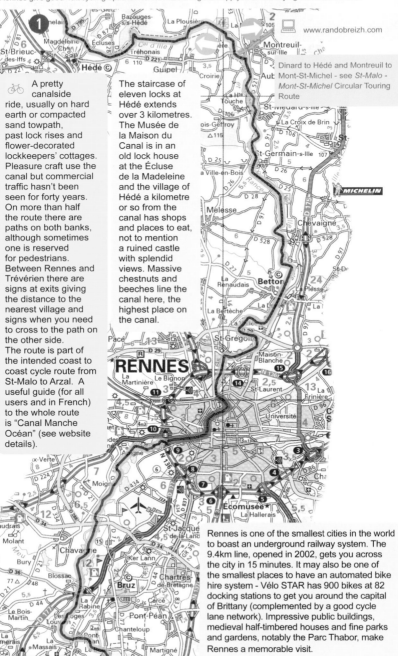

www.randobreizh.com

Dinard to Hédé and Montreuil to Mont-St-Michel - see *St-Malo - Mont-St-Michel* Circular Touring Route

A pretty canalside ride, usually on hard earth or compacted sand towpath, past lock rises and flower-decorated lockkeepers' cottages. Pleasure craft use the canal but commercial traffic hasn't been seen for forty years. On more than half the route there are paths on both banks, although sometimes one is reserved for pedestrians. Between Rennes and Tréverien there are signs at exits giving the distance to the nearest village and signs when you need to cross to the path on the other side. The route is part of the intended coast to coast cycle route from St-Malo to Arzal. A useful guide (for all users and in French) to the whole route is "Canal Manche Océan" (see website details).

The staircase of eleven locks at Hédé extends over 3 kilometres. The Musée de la Maison du Canal is in an old lock house at the Écluse de la Madeleine and the village of Hédé a kilometre or so from the canal has shops and places to eat, not to mention a ruined castle with splendid views. Massive chestnuts and beeches line the canal here, the highest place on the canal.

Rennes is one of the smallest cities in the world to boast an underground railway system. The 9.4km line, opened in 2002, gets you across the city in 15 minutes. It may also be one of the smallest places to have an automated bike hire system - Vélo STAR has 900 bikes at 82 docking stations to get you around the capital of Brittany (complemented by a good cycle lane network). Impressive public buildings, medieval half-timbered houses and fine parks and gardens, notably the Parc Thabor, make Rennes a memorable visit.

Greenway - unsealed   Greenway - sealed   Signed road route

8 The Rennes to Redon towpath

Rennes → Redon 89 km 55 mi

Mainly unsealed riverside path

Rennes, Bruz, Redon

www.tourisme-pays-redon.com
www.ille-et-vilaine.fr

| 0 | km | 5 |
| 0 | miles | 3 |

MICHELIN

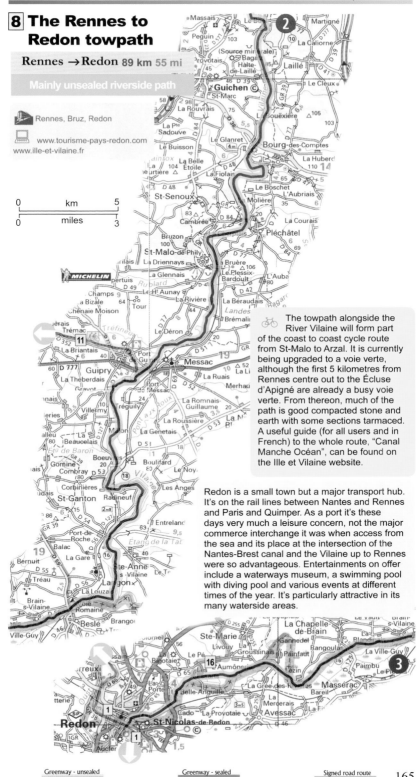

The towpath alongside the River Vilaine will form part of the coast to coast cycle route from St-Malo to Arzal. It is currently being upgraded to a voie verte, although the first 5 kilometres from Rennes centre out to the Écluse d'Apigné are already a busy voie verte. From thereon, much of the path is good compacted stone and earth with some sections tarmaced. A useful guide (for all users and in French) to the whole route, "Canal Manche Océan", can be found on the Ille et Vilaine website.

Redon is a small town but a major transport hub. It's on the rail lines between Nantes and Rennes and Paris and Quimper. As a port it's these days very much a leisure concern, not the major commerce interchange it was when access from the sea and its place at the intersection of the Nantes-Brest canal and the Vilaine up to Rennes were so advantageous. Entertainments on offer include a waterways museum, a swimming pool with diving pool and various events at different times of the year. It's particularly attractive in its many waterside areas.

Greenway - unsealed   Greenway - sealed   Signed road route

165

9 Dinard to Questembert

Dinard to Trévron -see St-Malo - Mont-St-Michel touring route (Days 1&2) on Touring Routes map

Dinard → Trévron 39 km 24 mi

Mainly unsealed tracks & railpath

Trévron → Médréac 18 km 11 mi

Unsealed railpath

Stations at St-Malo, Dinan and Questembert mean a rail return is an option. The station at Quédillac, about 7km from Médréac, allows shorter trips. Continue to the Atlantic coast and Vannes is on the same line as Questembert. If you would like St-Malo as a terminus there is the road over the barrage or a ferry during the summer across to Dinard which carries bikes

www.randobreizh.com

Near Trévron, join the voie verte along the old railway line which will take you south to meet the Médréac vélorail 3km east of the town. It's an unsealed surface of variable quality.
The 39km from Médréac to Mauron are a well-signed véloroute passing the end of the Voie Verte Chemin du Petit Train at Saint-Méen-le-Grand. It's a well signed route and there's a nice picnic area at La Crouais.

St-Méen-le-Grand has a distinctive little town hall and an ancient abbey church and for cyclists of a road racing persuasion there is the museum Louison Bobet, winner of the Tour de France from 1953-55.

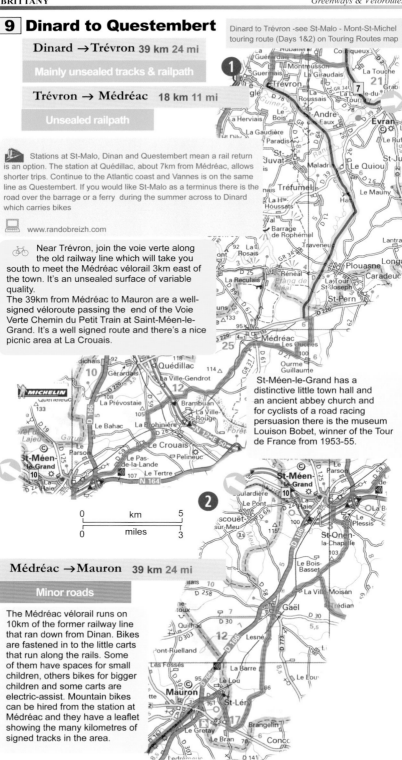

```
0        km        5
0       miles       3
```

Médréac → Mauron 39 km 24 mi

Minor roads

The Médréac vélorail runs on 10km of the former railway line that ran down from Dinan. Bikes are fastened in to the little carts that run along the rails. Some of them have spaces for small children, others bikes for bigger children and some carts are electric-assist. Mountain bikes can be hired from the station at Médréac and they have a leaflet showing the many kilometres of signed tracks in the area.

Greenway - unsealed   Greenway - sealed   Signed road route

Sealed railpath   Mauron → Questembert   53 km 33 mi

The voie verte between Mauron and Questembert is what you might call a high performance route. It's a smooth, 3 metre wide tarmac path with a supplementary 1 metre compact sand path alongside. There are helpful things such as seats and bins every couple of kilometres, plenty of picnic sites and a Relais Rando at Ploërmel which has toilets and water. Ploërmel itself is well-situated as a place to break and nearby, the Lac au Duc offers water sports and beaches. Here, the route links with the Nantes-Brest canal, allowing for a much longer off-road excursion.

At Molac, north of Questembert

This almost coast to coast route links to various other major cycle routes including the canal d'Ille et Rance which goes to Rennes, the chemin du Petit Train and the Nantes-Brest Canal. A link from Questembert through Muzillac to join the St-Armel to Port-Navalo véloroute sounds to be on the cards but, at present, a decent map and the network of quiet back roads covering the 20 or 30km between Questembert and the Presqu'île de Rhuys should get you to the coast.

Malestroit is a sleepy little village, enlivened by the unusual and often fun historic carvings on many of the buildings. Bagpipe-playing hares, acrobats and demons are to be found adorning the grey stone walls here, amongst many other unusual characters. It has the added attraction and convenience of being on the Nantes-Brest Canal route (pgs 154-157) Journey's end at Questembert is dominated by the spectacular and sizeable 16th century covered market.

Greenway - unsealed   Greenway - sealed   Signed road route   167

10 Voie Verte Chemin du Petit Train

Unsealed railpath   Carhaix-Plouguer → Saint-Méen   120 km 75 mi

Generally wide and reasonably well-maintained crushed stone path.

Carhaix-Plouguer to Mûr-de-Bretagne -see Brittany Coast to Coast Touring Route (Day 1)

Station at Carhaix-Plouguer. La Brohinière station, half an hour down the line from Rennes, is 5km from St-Méen-le-Grand and will lie on or near the projected cycle path to Rennes.

www.randobreizh.com

The rail line was a voie metrique, one of a number of lines in Brittany using a one metre wide track. These lines were all closed in the 1960s apart from the Carhaix to Guingamp line which was converted to standard gauge. The voie metrique was widely used in France and elsewhere for secondary lines and is the choice for many tramways also. This line closed to passengers in April 1967, carried goods for a short while but closed completely later the same year.

Wash away the dust of the trail. Les Aquatides is a leisure swimming pool at Loudéac, half way along the route. 25m swimming pool but also water slide, fountains, lagoons, jacuzzi and spa bath.

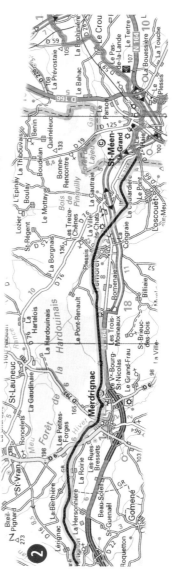

① ②

11 Ploërmel to Messac Voie Verte

Unsealed railpath   Ploërmel → Messac   47 km 29 mi

⚓ Messac is on the Rennes to Redon line with a reasonably frequent service.

🖥 www.ille-et-vilaine.fr for an overview map of routes in Ille et Vilaine and a downloadable leaflet for the Messac - Guer section of this route.

🚲 Linking the Rennes to Redon towpath alongside the River Vilaine to the Questembert-Mauron voie verte, this former railtrack can be difficult to find - it is generally not signed from the towns and the Ploërmel end is unsigned. The surface is also of varying quality.
There has been an extension from Ploërmel to Josselin on the Nantes-Brest canal and on to Réguiny, a pretty little town on the way to Pontivy. At the Messac end, the route is to be extended to Châteaubriant.

© Rob Glover Creative Commons

This route uses the old rail line, here at the former station building at Ploërmel

Greenway - unsealed   Greenway - sealed   Signed road route

12 Antrain to Louvigné-du-Désert Voie Verte

| Unsealed railpath | Antrain → Fougeres | 30 km 18.5 mi |
| Unsealed railpath | Fougeres → near St-Hilaire-du-Harcouët | 30.5 km 19 mi |

🚲 A railpath on packed sand/earth of variable quality, limited width (1.5 metres) and long stretches with frequent barriers. One of the least developed sections of this route is also one of the most picturesque - the path between Saint-Brice-en-Coglès and Antrain runs through a pretty wooded valley but is just two sandy ruts in places. Linking the route to the Vire - Pontaubault voie verte using quiet local roads allows a 120 kilometres circular route through Fougères and la baie du Mont-St-Michel of which some 70 kilometres are off-road.

Fougères is a small town with a big castle. The setting is memorable with little streets tumbling down steep slopes and great views of the ancient castle and the area generally from the public gardens. There's a magnificent, restored nineteenth century theatre and an attractive medieval quarter around the place du Marchix. The nearby Forest of Fougères has mountain bike trails but is also an attractive place to just wander with its megaliths and standing stones creating an air of mystery.

Quiet roads link to St-Hilaire and just to the north you can join the growing Normandy greenways network.

🛈 No railway stations on or near this route. Direct bicycle-carrying trains from Paris serve Vire to the north and it is possible to cycle from Vire to Antrain on greenways. Also, there's a link on quiet roads between St-Hilaire-du-Harcouët and Louvigné-du-Désert.

📖 www.ille-et-vilaine.fr has downloadable map leaflets covering Fougères - Louvigné-du-Désert and Fougeres - St Broladre.

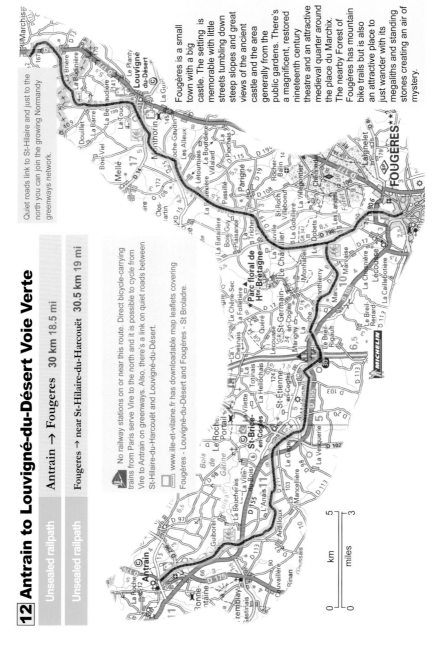

Greenway - unsealed   Greenway - sealed   Signed road route

Other Routes

13 Belle-Île

Minor roads and tracks	Island network 40km 25mi

Ferries all the year round from Quiberon (reservation by phone for bicycle spaces with Compagnie Océane. SMN don't carry bikes). Seasonal ferries from La Turballe, Vannes, Port Navalo and La Trinité sur Mer (none carry bikes).

www.randobreizh.com www.belle-ile.com

Largest of the Brittany islands at 17km by 9km. Le Palais and Sauzon are the main ports but there are also the little towns of Bangor and Locmaria and these four main settlements are linked by signed cycle routes which also pass through many of the villages across the island. Signed leisure routes give access to the beaches and tourist attractions of this lovely island. Whitewashed houses, green and undulating countryside, jagged cliffs and big beaches have attracted not only holidaymakers but artists, including Monet, and authors such as Flaubert and Dumas (Dumas had Porthos die here near Locmaria).

14 La Littorale Port Neuf - Roscoff - Plouénan & Île de Batz

Minor & Car-free roads	Port Neuf → Kerlaudy 34km 21mi

Roscoff is a major transport hub with ferries from Plymouth, Rosslare and Cork and a rail link to the main Paris-Brest TGV line.

www.roscoff-tourisme.com www.iledebatz.com

This route is a part of the "La Littorale" véloroute being developed right round the Brittany coast. For those who cannot wait for the full official route, Rando Éditions publishes, in French, a set of three spiral bound atlases covering a coastal route from Mont-St-Michel to Nantes. See www.editions-sudouest.com

A lesser known ferry out of Roscoff is the 15 minute crossing to the Île de Batz, a 3.5 kilometres long island with rocky coves, fine sandy beaches and the renowned Jardin Exotique Georges Delaselle which has over 2,000 species of plants and a collection of palm trees. Nice cycling on this car free island. Bike hire available or take your own on the ferry.

15 Plouasne to Mont-St-Michel and beyond

Mainly Minor roads	Plouasne → Roz-sur-Couesnon 113km 70mi

La Brohinière and Quédillac on the line from Rennes to St. Brieuc are at about 10km the nearest stations to Plouasne. Montreuil-sur-Ille station north of Rennes is near the véloroute on the line to Dol-de-Bretagne and Pontorson station is near the route spur up to Mont-St-Michel.

www.ille-et-vilaine.fr has a downloadable leaflet giving towns along the route from Plouasne to Antrain and basic supporting information. The section from Antrain to St-Broladre is included in a similar leaflet covering Fougères to St-Broladre and there's a separate leaflet for the Voie verte de la Baie du Mont-St-Michel. A good schematic map of routes in Ille-et-Vilaine is there too.

Quiet roads link Plouasne to the Voie verte du Baie Mont-St-Michel and the véloroute to Pontaubault, leading east to the Normandy greenway network (see opposite for more detail).

16 The Plouasne to Redon véloroute

Mainly Minor roads	Plouasne near Médréac → Redon 110km 68mi

Railway station at Redon. The nearest to the northern end of the route is La Brohinière (about 10km).

www.ille-et-vilaine.fr to download map leaflet "À vélo de Redon à St. Pern"

17 The Bay of Mont-St-Michel Voies Vertes

Dyke and causeway tracks	St-Broladre → Le Pas-au-Boeuf 12km 7.5mi Link to Mont-St-Michel 4km 2.5mi

 Pontorson station is about 3.5 hours from Paris and has good local connections to Normandy and Brittany

See the *St-Malo - Mont-St-Michel Circular* touring route for more detail. You can also link in to the Normandy cycle network - head east from the Mont-St-Michel causeway towards Pontaubault on a signed minor road route for some 26km.

18 Around the Quiberon Peninsula

Tracks and greenways	Kerhillio → Quiberon Peninsula 19 km 12 mi

 Auray lies to the north-east of this route, within easy cycling distance. Also see Tire-Bouchon below.

To the west of the Quiberon peninsula a greenway links the less touristy area south of Erdeven (Kerhillio beach area) and uses EnverrPaq for much of its length - an environmentally-friendly surface designed to blend in with the dune surroundings too.
Cyclelanes then take you south along the D768 west of Plouharnel then minor roads along the west of the peninsula link to a new voie verte at tiny Kerhivan for the rest of the west coast. A tourist train, the Tire-Bouchon, runs from Auray along the Quiberon peninsula from late June to the end of August and some weekends in June and September. It does carry bicycles, although cycle hire is available in Quiberon. Lovely beaches, a fishing port, marinas and ferries out to the islands of Belle-Île-en-Mer, Houat and Hoëdic make Quiberon a highly popular spot. See the *Brittany Coast to Coast* touring route for more detail.

19 St-Brieuc - Allineuc and Voie Verte Rigole d'Hilvern

Minor roads and greenway	St-Brieuc → St-Caradec 55 km 34 mi

 The nearest station is at Loudéac, a short ride down the voie verte from St-Caradec.

A section of the developing coast to coast route between St.Brieuc and Lorient. From St Brieuc follow minor roads to near Allineuc from where a recently extended voie verte uses a smooth, compacted earth path alongside an old canal feeder stream for the Nantes-Brest canal. It links to St-Caradec on the Voie Verte Chemin du Petit Train. From here you can follow the Chemin du Petit Train to Mûr-de-Bretagne and then head south along the Blavet towpath to Pontivy and the Voie Verte du Blavet towards the coast.
North of St-Brieuc there is also a 40km stretch of signed coastal route (25% traffic-free and 75% on quiet roads), from Hillion to near Pordic.

20 Saint-Méen-le-Grand to Vitré

Mainly Minor roads	Saint-Méen to Moutiers 125km 77.5 mi
Unsealed railpath	Moutiers → Vitré 30 km 18.5 mi

La Brohinière station, half an hour on the train from Rennes, is 5km from St.Méen-le-Grand. Vitré is about half an hour from Rennes. Two lines run south of Rennes with stations near the véloroute.

www.ille-et-vilaine.fr for useful leaflets on both the véloroute and the voie verte.

Vitré is a goal well worth aiming for - lovely old streets with ancient timber-framed houses, a dramatic castle housing a museum and a number of lakes nearby offering water sports, fishing and birdwatching. There are plans for cycle routes linking directly to Rennes and running south to Châteaubriant; see the North Centre / Pays-de-la-Loire greenways chapter for details.

Brittany's Signed Route Network

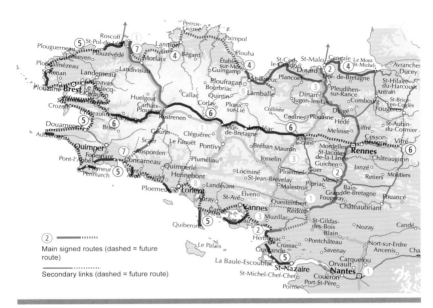

(2) ━━━━ ┄┄┄┄
Main signed routes (dashed = future
route)

┄┄┄┄┄┄┄
Secondary links (dashed = future route)

This schematic map shows the eight official long-distance routes across Brittany. They are signed as V1, V2 etc on the ground, although this is an ongoing project with many sections either only open to a basic standard or not yet available. The majority of these routes are covered by the routes in this chapter. Detailed French info at www.randobreizh.com
The eight routes are:

(1) **Roscoff-Nantes** Shares route V7 from Roscoff to south of Carhaix-Plouguer. Then it follows the magnificent Nantes-Brest canal all the way to Nort-sur-Erdre before using mainly minor roads into Nantes.

(2) **Saint-Malo - Arzal** Railpath from Dinard to Saint-Samson-sur-Rance then a short road link to the Rance / Rance-et-Vilaine canal which you follow all the way to Rennes. South of here the towpath is not official cycle way but can be cycled, nonetheless, all the way to Redon.

(3) **Saint-Malo - Sarzeau** As V2 to south of Dinan (écluse du Mottay) then its a mixture of minor roads and railpath all the way to Mauron where it picks up the superb tarmac greenway to just short of Questembert.

(4) **La Littorale (north)**

(5) **La Littorale (south)** Both V4 and V5, designed to run the entire length of the Breton coastline, are in the very early stages of development with only isolated sections complete.

(6) **Camaret - Vitré** Totally absent west of Châteaulin and east of St-Méen-le-Grand, otherwise almost entirely on greenways following either the Nantes-Brest canal or railpath.

(7) **Roscoff - Concarneau** Mainly minor roads from Roscoff to Morlaix where you pick up a railpath to Carhaix-Plouguer. South of here another railpath takes you over the Nantes-Brest canal then the route high point in the Black Mountains, before rolling into the current route end at Rosporden.

(8) **Saint-Brieuc - Lorient** Minor roads between St-Brieuc and Allineuc then off-road almost all the way to Hennebont, north of Lorient (note south of Pontivy the route isn't official greenway along the canalised river Blavet, though easily passable).

There are also numerous smaller linking routes - 'VD' routes - often but not exclusively on minor roads, detailed on the map on pgs 152-3 and in several of the entries in this chapter. National and international routes running through the area are:

Petit Tour de Manche Launched in 2012, the small Breton section runs east from St-Malo to Mont-St-Michel and into Normandy.

Tour de Manche With a projected launch in 2013, this will use V4 along the northern coast of Brittany, east of Roscoff.

Velodyssey (Vélodyssée) Shares V1 before heading off down the Atlantic coast
EuroVelo 4 (see pgs 8-9)

Normandy

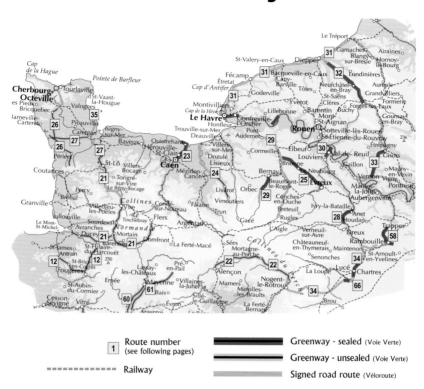

1 Route number (see following pages)	▬▬▬ Greenway - sealed (Voie Verte)
- - - - - Railway	▬▬▬ Greenway - unsealed (Voie Verte)
	▬▬▬ Signed road route (Véloroute)

With over 500 kilometres of voie verte available and a couple of signed long distance cycle routes largely completed, Normandy has much to offer. Some long-established high quality off-road routes make the Cotentin peninsula a great cycling area and the main north-south route is to be part of a signed circular tour into Brittany and along part of the English coast - the Petit Tour du Manche. A Paris to Le Mont St. Michel route goes through the Parcs Naturels Régionaux Normandie-Maine and du Perche of southern Normandy and a London - Paris route lands at Dieppe and follows an excellent railpath to Forges-les-Eaux and on to Paris. The little voies vertes and véloroutes dotted about the lovely department of the Eure are a delight and the scenic grandeur of some of the coastal cycle route is about as iconic as the white cliffs of Dover.

Organised Holidays

A good number of organised cycling holidays are available for Normandy. Some of the companies offering them are : www.thefrenchbike.com, www.brittanybordersbicycling.com, www.tripsite.com, www.frenchpedals.co.uk, www.freedomtreks.co.uk,
www.discoverfrance.com, www.frenchcyclingholidays.com, www.hfholidays.co.uk,
www.thechaingang.co.uk and www.utracks.com.

Culture, Food & History

Initially peopled by Celts and Belgians, the area that is now Normandy was conquered by the Romans in 98AD. Following the fall of Rome it was dominated by Franks and eventually became part of the Carolingian Empire. The Duchy of Normandy came into existence in 911 following various incursions by people from the north when the Viking leader Rollo was given a fiefdom there by the King of France. Normandy became a hugely powerful influence in Europe, ruling England after the conquest as part of an Anglo-Norman realm until the French king took the continental lands of the Duchy in 1204 and they became part of France. Today the Duchy of Normandy does survive, but only as the Channel Islands which went to the English as part of the Treaty of Paris in 1259. Queen Elizabeth II is the current Duke of Normandy. Independent-minded Normandy remained a thorn in the side of the central power for centuries thereafter but the gradual loss of powers and an increase in prosperity seemed to bring it into the fold and it was a stable and well-off area when the Second World War broke out. Following the German occupation and the Allied invasion, Normandy had 400 towns and villages destroyed and thousands of civilians killed. While the wounds may be healed, the experience is far from forgotten and as you cycle through the region it is brought home in the many museums and memorials, in the military cemeteries and in the street names given to commemorate fallen soldiers. Not that the region is bogged down in the past. You only have to look at the Pont de Normandie over the Seine near Le Havre to feel a sense of modern achievement. A region of varied landscapes. The 360 mile coastline ranges from towering cliffs to huge, open beaches, many used in the D Day landings. Inland, there are vast marshlands to the south of the gentle farmland of the Cotentin peninsula, hills and rivers in the Suisse Normande popular with climbers and canoeists and great walks through the forests and hill towns in the south of the region. The lush pastures of the Pays d'Auge and the Vire valley produce fabulous cheeses, creams, apples and ciders. The River Seine meanders through lovely countryside with attractive towns and villages alternating with white cliffs along its banks. The capital of Basse Normandie (the eastern part of Normandy) is Caen, busy and modern but still with some impressive medieval religious and military buildings and remains. Rouen is the capital of Haute Normandie. Much here also was destroyed in the second world war but extensive reconstruction has rebuilt the medieval old town and Rouen is classified as a 'City of Art and History' with over 200 protected sites. Much of Normandy is a land of half-timbered houses and there are many important castles and abbeys. One that may strike a chord with English visitors is the ruin of Château Gaillard overlooking the Seine and built by Richard the Lionheart.

Apple and dairy products have to be the best known aspects of Norman food and drink, from Calvados and Norman apple tart to Camembert and Pont l'Évêque cheeses. There is even a signed tourist "Cider Route" to the east of Caen. The famous "trou Normand" is a glass of calvados taken between meal courses with a view to improving appetite and making room for the next course. However, Norman seafood cuisine is also highly regarded boasting fine oyster and scallop dishes and delicious sole and turbot. Tripes à la mode de Caen is one of the best known dishes of the region and other specialities include duckling à la Rouennaise, tergoule (a spicy rice pudding) and the andouille de Vire, a chitterling sausage.

Access to Normandy

Normandy is well served by ferry with services from Portsmouth and Poole to Cherbourg, from Portsmouth to Caen and Le Havre and from Newhaven to Dieppe. Rail services via Paris are good with fast services to many towns and cities throughout Normandy, normally from Gare St. Lazare so you do have to get there from the Gare du Nord if using Eurostar. There's even a seasonal air service from London City airport to Deauville.

i More Info

www.normandie-cote-nature.com has downloadable leaflets covering the cycle routes of each of the departments of Normandy

www.normandie-tourisme.fr is the regional tourist website with a good cycling section

The Vire towpath (voie verte 27 and touring route *Around the Cotentin*) typifies the beautiful dairy farming landscape typical of much of Normandy

21 St-Lô to Mont-St-Michel or Flers

| Minor roads and unsealed greenway | St-Lô → Mont-St-Michel | 154.5 km | 96 mi |
| Minor roads and unsealed greenway | St-Lô → Flers | 143 km | 89 mi |

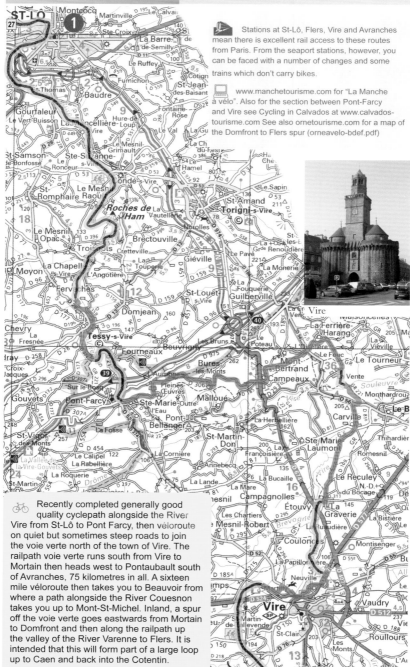

Stations at St-Lô, Flers, Vire and Avranches mean there is excellent rail access to these routes from Paris. From the seaport stations, however, you can be faced with a number of changes and some trains which don't carry bikes.

www.manchetourisme.com for "La Manche à vélo". Also for the section between Pont-Farcy and Vire see Cycling in Calvados at www.calvados-tourisme.com See also ornetourisme.com for a map of the Domfront to Flers spur (orneavelo-bdef.pdf)

Recently completed generally good quality cyclepath alongside the River Vire from St-Lô to Pont Farcy, then véloroute on quiet but sometimes steep roads to join the voie verte north of the town of Vire. The railpath voie verte runs south from Vire to Mortain then heads west to Pontaubault south of Avranches, 75 kilometres in all. A sixteen mile véloroute then takes you to Beauvoir from where a path alongside the River Couesnon takes you up to Mont-St-Michel. Inland, a spur off the voie verte goes eastwards from Mortain to Domfront and then along the railpath up the valley of the River Varenne to Flers. It is intended that this will form part of a large loop up to Caen and back into the Cotentin.

176   Greenway - unsealed   Greenway - sealed   Signed road route

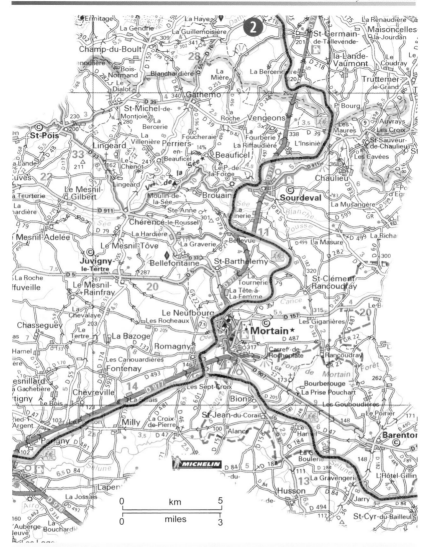

This route takes in many attractive towns and villages and includes one of the longest voies vertes in the area. St-Lô makes an excellent start or finish point being a good-sized town with plenty of facilities and good transport links. Built on a rocky outcrop, Vire is perhaps a bit less attractive than St-Lô. It was almost entirely rebuilt after the second world war but one or two older features do survive including the clocktower over a thirteenth century gateway and the church of Notre Dame. It's well known for the andouille de Vire, a large tripe sausage. Sourdeval is a pretty little "ville fleurie" with a small campsite near the centre and an aire de services for motorhomes. If you fancy a preview of where you're heading, take a short detour to Chaulieu where a viewing platform offers views of distant Mont-St-Michel on a good day. Mortain, where the spur to Flers leaves the route, is surrounded by woodland and waterfalls - the Grande and Petite Cascades are within walking distance of the town centre and are a lovely sight, especially in May / June time when rhododendrons are in flower. An ancient Cistercian abbey overlooks the town. Within walking distance of the centre of St.-Hilaire-du-Harcouët there's a lake with beach and swimming pool. More pretty villages and small towns lie along the route including St. Quentin-sur-le-Homme with its flower bedecked town hall and Ducey with its beautiful old stone bridge and its fine Château des Montgommery until you reach Pontaubault. From there a well-signed véloroute (great views of the mount in places) on quiet roads takes you the last 26 kilometres to Mont-St-Michel (the last two or three kilometres are not quiet unless you use the path alongside the River Couesnon).

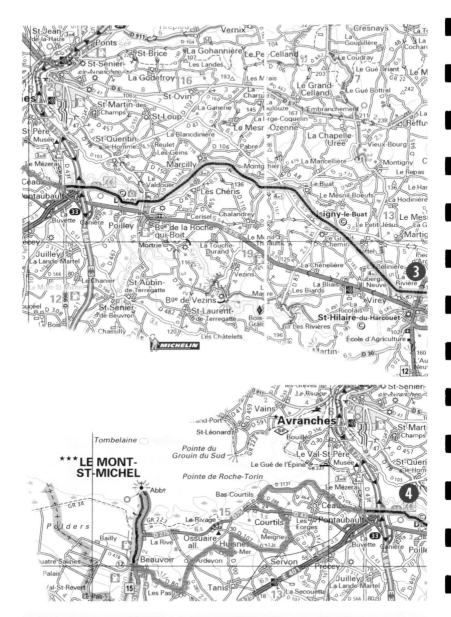

It is thought that a sanctuary was established on Mont-St-Michel, then Mont-Tombe, after three appearances by the Archangel Michael, the church being consecrated in 709. The Benedictine Abbey of Mont-St-Michel lies on a rocky island half a mile off the coast in the mouth of the River Couesnon near Avranches. This iconic structure, a marvel of engineering and a major pilgrim destination attracts well over two million visitors a year. It's a UNESCO World Heritage Site with a magic all its own and really not to be missed. Also see *St Malo - Mont-St-Michel Circular* touring route.

Greenway - unsealed   Greenway - sealed   Signed road route

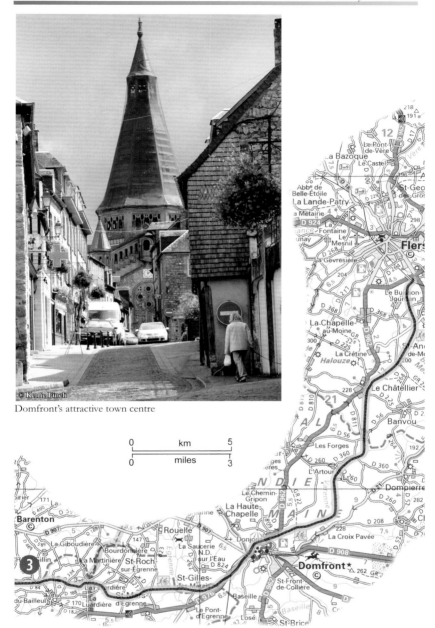

Domfront's attractive town centre

The spur from Mortain to Domfront and beyond is an unsealed railpath of variable quality through a variety of countryside. Domfront is a medieval hilltop town with half timbered houses and a castle. From Domfront, the path heads north east along the valley of the River Varenne, stopping slightly short of Flers, There is a lovely, photogenic castle at Flers containing a museum and surrounded by water and open to the public parkland.

Greenway - unsealed   Greenway - sealed   Signed road route   **179**

22 Voie verte from Alençon to Condé-sur-Huisne

Unsealed railpath   Alençon → Condé-sur-Huisne   67 km 41.5 mi

Stations at both ends of the path in Alençon and Condé-sur-Huisne mean a rail return is possible. However, it takes time as changes are needed and not all trains carry bikes. Similarly, rail access from Paris to either station involves changes and not all trains carry bikes.

www.ornetourisme.com has a detailed map (orneavelo-bdef.pdf) of the route and some supporting information (and lots of circular routes in the area). voievertealencon-conde.over-blog.com is useful and also see paris-le-mont-etape-1-10-01-12-pdf.pdf for a leaflet in English on the section between Condé-sur-Huisne and Mortagne-au-Perche.
A Topoguide for the route is available from ornetourisme.com or randonnees-normandie.com for five euros.

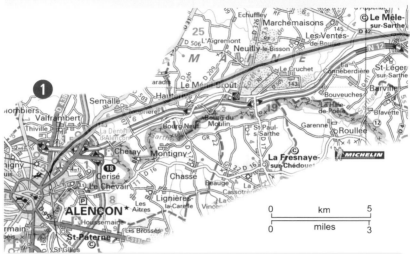

Generally well-signed unsealed railpath with a decent surface. Some barriers difficult for trailers, tandems and full panniers.
This long and relatively new voie verte is intended ultimately to form part of a Paris to Mont-St-Michel cycle route (see route 34) and currently links to a signed véloroute from Condé-sur-Huisne to Chartres. Several million euros have been spent on putting it in place on this former rail line, disused for over thirty years.

The route passes through the Parcs Naturels Régionaux Normandie-Maine and du Perche. The landscapes are varied with small towns and villages on or by the route. On leaving Alençon, the route is bordered by enormous fields as far as the fôret de Bourse, a wilder and more varied landscape. It's then back to prairie-size fields, more marshland than pasture at certain times, and on to the Sarthe valley with its stands of poplars. The hills of the Perche then take you up to Mortagne-au-Perche and on to a long, smooth descent across the Huisne valley to a world of cider-apple trees, dairy herds, rivers, hills and ancient farmsteads.

Le Mêle-sur-Sarthe is set round its hilltop church and is mainly known for its annual horse fair and for the nearby lakeside leisure facilities including swimming, sailing and fishing. Mortagne-au-Perche is also famed for an annual fair, but this time one celebrating black pudding, an international championship having been hosted there since 1963 by the Confrérie des Chevaliers du Goute Boudin and attracting over 20,000 enthusiasts to the town. Mortagne is, incidentally, a very nice little town anyway with a wealth of history and lots of interesting things to see and places to eat. The heavy horses you are likely to encounter around the area are Percherons, one of France's equivalents of the shire horse. Alençon is the capital of the Orne department and is a good-sized busy town where the manufacture of PVC windows has supplanted lacemaking as the prime earner. It's the birthplace of Ste. Thérèse of Lisieux , it has a substantial château (formerly a prison) and a museum covering the town's role and experiences in the second world war. Condé-sur-Huisne is a small place but with a railway station to speed you on your way or a véloroute to Chartres, or even Paris in the fullness of time (pg 222).

Greenway - unsealed   Greenway - sealed   Signed road route

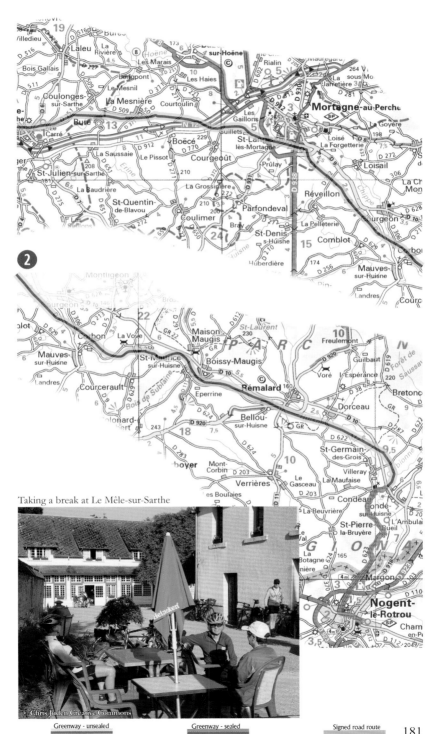

Taking a break at Le Mêle-sur-Sarthe

© Chris Juden Creative Commons

Greenway - unsealed   Greenway - sealed   Signed road route

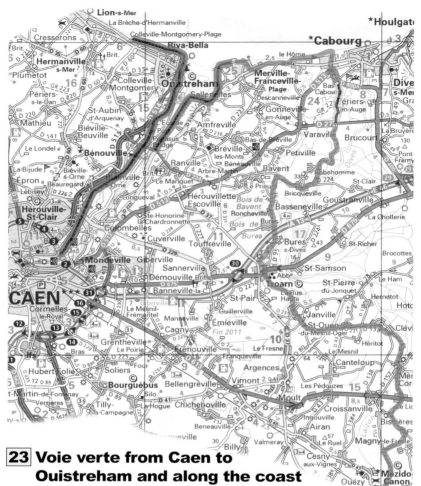

23 Voie verte from Caen to Ouistreham and along the coast

Sealed cyclepath   Caen → Ouistreham Coast **15 km** 9 mi

From the St Pierre canal basin, right next to the centre of Caen, there is an easy and well-surfaced direct link to Ouistreham, the seafront and the ferry to Portsmouth. (The path also heads out to the south of the city, changing from tarmac to an earth surface by the racecourse and continuing by the river and out into the countryside.) There is plenty of scope for exploring the coast either side of Ouistreham by bike. Branching off east at Bénouville, the cycle route to Cabourg is voie verte up to the coast at Merville-Franceville-Plage whilst heading west from Ouistreham itself cycle-lanes and dyke-top traffic-free riding will get you to Lion-sur-Mer, a further 5km on.

Stations at Cabourg and Mézidon-Canon. Signed cycle route from Ouistreham, where the Caen ferries from Portsmouth actually land, to Cabourg, much of it traffic-free.

Downloadable English language leaflet at www.calvados-tourisme.com gives a map and supporting information

The seaside resort of Cabourg has an atmosphere redolent of the elegant world of the late nineteenth and early twentieth centuries. The Grand Hotel (a setting for Proust's À La Recherche du Temps Perdu) and the Casino are a fine sight, as is the magnificent beach stretching over two miles where you sometimes see trotting horses training for races at Cabourg racecourse, famous for its night races.

Greenway - unsealed   Greenway - sealed   Signed road route

24 Véloroute Marais de la Dives

Roads and unsealed cyclepath   Cabourg → Vimoutiers   69 km 43 mi

🚲 Mainly véloroute on small, quiet roads from Cabourg through Bricqueville, Troarn and Mézidon-Canon to Le Mesnil-Mauger from where a railpath runs the 22 kilometres to Vimoutiers. Variable surface quality - roads are mainly tarmac but it's poor in places and some sections are crushed stone. Well signed including ground markings in Troarn and Mézidon. Passes through marshland and agricultural areas with attractive small towns and villages.

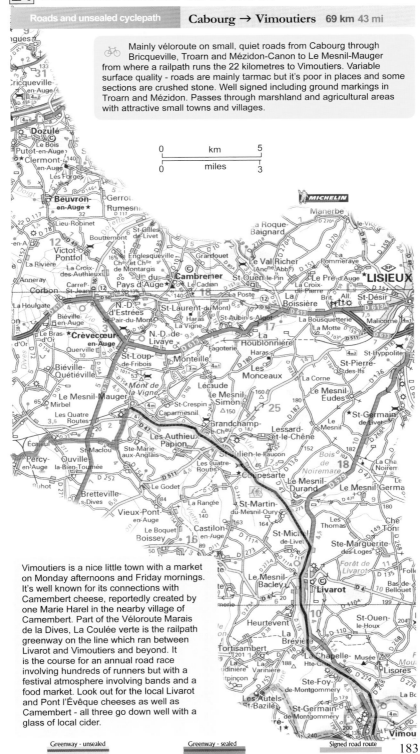

Vimoutiers is a nice little town with a market on Monday afternoons and Friday mornings. It's well known for its connections with Camembert cheese, reportedly created by one Marie Harel in the nearby village of Camembert. Part of the Véloroute Marais de la Dives, La Coulée verte is the railpath greenway on the line which ran between Livarot and Vimoutiers and beyond. It is the course for an annual road race involving hundreds of runners but with a festival atmosphere involving bands and a food market. Look out for the local Livarot and Pont l'Évêque cheeses as well as Camembert - all three go down well with a glass of local cider.

Greenway - unsealed   Greenway - sealed   Signed road route   183

25 Voie verte from Évreux to Pont-Authou

Sealed railpath Évreux → Pont-Authou 43 km 27 mi

The station at Évreux has direct bicycle-carrying trains from Paris Saint Lazare. Glos-Montfort station is a couple of kilometres to the north of Pont-Authou and has bicycle-carrying trains from Rouen and Serquigny.

www.eure-voiesvertes.fr has a schematic map and useful supporting information.

Pretty much a textbook example of a voie verte - continuous tarmac, 3 metres wide and barrierless access with well-controlled road crossings. Well signed.

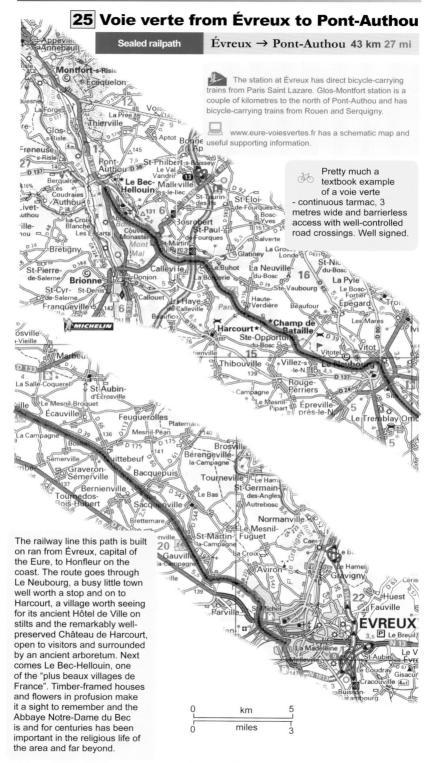

The railway line this path is built on ran from Évreux, capital of the Eure, to Honfleur on the coast. The route goes through Le Neubourg, a busy little town well worth a stop and on to Harcourt, a village worth seeing for its ancient Hôtel de Ville on stilts and the remarkably well-preserved Château de Harcourt, open to visitors and surrounded by an ancient arboretum. Next comes Le Bec-Hellouin, one of the "plus beaux villages de France". Timber-framed houses and flowers in profusion make it a sight to remember and the Abbaye Notre-Dame du Bec is and for centuries has been important in the religious life of the area and far beyond.

0 km 5
0 miles 3

Greenway - unsealed   Greenway - sealed   Signed road route

© Allie Caulfield Creative Commons

Le Bec-Helbuin has rightly earned the official classification of 'les plus beaux villages de France' - one of the most beautiful of French villages

Other Routes

26 The Cotentin Voie Verte

Unsealed railpath	Rocheville → Cambernon 68 km 42 mi

Direct trains from Paris, most of which will carry bicycles, serve Valognes and Cherbourg near the northern end of the path. Coutances near the southern end is similarly accessible with one change. Hop off the ferry at Cherbourg and the veloroute south will get you straight onto the Normandy cycle route network.

www.manchetourisme.com for "La Manche à vélo".

The signed véloroute link from Cherbourg (23 kilometres) is probably as scenic as much of the voie verte, crossing some very attractive countryside and passing the striking Château de Tourlaville. It is the start of the French side of the Tour and Petit Tour de Manche, two signed circular cross-channel routes being developed to encourage cycling visitors. For further detail on this and the voie verte itself, including mapping, see *Around the Cotentin* touring route. About halfway along the voie verte, near the junctions with the east-west Transcotentine voie verte between Portbail and Carentan, La Haye-du-Puits is a seemingly unremarkable little town. It has a decent range of shops and restaurants and a popular market on Wednesday mornings. Accommodation includes a rather nice campsite on the route at St -Symphorien le Valois just north of La Haye-du-Puits. But in July 1944, the invasion of Normandy was in progress and like most places in the Cotentin peninsula, there was heavy fighting here in the town itself and the other hillls in the area. The town was taken from the Germans on the 8th July with much loss of life. Memorials are at the northern and western gates of the town.

27 The Transcotentine and the Vire towpath

Unsealed railpath and roads	Portbail → St-Lô 91 km 56.5 mi

Stations at Carentan (direct trains from Paris) and St-Lô.

www.manchetourisme.com has an excellent booklet "La Manche à vélo".

A reasonably well surfaced path for the most part, although unsuitable for racing bikes, the Transcotentine is wide and well shaded. Unsealed railpath from Portbail to Carentan - the line ran between Carentan and Carteret, the section between Portbail and Carteret now being used as a heritage railway. The southern section is well-signed véloroute on quiet roads from Carentan to St.-Fromond and then a generally good, smooth hard earth and gravel towpath to St-Lô. Signage is not comprehensive and access from town centres can be fiddly to find. The ride from Carentan to St-Lô is particularly attractive, although some of the marshland areas west of Carentan, particularly around Baupte, quite take the breath away, when you can see them for the heavy vegetation along the path that is. For further detail, including mapping, see *Around the Cotentin* touring route.

28 Voie Verte d'Eure et Avre

Sealed railpath	Saint-Georges-Motel → Ivry-la-Bataille 18 km 11 mi

Bueil, 4 kilometres from Ivry-la-Bataille and Dreux, 6 kilometres from Saint-Georges-Motel have regular bicycle carrying trains from Paris, journey time around an hour.

For a map see www.eure-voiesvertes.fr

Nice new smooth 3m wide tarmac railpath along the Eure valley, taking in some pretty villages and the elegant Château d'Anet. It's only an hour or two's worth of riding but a very good quality path in a lovely area. The immediate plan is to extend it from Ivry-la-Bataille to Breuilpont taking it to 27 kilometres long and one day hopefully it will form part of a Rouen-Chartres route.

29 Véloroutes of the Risle and Charentonne valleys

Sealed railpath	Bernay → Broglie 13 km 8 mi
Minor roads	Le Petit Nassandres → Notre-Dame-du-Hamel 40 km 25 mi
Minor roads	Pont-Audemer → Rugles 80 km 50 mi

Access with a bike by rail is good on the direct trains from Paris to l'Aigle on the line a few miles south of Rugles and to Bernay. Just one or two bicycle carrying trains go from Rouen to Brionne, Serquigny and Bernay.

For a map of the véloroutes see www.eure-tourisme.fr and download the brochure D'Eure en Eure. For downloadable leaflets covering the voie verte see www.eure-voiesvertes.fr and www.bernaytourisme.fr.

The routes along the Risle and Charentonne valleys in Upper Normandy are on-road véloroutes, although part of the Charentonne valley route runs parallel to a high quality 13 kilometre Bernay-Broglie railpath. The fully signed Risle véloroute starts at Pont Audemer and goes south, 75% along lightly trafficked roads, the rest on busier ones, to Rugles. At Pont Authou it links to the excellent voie verte from Évreux and further south at Le Petit Nassandres the Charentonne véloroute heads eastwards and south to Notre-Dame-du-Hamel.
The half timbered buildings of Pont -Audemer stand on medieval streets and little canalised tributaries of the Risle. A heritage railway runs from the town to Honfleur. Bernay too has its share of half timbered buildings and is home to the 11th century church of Notre Dame, the oldest Romanesque church in Normandy.

30 Voie Verte from the Seine to the Eure

Sealed cyclepath	Pinterville → Poses 20 km 12.5 mi

Paris-Rouen Intercité service stops at Val-de-Reuil near the northern end of the ride.

www.eure-voiesvertes.fr for downloadable map with a little supporting information.

Mainly good, 3 metre wide multi-user smooth tarmac path although the section around Le Vaudreuil is less good and there are some sections open to motor vehicles. For the most part well signed. Very pleasant, meandering ride, much of it riverside, through lush countryside. Attractions along the way range from lovely Louviers with its museum, gardens, religious buildings and riverside walks to the leisure park at Léry-Poses offering water and other sports.

31 Véloroute du Littoral - Côte d'Albâtre

Minor roads	Le Tréport → Le Havre 172 km 108 mi

Rail links at Le Tréport, Dieppe, Fécamp and Le Havre. Dieppe and Le Havre are major ferry ports.

www.normandie-cote-nature.com for downloadable map. Includes options for mountain bikes and for bypassing some of the harder parts. Available also as a free brochure from www.seine-maritime-tourisme.com

The Côte d'Albâtre véloroute showcases the high white chalk cliffs of the area with some lovely seaside towns set by the estuaries of river valleys coming down to the sea. Places like Etretat and Fécamp are well known resorts but there are many smaller jewels and whilst Dieppe and Le Havre are probably first thought of as ferry ports, they too have their own charms. The restaurant-lined seafront of the still busy fishing port at Dieppe is captivating and the post war architecture of Le Havre is special enough to make it a World Heritage site. The route is great if you're a fairly fit sort of cyclist but doesn't make a good family tour as far as the riding's concerned, although this could change at least in part if plans for a railpath between Dieppe and Fécamp come to fruition. An electric bike would noticeably reduce the leg work on this route and might make the many ups and downs (with some climbs over 10%) more manageable. Mainly minor roads but occasional busier ones.

32 Pays de Bray Avenue Verte

Railpath — Arques-la-Bataille → Forges-les-Eaux 47 km / 29 mi

Newhaven to Dieppe ferries sail twice daily and take around 4 hours. www.ldlines.co.uk

www.avenuevertelondonparis.com

This superbly surfaced tarmac greenway is part of the *Avenue Verte & Seine Valley* touring route. It starts 8km south of Dieppe (signed road link straight off the ferry). Numerous circuits on quiet rural roads signed off the Avenue Verte. A luxurious 3 metre wide surface has interesting stop-offs at the château of Mesnières-en-Bray (including stylish 'gites' group accommodation) and the towns of Neufchâtel-en-Bray and Forges-les-Eaux. The *Avenue Verte* itself runs from London to Paris and was launched in summer 2012.

33 Epte valley voie verte

Railpath — Gisors → Gasny 26 km 16 mi

Station at Gisors with direct service from Paris but beware rush hour restrictions on bikes.

www.eure-voiesvertes.fr has downloadable leaflet on this route and others in the Eure. To find the start of the route near Gisors, see www.voiesvertes.com Also see www.avenuevertelondonparis.com

60 kilometres to the north west of Paris in the area known as the Vexin, this good, smooth tarmac railpath follows the Epte valley from Gisors to Gasny. It is only short but has plenty of stopping places and attractions. The once mighty fortifications at Gisors are still impressive, there are other châteaux along the route and the watermill at Forges is picturesque. The Epte valley was once the boundary between France and Normandy but was later a source of inspiration to impressionist painters. Giverny, home to Monet's house and gardens, is just a couple of miles west of Gasny near where the little River Epte flows into the Seine. It's part of the Avenue Verte & Seine Valley touring route.

34 Véloscénie - Paris to Mont-St-Michel

Minor roads and greenways — Montparnasse, Paris → Mont-St-Michel 386 km 240 mi

Downloadable maps covering the sections through Normandy at www.normandie-cote-nature.com For sections of the whole route see https://sites.google.com/site/parisnantesavelo/ www.veloscenie.com

Signed leisure route on greenways and quiet roads, planned for completion in the near future. Much of this route is in fact available now with the majority of it running through Normandy. The sections between Domfront and Mont-St-Michel (route 21) and between Alençon and Condé-sur-Huisne (route 22) are covered in this chapter and Condé-sur-Huisne to Chartres and on to Maintenon is largely in place. The Coulée Verte du TGV Atlantique that starts near Montparnasse station and runs 15 kilometres to Massy (route 53) is also part of it, just leaving the section from here to near Chartres and the one between Domfront and Alençon to be completed (interim routes available on the Véloscénie website).

35 Normandy beaches to Mont-St-Michel

Minor roads and greenways — Ste-Marie-du-Mont, Port-en-Bessin and Arromanches → Mont-St-Michel

Downloadable maps at www.normandie-cote-nature.com

About to be launched at the time of writing, this series of long-distance routes will initially link Utah beach (just north of Carentan) to Mont-St-Michel. In the long term there are plans for a route from Omaha beach to north of Vire, via Bayeux.

Picardy

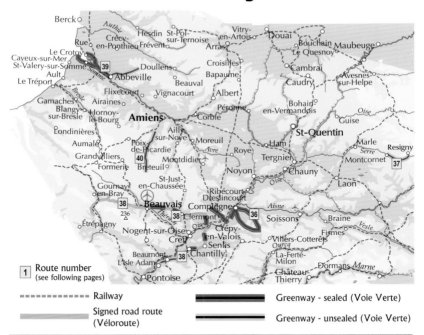

1 Route number
(see following pages)

▬▬▬▬▬▬ Railway

Signed road route
(Véloroute)

Greenway - sealed (Voie Verte)

Greenway - unsealed (Voie Verte)

The cycle network in Picardy has great potential, particularly in the Aisne département which has a rich legacy of waterways and disused railways. Hopefully the opening of the Avenue Verte in 2012, linking London to Paris and passing through Picardy, will provide a boost to further development; there are many fine sites waiting to be explored by bike, including some fine historic towns and cities and beautiful rivers and coast.

Culture, Food & History

Picardy is known for its massive cathedrals that competed with each other for size throughout the middle ages; today they dominate the centres of Amiens, Beauvais and Laon. Gourmets will head for Champagne, not just to drink its bubbly but to try a variety of dishes that use it! Picardy cuisine may not be world renowned but has its own distinctive dishes including ficelle picardie, a ham and mushroom crêpe sometimes containing the pungent local cheese Maroilles. Sweet macaroons are a speciality of Amiens and gâteau battu is a little brioche shaped cake from around Ponthieu and Abbeville. You may even occasionally hear the Picard language. But for many people the big association is the two world wars. Picardy bore the brunt of much action and is especially known for First World War. trench warfare There are many cemeteries, monuments and battlefield sites. Some see Picardy as a featureless area of prairie style farming but it is also an area with wooded river valleys, large forests and long sand beaches on the Somme estuary - all pretty dramatic.

Organised Holidays

For Somme battlefields tours see www.cyclingthewesternfront.co.uk For a three day Champagne Vineyard bike tour see www.weekend-picardy.co.uk www.aisne-a-velo.com has weekend rides.

Access to Picardy

Direct trains from Calais and Lille to Amiens give ready access to the heart of Picardy by ferry or Eurostar. The airport at Beauvais has flights in from Manchester, Glasgow, Dublin and Knock.

i More Info

www.picardietourisme.com www.aisne-a-velo.com www.oise-randonnee.com which includes an excellent section on voies vertes long and short. **www.oisetourisme.com**
www.baiecyclette.com www.somme-nature.com

36 Compiègne & around

Sealed railpath   Compiègne and Pierrefonds (circular)   26 km   16 mi

Lacroix-Saint-Ouen → Compiègne Forest Armistice Clearing   17 km   11 mi

Compiègne is about an hour, or less on some trains, from Paris.

www.oise-randonnee.com and for a good map of all the cycle paths in the area see www.au5v.fr/IMG/pdf/plan_pistes_compiegne.pdf

Surfacing is generally tarmac, sometimes excellent, sometimes poor. Inadequate signage and some junctions needing care. Popular with both cyclists and skaters.
Compiègne is relatively flat and is surrounded by ancient and beautiful forest which goes to make for a couple of rather nice cycle paths forming a circular ride of some 26 kilometres between Compiègne and Pierrefonds. In fact the area has some 57 kilometres of cycle path including the riverside path from Compiègne to La-Croix-St-Ouen and Le Meux. A new path between Le Meux and Rivecourt links the Compiègne Forest network to the Plaine d'Estrées railpath.

Sixty kilometres north of Paris, the Forest of Compiègne is big, about nine miles in diameter, and has always been well-used one way or another. What is now a haven for cyclists, walkers and horse-riders was once the hunting ground of kings and emperors and is still home to deer and wild boar. Both ancient and recent beech and oak trees are the dominant species and the lush forest is well irrigated by the Rivers Aisne and Oise and their tributaries. The villages of Vieux-Moulin and Saint-Jean-aux-Bois are particularly attractive and the Château de Pierrefonds is a spectacular sight. The Rethondes Armistice clearing is where the First World War officially ended and has a replica of the carriage where the signing took place. The whole forest is a delight but is especially seductive in autumn. Just outside the city of Compiègne there is a grand entrance to the forest at the remarkable former royal château of Compiègne (collection of bicycles in the national motor museum here). Much of the city of Compiègne was destroyed in WWII so it's not what it might have been but does nonetheless attract large numbers of day visitors from Paris.

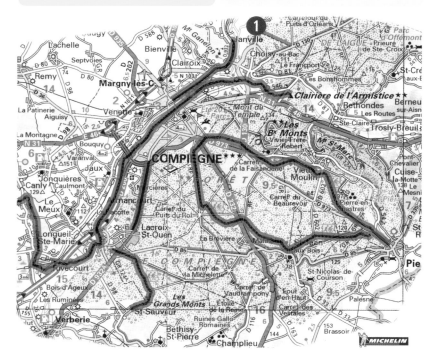

Greenway - unsealed   Greenway - sealed   Signed road route

Sealed railpath   Estrées-Saint-Denis → Longueil-Sainte-Marie 13 km 8 mi

Direct trains between Compiègne and Estrées-Saint-Denis and Longueil-Sainte-Marie give a number of rail return options.

For a map of the route see http://www.au5v.fr/IMG/pdf/Plaine-Estrees.pdf

Wide railpath from Estrées-Saint-Denis to Longueil-Sainte-Marie surfaced with coated gravel making it OK for most bikes but a bit doubtful for those with narrow tyres. It's 13 kilometres long but then there is a 6 kilometre signed véloroute link from Longueil-Sainte-Marie to Lacroix-Saint-Ouen and the 17 kilometre path alongside the Oise to Compiègne and on to the Armistice Clearing.

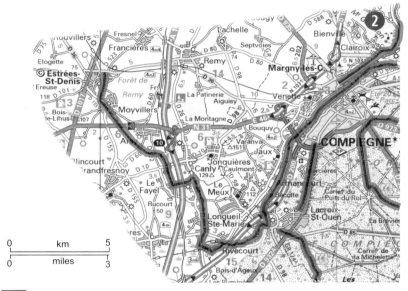

37 | Voie verte of the Serre Valley

Unsealed railpath   Montcornet → Résigny 16 km 10 mi

 This unsealed railpath is not that suitable for narrow tyres.

 The nearest railway stations are at Laon and Liart, both quite a long way from the ride. However, there is an SNCF coach service between the two places serving the whole of the ride, so if you have a folding bike or a sparklingly persuasive nature, you may be able to get on that. Also, from the northern end, a mountain bike may let you continue along the old railtrack to La Férée from where quiet roads lead to Liart.

www.randonner.fr www.tourisme-thierache.fr

Some thirty miles or so north of Reims, the Val de Serre is a lush area of pasture and wetlands with the railpath voie verte something of a feature there. It has three signed mountain bike circuits off it and has the potential for being developed into a much longer ride. The path starts at the village of Montcornet with its remarkable fortified church of St. Martin, one of about sixty churches in the area which have had keeps, watchtowers etc. built into them as protection against marauders of old. There are information boards about the circular mountain bike routes and others about the flora and fauna of the wetland areas. Picnic tables have been provided and if you're looking for a quiet, bucolic ramble, this little route might well suit.

Parfondeval, about 5km north of the trail at Rozoy-sur serre, is a beautiful redbrick, village amidst orchards and pastureland and is certainly worth the detour.

This route option is part of the larger *Avenue Verte* London to Paris route inaugurated in 2012, the French section between Dieppe and Paris being covered in more detail in the touring route *Avenue Verte & Seine Valley*.

This eastern option gives you the choice to split off near Gournay (where there are plans to open up the disused railway to Beauvais as a railpath for cyclists) and head past Beauvais' magnificent cathedral before heading to the sumptuous ancient towns of Senlis and Chantilly.

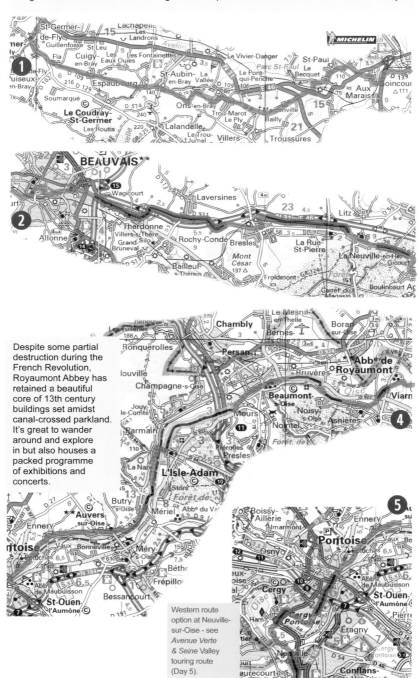

Despite some partial destruction during the French Revolution, Royaumont Abbey has retained a beautiful core of 13th century buildings set amidst canal-crossed parkland. It's great to wander around and explore in but also houses a packed programme of exhibitions and concerts.

Western route option at Neuville-sur-Oise - see *Avenue Verte & Seine* Valley touring route (Day 5).

Greenway - unsealed   Greenway - sealed   Signed road route

38 Avenue Verte Eastern Option

Minor roads and tracks · St-Germer / Gournay → Neuville 168 km 105 mi

🚲 Initially following minor roads through hilly country (until the arrival of the Gournay to Beauvais railpath) things get flatter and more traffic-free as you cross the Oise and then join its banks for the final stretch to rejoin the shorter western option of the *Avenue Verte* at Neuville-sur-Oise. The *Avenue Verte* then follows the Seine into Paris (again, see the *Avenue Verte & Seine Valley* touring route for this section).

Stations en route at Beauvais, Clermont de l'Oise, Pont-Sainte-Maxence, Chantilly, Persan, Beaumont, L'Isle Adam, Valmondois, Auvers-sur-Oise and Pontoise.
Times to Paris range from around 1 hour 10 mins (Beauvais) to around 40 mins (Pontoise).

💻 www.randonner.fr www.tourisme-thierache.fr

Senlis has preserved its impressive, ancient encircling walls and Notre-Dame Cathedral is impressive enough itself, but is surrounded by a warren of ancient streets and buildings. Chantilly is on a grander scale altogether, with magnificent stable blocks and a stately home on the edge of town which the route goes right past.

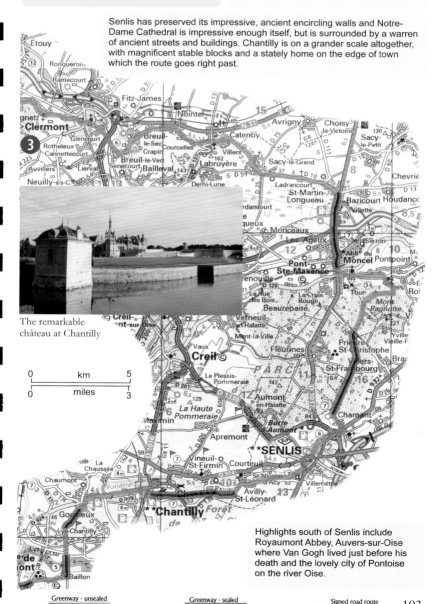

The remarkable château at Chantilly

0   km   5
0   miles   3

Highlights south of Senlis include Royaumont Abbey, Auvers-sur-Oise where Van Gogh lived just before his death and the lovely city of Pontoise on the river Oise.

Greenway - unsealed   Greenway - sealed   Signed road route

39 Somme bay cycle paths and around

Sealed paths	St-Firmin → Le Hourdel	24 km 15 mi
Sealed paths	Parc de Marquenterre → Quend-Plage	13 km 8 mi

These routes are mainly tarmac or concrete paths, with the Traverse du Ponthieu between Abbeville and Bernâtre being smooth compacted grit and with a short section of quiet road towards the north eastern end of the system. Excellent system of quiet linking minor roads used for small loops rides; see websites opposite.

Greenway - unsealed   Greenway - sealed   Signed road route

Sealed paths	**Saint-Valery-sur-Somme → Abbeville** 15 km 9 mi
Unsealed path	**Abbeville → Bernâtre** 25 km 15.5 mi

The cyclepath around the Bay of the Somme runs alongside the main road round the estuary, although in some places at a distance and in some separated by a large hedge. To the north eastern end, a short distance on a quiet road leads to the 13 kilometres of voie verte between Marquenterre and Quend-Plage. There is a good number of circular rides off these two cyclepaths. The towpath alongside the Canal de la Somme runs south from Saint-Valery-sur-Somme on the Bay of the Somme path to Abbeville from where there is a railpath link to Bernâtre.

Stations at Abbeville and Noyelles on the Paris to Boulogne line with a heritage railway (www.cfbs.eu) round the bay which carries bikes free.

www.baiedesomme.fr www.baiecyclette.com
www.sommenature.com

The huge estuary that forms the Bay of the Somme is an area of marshes, sand dunes, saltwater meadows and pebble or white sand beaches. Saint-Valery-sur-Somme is a pretty place with a harbour full of boats and a town that's a mix of medieval citadel, brightly painted cottages and elegant nineteenth century villas. The Parc du Marquenterre is a bird reserve with a dozen hides and support in the form of guides, tours and horse-drawn cart rides along the beach.

Greenway - unsealed   Greenway - sealed   Signed road route

40 Amiens to Beauvais coulée verte

Unsealed railpath · Bacouël-sur-Selle → Crèvecoeur-le-Grand · 29.5 km · 18 mi

There are railway stations in Beauvais and Amiens but the journeys between these two town centres and the railpath access points are fairly lengthy.

There are a couple of useful downloadable map leaflets on www.somme.fr and a more schematic one on www.sortir-amiens.com and www.cccconty.com

Surfaces vary widely and can include grass, so a suitable bike is needed.

This voie verte does not itself link Amiens and Beauvais and requires road riding at each end, about 8 kilometres to Amiens and about 23 kilometres to Beauvais. It was opened in 1997 along a section of the former railway between the two cities. For the most part it follows the valley of the River Selle, popular with fishermen because of its lakes fed by the river and popular with equestrians also. There are several charming villages along the tree-lined coulée verte including Prouzel with its magnificent 17th century castle, Wailly, Loeuilly, Conty and Monsures.

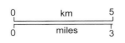

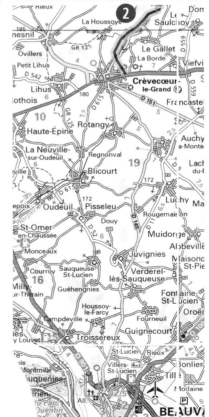

0 — km — 5
0 — miles — 3

Greenway - unsealed · Greenway - sealed · Signed road route

Nord-Pas-de-Calais

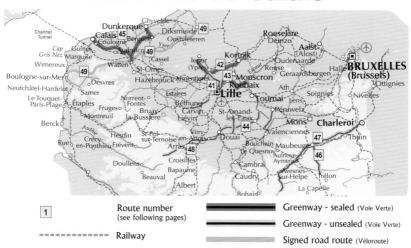

1	Route number (see following pages)
	Greenway - sealed (Voie Verte)
--------------	Railway
	Greenway - unsealed (Voie Verte)
	Signed road route (Véloroute)

France's northernmost region undoubtedly benefits from being Belgium's neighbour - in terms of cycle routes at least. Indeed many of the routes in the French Flanders area link directly into the Belgian RAVEL network of traffic-free cycle trails, making for countless cross-border trip opportunities.

Culture, Food & History

The Flemish influence in the far north of this area is overwhelming and in border towns you will even find some inhabitants preferring to speak Flemish over French. Architecture is distinctive too, most notably the ubiquitous 'stepped' Flemish brickwork on buildings' facades. The riches generated by the role of Flanders in the medieval cloth trade in particular have left a fine heritage of opulent and attractive civic buildings.

Even more unusual for France is the fact that locals often prefer the local Pelforth beer (choose from light blonde or heavier, darker brune or even the rich and golden-coloured ambrée) to wine. Estaminets are local brasseries that often specialise in various dishes cooked in beer, the best-known being carbonade à la flamande. You'll also be able to refuel with plenty of crêpes, waffles and the often-strong local cheeses.

Access to Nord-Pas-de-Calais

Unfortunately ferries from the UK to Boulogne had ceased at the time of writing. By way of compensation, Eurostar can now carry bicycles on the same train as the passenger and gets you to the region's heart and one of its most attractive cities, Lille, in only an hour and a half or so from

London. If you take the le Shuttle train from Folkstone to Calais, you will travel with your bike, you in a minibus and your bike on a trailer behind. Ferries from Dover to Calais are frequent. Le Touquet airport is about 20 kilometres south of Boulogne with a good number of flights in from the UK. Bike hire is available at the airport.

i More Info

For a broad schematic map of major cycle routes through Nord-Pas-de-Calais, see
www.nordpasdecalais.fr

Although much of this area is flat there are plenty of hills too if you know where to go.

197

41 The Deûle Valley greenway

Unsealed Towpath   Marquette-lez-Lille → Deûlémont   12 km   8 mi

42 River Lys voie verte

Unsealed and sealed towpath   Armentières → Halluin   27 km   17 mi

🚲 The coulée verte de la Deûle is 12 kilometres of well signed compacted surface towpath through pleasant countryside with plenty of picnic stops. It starts in Marquette-lez-Lille about 5 kilometres out of Lille and goes to Deûlémont where you join the voie verte de la Lys, a good tarmac surfaced towpath running out to the Belgian border where it joins an excellent voie verte to Courtrai. There are local railway stations at various places on these routes with services (not always that frequent) from the centre of Lille, although it's not far out anyway and a cycle route link has been planned. Also see *Boulogne to Lille* touring route.

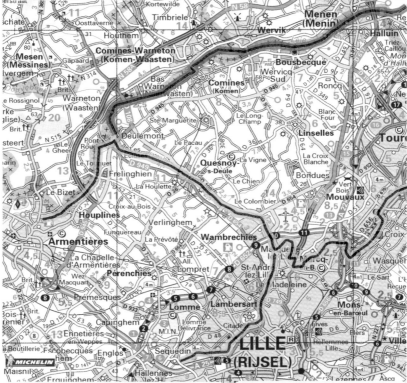

The eastern end of the voie verte de la Lys is Armentières, famous for the World War 1 song "Mademoiselle from Armentières". In contrast with the cheeriness of the tune, the town had a hard time of it in the first war being shelled with mustard gas and suffering much destruction. The nearby cité Bonjean military cemetery is extensive.

The little tourist tramway along the 3 kilometres between Marquette and Wambrechies makes a pleasant entertainment. Its colourful carriages are an elegant accompaniment to the collection of buses, trolley buses and other working vehicles.
www.amitram.asso.fr

Lille knows how to look after its cyclists - there's a network of cycle lanes and a number of traffic-free paths along with a public bike hire system,electric bike hire (and Segways) and plenty of cycle parking. Bikes are allowed not just on local trains but on the trams also, although sadly not on the metro lines. And of course there's the Eurostar service into Lille which will carry your bike on the same train. There is no cycle parking at the Lille Europe station. For a detailed town plan of Lille see *Boulogne to Lille* touring route on the *Touring Routes* map.

43 The Roubaix Canal

Unsealed Towpath　　Marquette-lez-Lille → Belgian border (Leers)　22 km　13.5 mi

Extensive local system but with also extensive TGV and Eurostar connections.

www.mairie-lille.fr for a downloadable map leaflet of cycling routes and facilities in the city. Also www. lilletourisme.com has one covering a wider area and zoom facilities for Lille and Roubaix/Tourcoing.

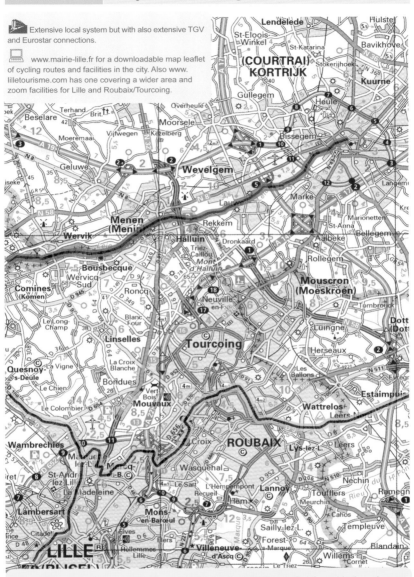

🚲　Yet another waterside path runs from Marquette-lez-Lille into Belgium, this time along the Marque and the canal de Roubaix, using a wide, level surface of crushed stone.

```
0        km        5
├─────────────────┤
0       miles       3
```

La Piscine or the Musée d'Art et d'Industrie is a recently opened museum in Roubaix, housed in a delightful 1930s swimming pool, with excellent collections of mainly 19th and early 20th century sculpture and painting with some fashion and textiles.

Greenway - unsealed　　　　　　　Greenway - sealed　　　　　　　Signed road route　　199

44 Voie Verte de la Scarpe and Voie Verte de la plaine de la Scarpe

Unsealed Path	Douai → Mortagne-du-Nord 37 km 23 mi
Unsealed Path	Fenain → Orchies 12 km 7.5 mi

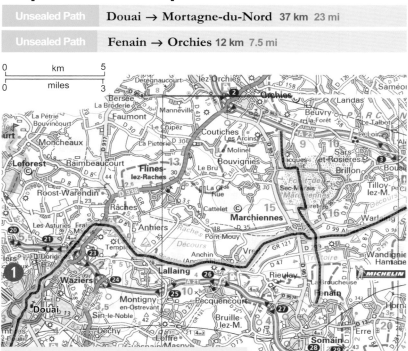

Towpath continues to Arras; cycleable though not an official route

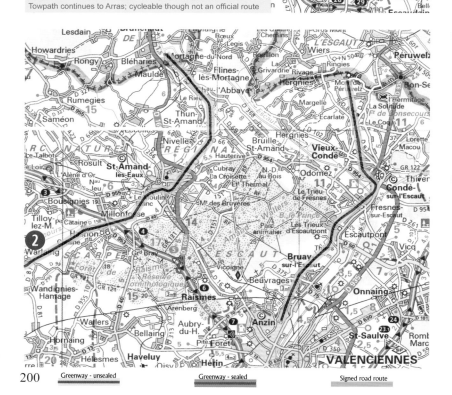

Greenway - unsealed   Greenway - sealed   Signed road route

Rail access to and around the area is good with plenty of bicycle carrying trains from Lille to Valenciennes, Douai, Somain, Orchies and Saint-Amand-les-Eaux.

www.rando-nord.fr has a downloadable leaflet on the voie verte de la plaine de la Scarpe.

The voie verte de la Scarpe is a pleasant, rural path with a compacted surface but no signage or rest areas.The cycle path section alongside the heritage railway at Saint-Amand-les-Eaux is narrow and difficult. Although the western end of this voie verte is at Douai, the cyclable towpath actually comes in from Arras. At the eastern end, it finishes at Mortagne-du-Nord near the Belgian border, just across which you can join the Belgian RAVeL system of cycle paths and head off to Tournai or various other places.

At Rieulay about 10 kilometres from Douai it passes the parc des Argales, where there is an artificial beach and a bird reserve and at Saint-Amand-les-Eaux there is a little heritage railway with steam trains running mainly on Sundays in July and August.
Saint-Amand is a small attractive spa town with a magnificent tower from a former abbey as its most visible feature although it's probably best known for its mineral and thermal waters.

The Voie Verte de la plaine de la Scarpe is a 12 kilometre railpath of variable width with a decent compacted surface. It passes through much woodland and forest offering rides off the la Scarpe towpath which it crosses near Marchiennes.

There are other voies vertes in the area, not least of which is the Gueules Noires voie verte which runs from Péruwelz, just across the border in Belgium, to Anzin, just outside Valenciennes. It's unsigned and a bit rough in places but it does form a link between Valenciennes and the Belgian RAVeL network. For a pretty extensive view of these many other routes in this area and the rest of the Pas-de-Calais, see www.velo-ravel.net which has photos of a lot them so you can get an idea of what they might be like.

A Parc Naturel Régional is an area where the landscape, cultural or historic heritage of the area is preserved and is in some ways similar to Britain's National Parks. The first one, in 1968, was the Parc Naturel Régional Scarpe-Escaut north of Valenciennes.It is crossed east - west by the towpath voie verte alongside the River la Scarpe and north - south by the plaine de la Scarpe railpath.

45 Canal network between Dunkirk and Calais

Canals de la Bergue and Haute Colme

Towpath & road	Dunkirk → Watten → Calais 67 km 42 mi

An attractive ride in itself but even more appealing as it's effectively a day trip from the UK for those who are within striking distance of Dover, which has regular ferry services to both Dunkirk and Calais. Another option would be to take the Eurostar from London St Pancras International to Lille then a local train of about 1hr 20mins from Lille Flandres station to Dunkirk (30mins), Watten-Eperleques (1hr) or Calais (1hr 20mins)

Good quality cycle lane, canal towpath and usually quiet roads.

From Dunkirk there are reasonable cycles lanes paralleling the canal up rue de Lille, which starts a couple of blocks south-east of the train station. Follow these all the way up route de Bergues and route de Dunkerque to pretty Bergues. Here cross the D352 and pick up the towpath along the south side of the canal de la Haute Colme, staying on this bank all the way to Watten. Here you can join the touring route, *Boulogne to Lille*.
To get back to the coast at Calais follow the D3 north-west, alongside the pretty river Aa, to cross it and immediately pick up the towpath road on the west side. This leads off onto the canal de Calais a St-Omer. You can follow small roads or reasonable quality towpaths all the way to Calais to hop on a ferry back to Dover.

46 Avesnois voie verte

Unsealed Towpath   Maubeuge → Trélon 30 km 18.5 mi

47 River Sambre voie verte

Unsealed Towpath   Jeumont → Hautmont 21 km 13 mi

Trains run from Jeumont to Maubeuge and from Fourmies, 7 kilometres south of Trélon.

www.ville-maubeuge.fr www.noirdpasdecalais.fr

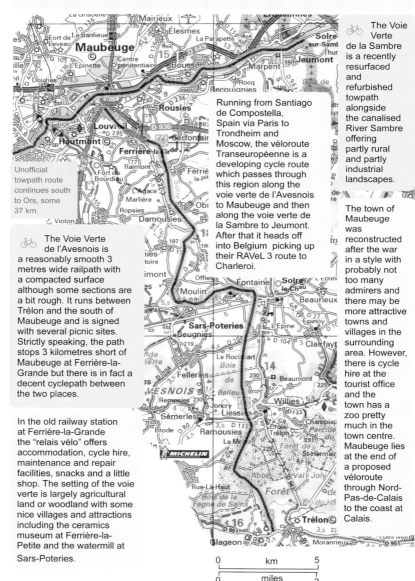

Running from Santiago de Compostella, Spain via Paris to Trondheim and Moscow, the véloroute Transeuropéenne is a developing cycle route which passes through this region along the voie verte de l'Avesnois to Maubeuge and then along the voie verte de la Sambre to Jeumont. After that it heads off into Belgium picking up their RAVeL 3 route to Charleroi.

The Voie Verte de la Sambre is a recently resurfaced and refurbished towpath alongside the canalised River Sambre offering partly rural and partly industrial landscapes.

The town of Maubeuge was reconstructed after the war in a style with probably not too many admirers and there may be more attractive towns and villages in the surrounding area. However, there is cycle hire at the tourist office and the town has a zoo pretty much in the town centre. Maubeuge lies at the end of a proposed véloroute through Nord-Pas-de-Calais to the coast at Calais.

The Voie Verte de l'Avesnois is a reasonably smooth 3 metres wide railpath with a compacted surface although some sections are a bit rough. It runs between Trélon and the south of Maubeuge and is signed with several picnic sites. Strictly speaking, the path stops 3 kilometres short of Maubeuge at Ferrière-la-Grande but there is in fact a decent cyclepath between the two places.

In the old railway station at Ferrière-la-Grande the "relais vélo" offers accommodation, cycle hire, maintenance and repair facilities, snacks and a little shop. The setting of the voie verte is largely agricultural land or woodland with some nice villages and attractions including the ceramics museum at Ferrière-la-Petite and the watermill at Sars-Poteries.

Unofficial towpath route continues south to Ors, some 37 km.

```
0            km           5
|----|----|----|----|----|
0          miles          3
```

Other Routes

48 Around Arras

A towpath and a railpath   Arras → Fampoux and Saulty → Dainville   **25 km** 15 mi

Arras is a great rail centre with TGV services to Lille and Paris and a good range of services on other lines including to Calais.

www.arrasavelo.com about electric bike hire and in English. www.pasdecalais.fr or www.ccvertesvallees.fr for railpath leaflet

Two short but good quality voies vertes, one a canal towpath with a smooth compacted surface from Arras to Fampoux, the other a 12 kilometre tarmaced railpath between Saulty and Wailly a few kilometres south west of Arras. Around 2 kilometres of the canal de la Scarpe towpath at Saint-Laurent-Blangy are lit. The path is unsigned. From the Fampoux end, there is a path which continues to join the voie verte de la Scarpe at Douai. The tarmac voie verte between Saulty and Wailly, the first tarmac voie verte in Nord-Pas-de-Calais, will become part of the Véloroute de la Mémoire which will ultimately link the battlefields of the First World War. Arras is a fine city with grand squares and some splendid buildings but one of its top cycling features has to be Arras à Vélo, an electric bike hire enterprise operating from four centres in the city.

49 Route de la Mer du Nord (LF1)

Mainly Minor roads   Oost-Cappel → Boulogne   **95 km** 60 mi

A rail return is possible using the station at Esquelbecq about 15 kilometres short of the border or the one at Watten-Eperlecques about half way along the route. Both involve changes.

For information on the route topoguide see jderoi.free.fr/datas/dossierpresse/lf/f/html/LF1.htm

This is part of a 470 kilometre cycle route from Den Helder in The Netherlands to Boulogne. In The Netherlands and Belgium it follows all traffic-free trails but in France, it follows quiet minor roads avoiding big towns and landing at the coast about 3 kilometres north of Boulogne. For navigation, the topoguide for the route would probably be extremely useful. For a copy of this see jderoi.free.fr/datas/dossierpresse/lf/f/html/LF1.htm Despite the name this is not a coastal route, passing through green and gentle countryside. In the fullness of time it is likely it will be replaced by a currently developing coastal route. The touring route *Boulogne to Lille* uses part of this route.

Some less well-known voies vertes in Pas-de-Calais and the RAVeL network in Belgium

Various Greenways   Pas-de-Calais and Belgium

www.ravel.wallonie.be and www.velo-ravel.net

A number of voies vertes in the Pas-de-Calais cross the border and link in to the traffic-free RAVeL cycle path network in Belgium and there are also a number of voies vertes in the Pas-de-Calais not included in this book as the quality is highly variable. For information on these, www.velo-ravel.net is useful as it has information and photos for many of them. One example within France itself is the voies vertes de la Pévèle and du Sucre lying between Douai and Lille and linking Roost-Warendin north of Douai to Pont-à-Marcq. There are breaks and obstructions according to the website and in places the surface looks more mountain bike territory; however there are plans to improve the route so it may worth be checking out.
For the routes of the truly impressive Belgian RAVeL network see www.ravel.wallonie.be

Paris & Île-de-France

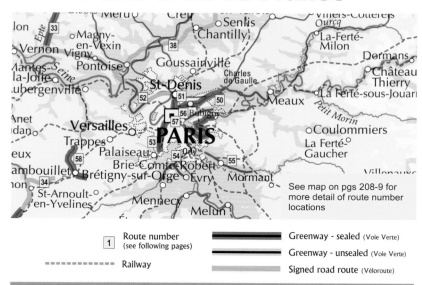

1 Route number (see following pages)	Greenway - sealed (Voie Verte)
	Greenway - unsealed (Voie Verte)
▬▬▬▬▬▬ Railway	Signed road route (Véloroute)

See map on pgs 208-9 for more detail of route number locations

You might think a city known for it's traffic-choked streets was no place for cycling - but you'd be wrong. Whereas London has suffered a slew of cycling fatalities in recent years Paris has an exemplary safety record by comparison. Often well-segregated cycle-lanes and the huge popularity of the free bike hire scheme Vélib' no doubt have contributed, as has a distinct lack of HGVs compared to London. There are also official and often traffic-free entries into the city's heart; the Avenue Verte from the west and the canal de l'Ourcq from the east, making it a cinch to avoid the traffic and explore some of Paris's fine surrounding attractions. Developments include Véligo, a system of secure cycle parking facilities currently being installed at some suburban stations, and a journey planning website planned to start soon.

Culture, Food & History
Few places on earth could claim to rival Paris for culture, food or history. With its compact centre stacked with museums and fine restaurants and a myriad of spectacular landmarks it's not surprising it claims the number one spot in the league of worldwide tourist attractions.

Organised Holidays
www.frenchmystiquetours.com for day rides from Paris into the countryside.

Access to Paris
Eurostar is the easiest way to arrive from the UK with a bike; it delivers you and your trusty steed into the heart of the city at Gare du Nord in around only 2 hours 20 mins from St Pancras International station. Arriving at Charles de Gaulle or Orly airports is likely to be more problematic, entailing getting your bike some 25km or 15 km respectively across the suburbs.

i More Info
There is a map available of cycle infrastructure in the whole of the Île-de-France area, both on paper (available locally) and downloadable at **www.iau-idf.fr** (though extremely difficult to find).
For Paris both the IGN Paris Plan de Ville and the vélib' maps are good. Éditions le Petit Futé publish 52 balades à vélo en Île-de-France. **www.paris.fr** has a downloadable schematic map of the city cycle lane network.

50 Canal de l'Ourcq see pgs 206-9 for maps

Sealed Towpath	Place de Stalingrad, Paris → Claye-Souilly 25 km 15.5 mi

Sevran, Le Vert-Galant and Villeparisis stations on the RER are all close to the Ourcq canal route with frequent bicycle-carrying trains (not peak hours though).

www.paris.fr www.avenuevertelondonparis.com

Sections of the route pass through some of the possibly less elegant areas of Paris but as a cyclepath with a very good surface and few barriers to progress, it is superb. Beyond Claye-Souilly the towpath is unsurfaced and is cycled by many, though not an official route.

The busy cycle route by the Ourcq canal is the main exit from north-east Paris and is part of the developing Paris - Moscow cycle route. It's a route of contrasting halves. The first is urban but with open spaces such as the parc de la Villette at the beginning with its walkway over the canal, the giant geodesic dome and various eye-catching structures. Further on, the parc de la Bergère at Bobigny has wide open spaces. About 15 kms out the second half starts, the landscape becoming more pastoral and the route leaving the canal to pass through the forest of the parc de la Poudrerie, where there is a gunpowder museum before rejoining the waterside. Then, on to Villeparisis and the route end at Claye-Souilly.

51 Canal Saint-Denis see pgs 206-9 for maps

Sealed Towpath	Bassin de la Villette, Paris → Gare de Saint-Denis 5 km 3 mi

There's a decent link from the canal de l'Ourcq through the parc de la Villette to the canal Saint-Denis, the voie verte proper starting about 2 km after joining the towpath. Path width, surface quality and the interest of the surroundings are quite variable.

Rueil-Malmaison station on the RER-A line.

www.avenuevertelondonparis.com

The Cathedral Basilica of Saint-Denis, a masterpiece of Gothic architecture, dates back to the days of Charlemagne. It's the burial place of many, many kings of France, not to mention assorted queens, princes and princesses. The canal Saint-Denis path is the end of the London - Paris Avenue Verte, 100 miles of signed largely traffic-free route which has just been completed. See *Avenue Verte & Seine Valley* on the Touring Routes map.

52 Promenade bleue see pgs 206-9 for maps

Off road paths	Rueil-Malmaison → Colombes 9km 5mi

Rueil-Malmaison station on the RER-A line.

http://promenades.hauts-de-seine.net/

The path itself is wide with a mostly very good surface, some grit, some tarmac and passes through quite a bit of parkland with benches and picnic tables.

This restful, easy path along the south bank of the Seine runs from the parc Pierre Lagravère at Colombes to the pont de Chatou at Rueil-Malmaison and is part of the London - Paris Avenue Verte. In time, a longer promenade bleue is expected to run 39 kilometres along the river out to Issy-les-Moulineaux. There are one or two industrial bits on the route but mostly it's lush green river bank. This ride can be extended to more of a day ride by following the *Avenue Verte* further along the Seine's banks on a mixture of off-road paths and quiet roads past St.-Germain-en-Laye then through the attractive town of Maisons-Laffitte and the Forest of St. Germain to the confluence of the Oise and the Seine at Conflans-Sainte-Honorine, an attractive port town. For route details beyond here see *Avenue Verte & Seine Valley* touring route.

205

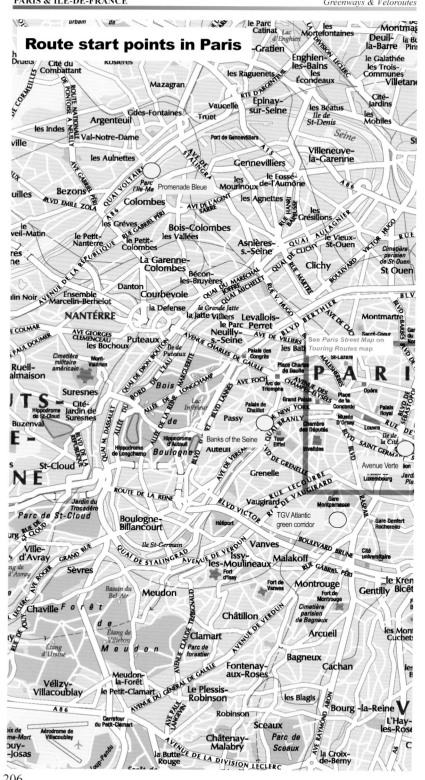

Route start points in Paris

Paris routes

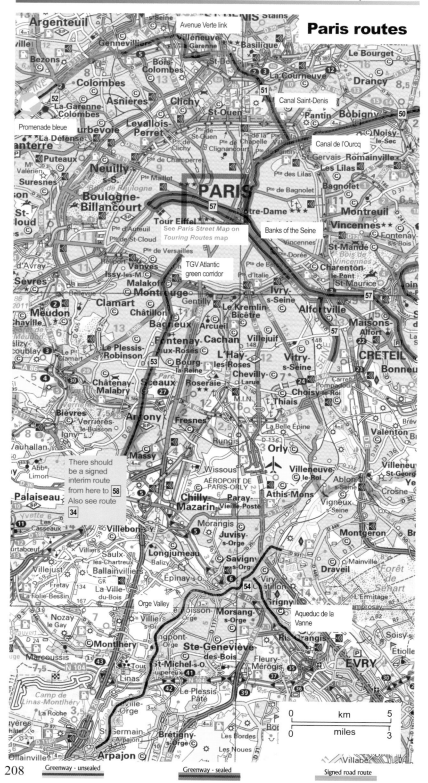

Avenue Verte link

Canal Saint-Denis

Promenade bleue

Canal de l'Ourcq

See *Paris Street Map* on *Touring Routes* map

Banks of the Seine

TGV Atlantic green corridor

There should be a signed interim route from here to 58 Also see route 34

Orge Valley

Aqueduc de la Vanne

| 0 | km | 5 |
| 0 | miles | 3 |

Greenway - unsealed   Greenway - sealed   Signed road route

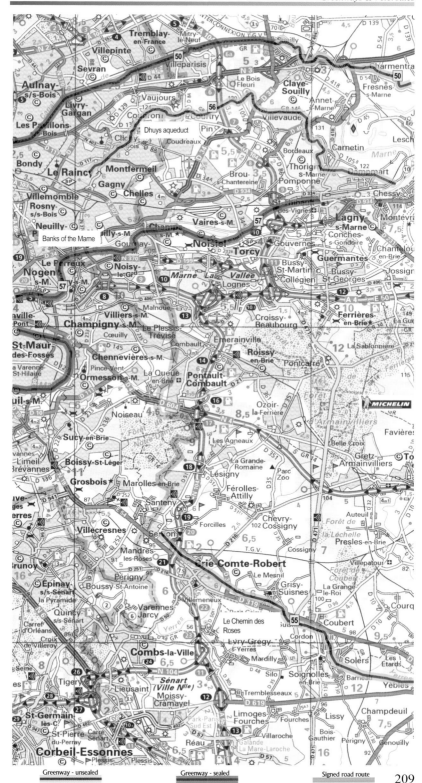

Dhuys aqueduct

Banks of the Marne

Le Chemin des Roses

53 TGV Atlantic green corridor (coulée verte du sud parisien)
see pgs 206-9 for maps

Mainly sealed tarmac path	Place de Catalogne, Paris → Massy 12 km 7.5 mi

Stations at Fontenay-aux-Roses and Sceaux-Robinson on RER B and Massy-Verrières on RER B and C.

Good map on www.af3v.org Paper map from tourist office in Verrières-le-Buisson. Map and website at http://perso.orange.fr/marcoussis-thurion/couleeverte/couverte_accueil.htm

This route has good signage and well set out junctions with good facilities along the way. It's all lit between Paris and Sceaux. However, it can get busy and there are one or two short but steep climbs around Sceaux and Fontenay-aux-Roses. It can be tight with a trailer or large panniers in places. Access from Paris starts at place de Catalogne behind Montparnasse station, continues along rue Vercingétorix and then crosses place de la République with the greenway proper starting at Malakoff. From there it is well signed out to Massy.

Known variously as the Coulée verte du Sud Parisien, Coulée verte du TGV Atlantique and in part La Promenade des vallons de la Bièvre, this linear urban park route runs alongside or over the TGV Atlantique line, linking some of the parks of southern Paris and passing through the green spaces of various residential areas. As greenways go, it is pretty green. Highlights are probably the château and parkland of Sceaux.

54 Banks of the River Orge and the voie verte de l'aqueduc de la Vanne see pgs 206-9 for maps

Unsealed Path	Athis-Mons → St-Germain-lès-Arpajon 18 km 11 mi
Unsealed Path	Savigny-sur-Orge → Ris-Orangis 5 km 3 mi

Well served by the RER line C to Dourdan although weekday peak hour restrictions apply to bikes.

www.sivoa.fr for downloadable map leaflet "La Promenade de l'Orge".

Twenty miles to the south of Paris, the pretty little River Orge hosts a decent quality unsealed cycle path from Athis Mons, where the Orge joins the Seine, to St-Germain-lès-Arpajon. There are one or two bits of road riding but some decent facilities along the way including toilets and water points, some signage and some information boards. The length of cycleable path available is in reality around 40 kilometres as there are paths on both banks and circuits off the main route in places.
From Savigny-sur-Orge, a short length of voie verte leaves the river route and follows a little of the remarkable Vanne water conduit, just 5 of its 173 kilometres in fact. It's not tarmac, but it's a very good, smooth surface. For most of its way it runs parallel to the A6 autoroute.

A number of attractions along the way include the Camille Flammarion observatory at Juvisy (closed to the public but an interesting sight) and the tower at Monlhéry where in 1822 François Arago calculated the speed of sound using a canonball shot. In 1874, Alfred Cornu tried to calculate the speed of light between the tower and the Observatory in Paris. Probably the biggest delight on the little spur at Savigny-sur-Orge is the aqueduct itself.

55 Le Chemin des Roses see pgs 206-9 for maps

Railpath   Servon → Yèbles   18 km 11 mi

 The nearest station is at Boissy-St-Léger 7 kilometres from Servon.

 Crushed stone railpath apart from a 1km road cycle lane by Brie-Comte-Robert. Good width plus seats and information boards.

It's called Chemin des Roses as trains used to carry flowers to Parisian markets along it, although the countryside isn't especially attractive. However, the path itself is a hive of natural activity with over 200 different plant species and various fauna. The towns are very pleasant and the castle at Brie-Comte-Robert an impressive sight.

56 Along the Dhuys aqueduct see pgs 206-9 for maps

Off road tracks   Le Raincy → Dampmart   27 km 17 mi

 Trains run from Paris gare de l'Est to Lagny-Thorigny station.

This voie verte is not of the same level of development and sophistication as many of the others in the Île de France. It's more of a mountain bike route really but even then you need to know where you're going and take a good deal of care. Signage is nil, the limestone surface is crude in some areas and there are some road intersections to be wary at. A good map such as the Michelin 1:53 000 Banlieue de Paris would be a help. However, there are some good scenic views and it has a link to the Canal de l'Ourcq, if you can find it. Popular with trials bikes and quad bikes.

Follows the line of a section of the aqueduc de la Dhuys, a nineteenth century water conduit supplying water to the metropolis but now supplying it to Disneyland with only any excess going to Paris. Much of this voie verte is along the Grande Randonnée 14A route.
Bits of WW2-bombed aqueduct have gone towards the construction of some forty unusual and interesting sculptures further down the river on the south bank in the riverside sculpture park near Chessy - cross the river at Thorigny-sur-Marne.

Good quality cyclepaths approach Paris along the Seine from the south (see route 57, following page)

57 Banks of the Seine and Marne rivers

Mixture of paths and 'slow' roads   Pont Charles de Gaulle → Lagny-sur-Marne **47 km** 30 mi

 RER stations on or near the route make a rail return or a partial one possible as long as you avoid rush hour restrictions on bikes.

 See the IAU map as described on pg 204

This excellent three metre wide tarmac path runs for 10 kilometres out of Paris by the Seine as far as Saint-Maurice. It then changes to a mix of sections of good quality voie verte interspersed with quiet local roads, many residents only, some with contra flow cycle lanes and all well-served with facilities along the way such as bars and cafes, picnic tables and drinking fountains.

One minus for the route is the inadequate signage. Whilst route guides are available, they're not that helpful for navigation - the direction tips on the AF3V website are probably the best thing to use. A recently opened voie verte with a good smooth compacted limestone surface alongside the canal de Vaires and some more of the Marne extends the route by 9 kilometres out as far as Pomponne, near Lagny.

If you want to shorten the route, it is possible at Saint-Maurice to shortcut the 15 kilometre loop of the Marne that goes around Saint-Maur-des-Fossés. If you want to lengthen it, it may be possible to cycle along the canal path to Meaux. Just along the river from Pomponne the canal de la Dhuys route joins the river at Thorigny-sur-Marne. Cross the river here and you can go down to the sculpture park on the next river bend at Chessy.

If you fancy a bit of Belle Époque atmosphere in the form of a leisurely ride out for food and possibly music, pick one of the waterside cafes or restaurants known as guinguettes which have come back into fashion in this area over the last twenty or thirty years and try it out. Originally, guinguettes were suburban open air drinking establishments and dance halls popular with Parisians wanting to escape the city on Sundays and holidays and some of the modern guinguettes have maintained these traditions. Some of the best known modern guinguettes are La Goulue and Chez Gégène or the island guinguette of Martin-Pêcheur set in a large area of parkland. But it wasn't just the guinguettes people came for ; a train ride from Paris to Nogent would allow you to hire a bike and ride down to the river to fish, swim or go boating.

Sealed paths   Eiffel Tower → Villeneuve-St-Georges **27.5 km** 17 mi

 All central Paris stations are within easy cycling distance of the Seine

 See Paris Street Map on accompanying Touring Routes map and cycle route map at www.paris.fr

Despite being a major artery for motor transport the Seine has some fine cyclepaths

 Generally good quality riverside paths

Take in classic Parisian landscapes alongside the Seine from near the Eiffel Tower to the ringroad just before the Marne in the east.
You can follow the Seine's north bank from the ring road (*la périphérique*) to the traffic-free bridge, the Passerelle d'Ivry -Charenton, just before the confluence with the Marne and cross it to see if the new section of Euro-velo 3, following the western bank of the Seine as far as Villeneuve-St-Georges, is built (under construction at the time of writing).
Cycle lanes on the opposite, eastern bank link Choisy-le-Roi back to the confluence with the Marne.

58 Rambouillet forest

Forest network (circular route based on Rambouillet)

50 km 31 mi **(41 km** 25 mi traffic-free)

Stations at Rambouillet and Montfort l'Amaury.

www.rambouillet-location-velos.fr for info on cycle hire but also for a good schematic map of routes in the forest.

Many of the towns and villages in the magnificent Rambouillet forest are linked by cycle paths or cycleable forest roads. Montfort l'Amaury, Les Essarts-le-Roi, Le Mesle, Poigny-en-Forêt and Rambouillet itself all stand on cycle routes and there is a lovely 4 kilometre path around the Étang d'Or near Rambouillet.

Quiet roads can be used to form a circular route of some 50 kilometres based on Rambouillet. The width of the paths varies between about 2 and 2.5 metres. Generally a good smooth surface but the paths are old so there can be potholes and roots. Signage is good at junctions giving place names and distances and the distance to the end of the path. The 20 kilometre Rambouillet to Montfort l'Amaury path has the best facilities, with shelters and cycle hire (Loca Cycles) and is probably the best surfaced overall.

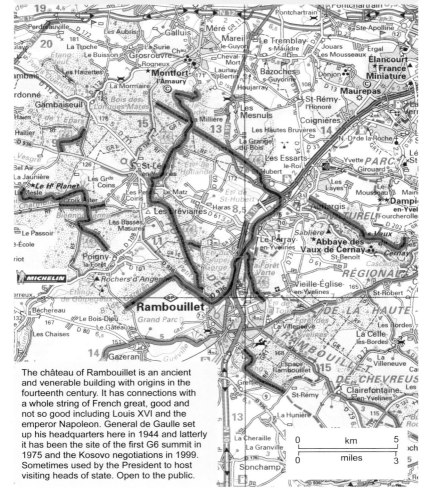

The château of Rambouillet is an ancient and venerable building with origins in the fourteenth century. It has connections with a whole string of French great, good and not so good including Louis XVI and the emperor Napoleon. General de Gaulle set up his headquarters here in 1944 and latterly it has been the site of the first G6 summit in 1975 and the Kosovo negotiations in 1999. Sometimes used by the President to host visiting heads of state. Open to the public.

Greenway - unsealed   Greenway - sealed   Signed road route   213

North Centre & Pays-de-la-Loire

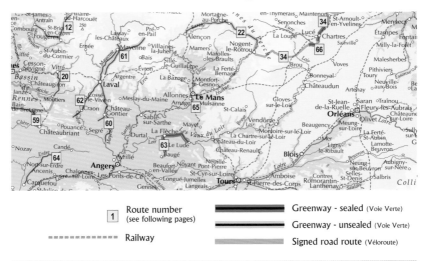

1 Route number (see following pages)	Greenway - sealed (Voie Verte)
	Greenway - unsealed (Voie Verte)
============ Railway	Signed road route (Véloroute)

In the area covered by this section - north of but not including the River Loire (with its incredible cycle route covered in our book *Cycling Southern France*) official cycle routes are rather scant with the exception of the area around Mayenne and Laval, which boasts over 200km of often quite beautiful traffic-free riding. Not only that, but this system of routes in the Mayenne is all either railpath or river towpath and hence great for easy touring. In time, the Mayenne towpath will form part of a major national route from the channel coast at Ouistreham near Caen to the Loire near Angers and on to the Atlantic coast at La Rochelle. Whilst the Loire à Vélo cycle route to the south is deservedly well-known and popular, there is much excellent cycling to be had around the lovely smaller rivers in the area - the Mayenne, Loir, Sarthe and Eure. There are nice towns and villages to stay in and organised holidays are available. Although the area is maybe not as well-known as Brittany or Normandy or the Loire, it still has much to offer.

Culture, Food & History

One of the few official cycle routes in the area begins at the remarkable town of Chartres, known for its hugely imposing cathedral and elevated in importance in religious history as it contains (still) the Sancta Camisia, supposedly part of the clothes worn by the Virgin Mary when she gave birth to Jesus. Elsewhere, Le Mans has the Cathedral of St. Julien which forms part of the spectacular light show put on in the streets of the old town most evenings in July and August. Foodwise the Loire region is renowned for its fecundity in producing fruit, vegetables and fish as well as delicious white wines.

Organised Holidays

Cycling for Softies offer "self-guided, tailor-made luxurious, cycling holidays through rural France". They've been organising holidays in the Mayenne for over 30 years and describe it as "that rural world that you thought had vanished". www.cycling-for-softies.co.uk   Safran also offer cycling holidays along the Mayenne, describing it as "perfectly suited to those who enjoy peddling safely along on practically flat terrain, adults and children alike". www.safrantours.com

Access to North Centre and Pays-de-la-Loire

There are fast bicycle-carrying rail services into the area from Paris, although rail transport from the channel ferry ports involves changes and many trains do not carry bicycles. Airports at Angers and Tours both have flights from the UK

i More Info

Excellent downloadable map leaflet showing the whole system of greenways in the area on **www.mayenne-tourisme.com** along with an orderable paper version and other leaflets.

59 From Châteaubriant into Brittany

Châteaubriant paths **28 km** 17 mi

A spur line from Rennes terminates at Châteaubriant and carries bikes. The journey takes a good hour and there are two or three trains a day. The bike-carrying TGV service from Paris to Rennes takes around 2 hours 10mins.

A smooth tarmac railpath from Châteaubriant to Rougé with excellent signage, generally good junction controls and a 2 kilometre unsealed extension northwards through the forest of Teillay and then more beyond to the marina at Bain de Bretagne. This is currently linkable to the voie verte at Messac Guipry using about 50% main road and 50% voie verte and quiet roads and should soon be all voie verte. The section between Châteaubriant and Rougé is of a remarkably high quality with good facilities.

Châteaubriant has a magnificent Renaissance castle, a well-known racecourse, a velodrome and a theatre amongst its attractions. The second week every September sees some 40 or 50 thousand visitors coming to the Foire de Béré at Châteaubriant, a huge regional show and knees-up.

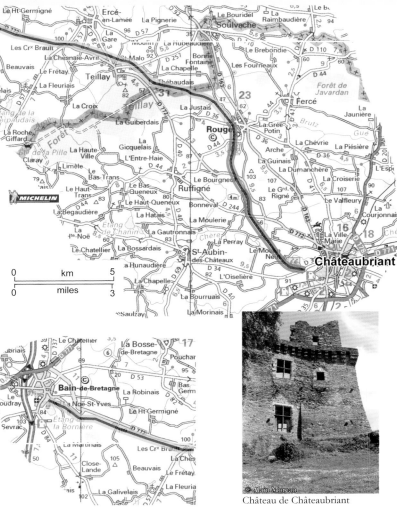

Château de Châteaubriant

Greenway - unsealed   Greenway - sealed   Signed road route

60 The Mayenne Towpath

Unsealed towpath   Mayenne → Le Lion-d'Angers **100 km** 63 mi

Station at Laval with some bicycle-carrying services from Paris, some direct, some not. Line goes on through Vitré to Rennes.

www.anjou-velo.com www.anjou-tourisme.com

The Mayenne towpath is a good quality, unsealed flat riverside towpath with a good, smooth unsealed surface suitable for family touring with plenty of interest. The northern section between Mayenne and Laval can be combined with the railpath route between the two towns to make an excellent circular ride of some 80 kilometres or so. Places and attractions are signposted with distances and there are information boards. There is a number of stops with tables and benches, ten with toilets and a water point.

Mayenne, Laval and Château-Gontier are three delightful flower-bedecked towns with plenty of eating places, accommodation and things to see and there are plenty of nice villages on and near the route worth stopping at. The lovely town of Mayenne, on the River Mayenne in the département of Mayenne has a medieval castle (now a museum, open to the public) and the basilica church of Notre-Dame-des-Miracles. Fun on the river comes in the form of pedalos, little electric boats or a cruise on a larger boat, possibly with a meal.

The river is not the commercial highway it once was and is these days used more for leisure. It passes through scenic and varied countryside, sometimes below cliffs, sometimes looking out over broad acres of farmland, and is punctuated with many picturesque locks, often as not with an appealing cottage by it. There are riverside and hilltop châteaux, old watermills and a variety of historical ruins.

Greenway - unsealed   Greenway - sealed   Signed road route

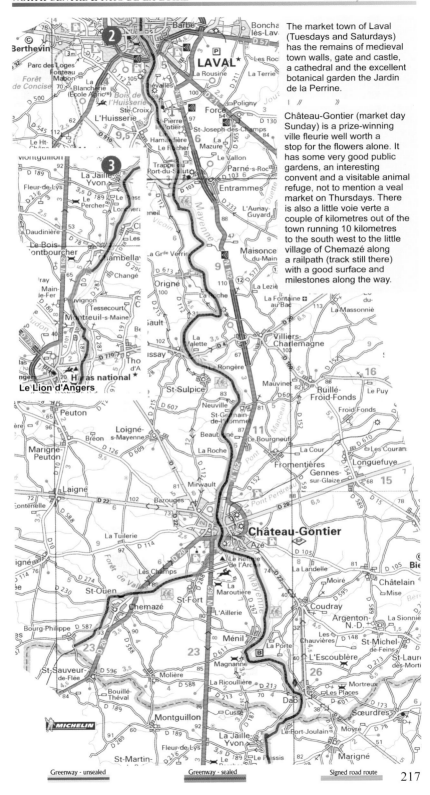

The market town of Laval (Tuesdays and Saturdays) has the remains of medieval town walls, gate and castle, a cathedral and the excellent botanical garden the Jardin de la Perrine.

Château-Gontier (market day Sunday) is a prize-winning ville fleurie well worth a stop for the flowers alone. It has some very good public gardens, an interesting convent and a visitable animal refuge, not to mention a veal market on Thursdays. There is also a little voie verte a couple of kilometres out of the town running 10 kilometres to the south west to the little village of Chemazé along a railpath (track still there) with a good surface and milestones along the way.

Greenway - unsealed   Greenway - sealed   Signed road route

61 Around Mayenne

Unsealed railpath — Ambrières-les-Vallées → La Chapelle-Anthenaise 40km 25mi

Unsealed railpath — Mayenne → Javron 33km 20.5mi

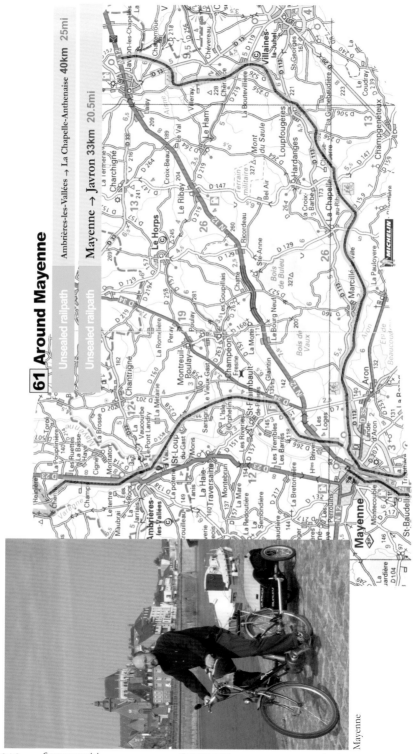

Mayenne

Greenway - unsealed   Greenway - sealed   Signed road route

62 Laval to Renazé

🚲 These three voies vertes are all railpaths with a good unsealed surface suitable for maintaining a decent pace. If you're looking for suitable family riding these routes would be worth considering - they're not terribly strenuous, they're easy to follow and there are one or two interesting diversions.

The vélorail at Saint-Loup-du-Gast runs alongside the voie verte to the dairy museum at Vilaines-la-Juhel on the Mayenne- Javron route. On the Laval - Renazé voie verte, the neoclassical Château de Craon of 1770 has fine gardens,a greenhouse and extensive parkland open to the public although the château is only visitable by group booking. They do bed and breakfast as well. The village of Cossé-le-Vivien is home to the Musée Robert Tatin where you will find a selection of strange and colossal sculptures set out in delightful gardens. Renazé has a slate museum dedicated to a local industry only recently lost. Whilst the area is rural and agricultural and 'away from it all', there's no shortage of accommodation, things to see and every town and village is worth a stop.

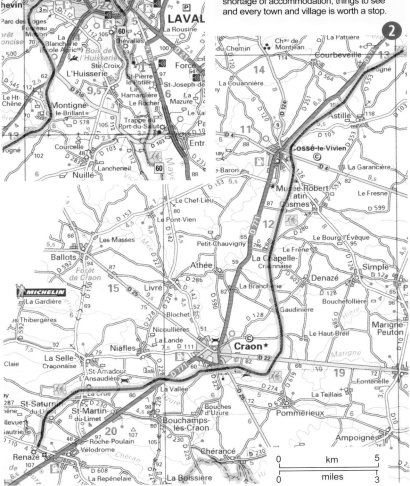

Greenway - unsealed   Greenway - sealed   Signed road route

The market town of Laval (above) is one of the highlights on the Mayenne towpath (below), detailed on previous pages.

63 De Loir en Loire

Sealed railpath and roads   **Le Lude → La Flèche → Baugé**   **45 km** 28 mi

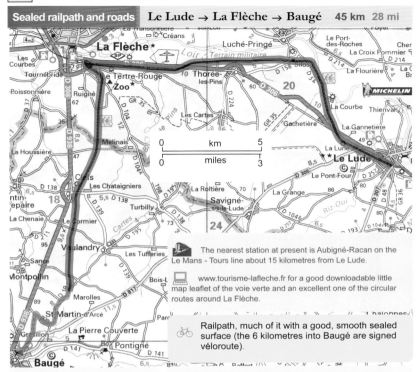

The nearest station at present is Aubigné-Racan on the Le Mans - Tours line about 15 kilometres from Le Lude.

www.tourisme-lafleche.fr for a good downloadable little map leaflet of the voie verte and an excellent one of the circular routes around La Flèche.

Railpath, much of it with a good, smooth sealed surface (the 6 kilometres into Baugé are signed véloroute).

Midway between Le Mans and Angers the River Loir (a different one to the Loire) crosses the department of la Sarthe running through the small towns of Le Lude and La Flèche which are also linked by a voie verte along a former rail corridor. There is then a further railpath running south from La Flèche followed by 6 kilometres on-road into Baugé with the prospect that a southern véloroute extension will be completed very shortly to link the route into the major Loire à Vélo cycle route.

Whilst this route may be awkward to get to by train at the moment and parts are near a busy road, it does have its rewards. There are a number of villes and villages fleuris, the Château du Lude and its gardens are well worth visiting, as is the characterful little village of Luché-Pringé with its nice outdoor swimming pool and riverside leisure park with tennis etc. and boating on the river Loir. La Flèche too has a nice leisure park, this one by a lake, not to mention a watermill and an extensive and renowned zoo and Baugé has plenty to see and do. There is a number of circular cycle routes off the voie verte and some around La Flèche. It is something of a holiday area, with good facilities whether you're camping, in a motorhome or caravan or wanting accommodation.

Other Routes

64 North-east of Nantes

Railpath of uneven quality   **Carquefou → Saint-Mars-la-Jaille**   36 km 22 mi

No nearby stations but several run south of the route along the Loire to Ancenis, allowing numerous greenway plus road plus train return trips.

www.af3v.org.uk

Part of the disused railway that ran between Nantes and Segré to the north-east. There are still lengthy sections of the old railway available and there is a long term plan to construct a route between Nantes and the extensive network around Laval and Mayenne.

Greenway - unsealed   Greenway - sealed   Signed road route   221

65 Le Mans

| Riverside paths | Le Mans → Arnage & Changé   26 km 16 mi |

Le Mans is less than an hour from Paris by bicycle carrying TGV. Trains from the channel ferry ports to Le Mans normally involve changes and many do not carry bicycles although there is the occasional direct one from Saint Malo and those do carry bicycles.

www.lemans.fr has good maps and leaflet for cycle paths and lanes in Le Mans

Le Mans has a couple of good riverside voies vertes. The 14 kilometre path alongside the River Sarthe from the centre out to Arnage is a high quality one. It's not tarmac, but it's still smooth and is pretty much free of road crossings. Towards the southern end, the lac de la Gémerie has swimming and sailing and other sports and games. A chunk of this voie verte will form part of the "boulevard Nature," a 72 kilometre voie verte network for the city in the early stages of development. The 12 kilometre voie verte largely of a similar high quality running alongside the River Huisne and through forest from the south east of the city to Changé is a tranquil affair only a stone's throw from the busy city. It too is to be part of the "boulevard Nature".

Le Mans is well worth a visit - it has a thriving modern area but also a completely separate old town high above it full of narrow streets and medieval houses, not to mention the breathtaking cathedral.

66 Chartres green corridor & Véloscénie

| Sealed & unsealed tracks & roads | Chartres → Nogent-le-Rotrou   81 km 50.5 mi |

Chartres is a good hour from Paris. The trains carry bikes and there is secure parking at the station in Chartres. Villette-Saint-Prest station is only 5 minutes out of Chartres.

www.chartres-metropole.fr for plan vert map leaflet of the green corridor and plan des pistes cyclables for all cycle paths in Chartres. www.veloscenie.com for the entire Véloscénie route (including interim sections)

The cathedral has to be the jewel of Chartres and the surrounding area. A masterpiece of French Gothic art, its statues, stained glass and vast nave are a wonder and the view from the towers is breathtaking. Having said that, Chartres has much else to commend it - cobbled streets with half-timbered houses, steep lanes and steps leading through the old town to a walk alongside the River Eure past humpbacked bridges, wash-houses and water mills. Other entertainments on offer include Segway hire, a racetrack (horses), a swimming pool, an ice rink and some very nice walks and bike rides, especially around the town at night when many fine buildings and monuments are illuminated.

The Chartres coulée verte is a high quality path, part tarmac, part high quality unsealed surface mainly alongside the River Eure. Sadly, there is a 400 metre break in the path in the city centre but it is on quiet roads and cycle lanes. The northern section runs 4.5 kilometres out of town to near the station at Saint-Prest but it is then possible to follow a véloroute (part of the developing Paris - Mont St. Michel route known as Véloscénie) along the Eure valley to Épernon another 10 or 15 kilometres further north. To the south, the coulée verte goes 3.5 kilometres to Luisant then across Lucé picking up traffic-free paths down to Fontenay-sur-Eure and the véloroute to Nogent-le-Rotrou. (This goes on to Condé-sur-Huisne and the voie verte to Alençon). The véloroute leaves Chartres and passes between large open fields, moving on to the wooded landscape of the Perche. It's an easy ride on quiet roads although the last 10 kilometres into Nogent-le-Rotrou can be quite hairy. It's well signed, even the 7 kilometres beyond Nogent leading to the voie verte to Alençon.

Champagne-Ardennes

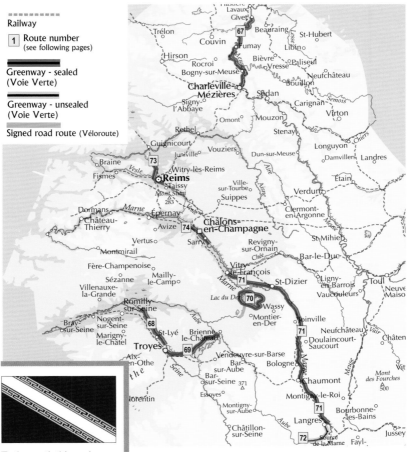

Railway

1 Route number
    (see following pages)

Greenway - sealed
(Voie Verte)

Greenway - unsealed
(Voie Verte)

Signed road route (Véloroute)

To the north this region
boasts the magnificent greenway along the Meuse valley as it winds its way through
the densely wooded hills of the French Ardennes, a route that connects to the RAVeL
network of Wallonia (French-speaking Belgium). South, in Champagne country, the epic
Champagne to Burgundy canal provides a cycling holiday in itself.

Culture, Food & History
One region but two notably distinct areas; to the south are the Champagne vineyards which dominate
the economy around Reims and Épernay. To the north the French Ardennes, a small outlier of the
main Belgian hills, are one of the country's best kept secrets. The terrain and lack of agriculture have kept the
area's steep wooded hills isolated for much of their history and with a rich natural environment.

Organised Holidays
Cycling for Softies (www.cycling-for-softies.co.uk) offer all-in holidays. Bikes are provided
including trail-a-long bikes and child seats along with hotels and restaurants.
www.frenchpedals.co.uk offer organised cycle holidays here and shorter tours are available locally
eg through the Charleville-Mézières tourist office.
Also see www.discoverfrance.com wheel2wheelholidays.com www.freedomtreks.co.uk

Access to Champagne-Ardennes
Paris Est to Reims by TGV takes around 45 mins (note there's a TGV station 8km from Reims centre).
Paris to Troyes is around 1 hour 35 mins and Paris to Charleville-Mézières 1 hour 30 mins by TGV.

i More Info
www.tourisme-champagne-ardenne.com for a downloadable map of routes and supporting
information. www.aube-champagne.com for good info and map for that department.

223

67 Trans-Ardennes Voie Verte

Sealed railpath   Givet → Charleville-Mézières   86 km 53.5 mi

Charleville-Mézières has high speed TGV access from Paris (two trains daily) and a train line parallels the Trans-Ardennes greenway with many local stations and free bike carriage.

www.ardennes.com for a detailed map leaflet in French and English. Also nice schematic map on same site and detailed maps and info in English on www.voiesvertes.com

Towns such as Fumay and Revin have an industrial past (slate extraction in particular at Fumay) but today they are low key tourist centres both with ancient and attractive centres, and all the more pleasant for it.

Approaching Givet to the north the valley opens out somewhat and you pass the impressive Fort de Charlemont. Built in the 16th century and subsequently reinforced, it was once the training centre for French commandos, but today is open to all visitors.

86 kilometres of fabulously easy leisure riding alongside the Meuse from near the Belgian border to just outside Charleville-Mézières, the route has only been open in its entirety since 2008. 12 railway stations along the rail line which parallels this popular, high quality route give huge flexibility for rail returns, although mainly it runs on the opposite bank to the cycle route so beware the four stations not near any bridges. Signage is clear and informative (bilingual information boards are a nice touch) and there is a number of picnic areas and plenty of bench seats. Shade is limited. A major project will extend the route some 50 more kilometres south along the Meuse as far as Mouzon.

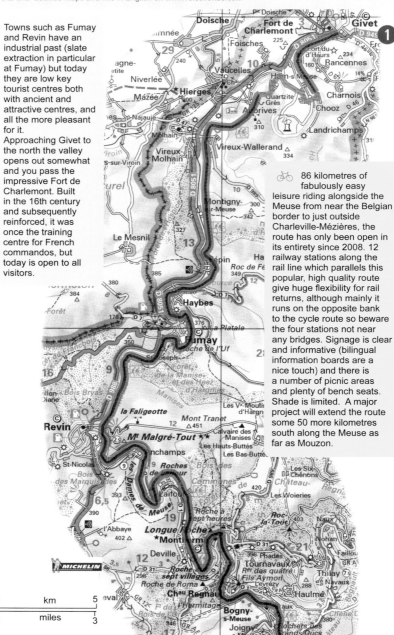

0 ___ km ___ 5
0 ___ miles ___ 3

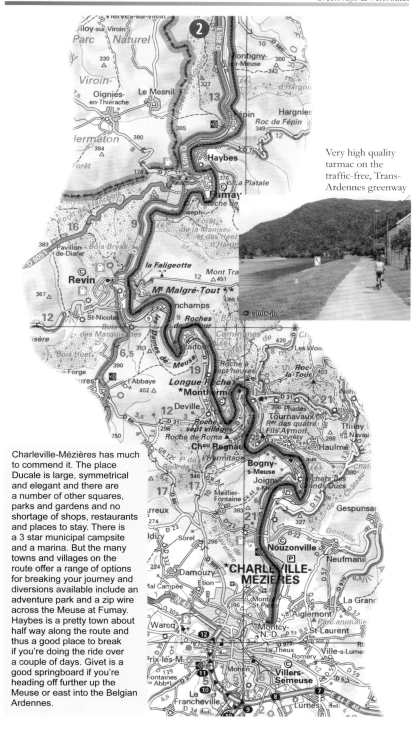

Very high quality tarmac on the traffic-free, Trans-Ardennes greenway

© cdl08-jh

Charleville-Mézières has much to commend it. The place Ducale is large, symmetrical and elegant and there are a number of other squares, parks and gardens and no shortage of shops, restaurants and places to stay. There is a 3 star municipal campsite and a marina. But the many towns and villages on the route offer a range of options for breaking your journey and diversions available include an adventure park and a zip wire across the Meuse at Fumay. Haybes is a pretty town about half way along the route and thus a good place to break if you're doing the ride over a couple of days. Givet is a good springboard if you're heading off further up the Meuse or east into the Belgian Ardennes.

68 Haute-Seine Canal

Sealed canal path	Troyes → St Oulph 27 km 17 mi

69 Through the Lakes of Champagne

Mainly sealed paths	Troyes → Dienville 42 km 26 mi

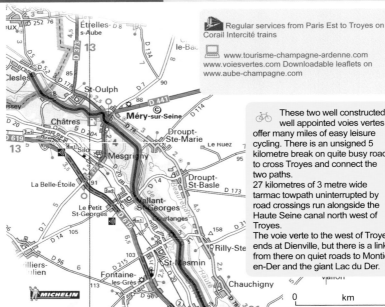

Regular services from Paris Est to Troyes on Corail Intercité trains

www.tourisme-champagne-ardenne.com
www.voiesvertes.com Downloadable leaflets on
www.aube-champagne.com

These two well constructed, well appointed voies vertes offer many miles of easy leisure cycling. There is an unsigned 5 kilometre break on quite busy roads to cross Troyes and connect the two paths.

27 kilometres of 3 metre wide tarmac towpath uninterrupted by road crossings run alongside the Haute Seine canal north west of Troyes.

The voie verte to the west of Troyes ends at Dienville, but there is a link from there on quiet roads to Montier-en-Der and the giant Lac du Der.

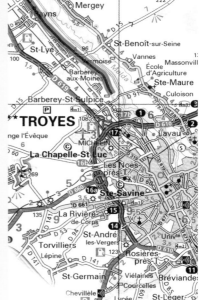

The Haute-Seine canal offers a lush green thread through a fairly monotonous agricultural landscape. Just outside Troyes, the château de Barberey-Saint-Sulpice is an elegant 17th century affair with notable park, gardens and orchard open to the public. Near the other end of the ride, the château de Droupt-Saint-Basle is an equally attractive prospect offering guided tours and a small museum and along the way there are a good number of small churches nearby which are worth a visit. Although the canal was decommissioned over 50 years ago, the voie verte is part of a programme to revitalise this section of it.

Troyes is a fine city and a great way to see it is by joining one of the free, guided, 20 kilometre evening cycle rides. Sadly these only take place twice a year with a roller equivalent happening 5 times a year. Otherwise, it's still a nice place to explore by foot or wheel; not having suffered in the world wars, there's still much older style architecture, especially half-timbered houses and churches.
A major project recently has been the restoration and re-opening of the town centre sections of the canal de la Haute Seine.

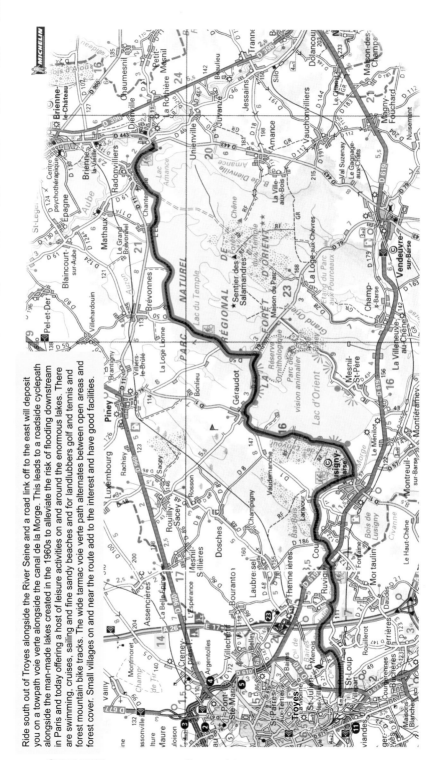

Ride south out of Troyes alongside the River Seine and a road link off to the east will deposit you on a towpath voie verte alongside the canal de la Morge. This leads to a roadside cyclepath alongside the man-made lakes created in the 1960s to alleviate the risk of flooding downstream in Paris and today offering a host of leisure activities on and around the enormous lakes. There are swimming, cruises, sailing and fine sandy beaches and for landlubbers golf and tennis and forest cover. The wide tarmac voie verte path alternates between open areas and forest cover. Small villages on and near the route add to the interest and have good facilities.

Greenway - unsealed   Greenway - sealed   Signed road route

70 Lac du Der

| Sealed path | Circular route with spurs | 83 km 52 mi |

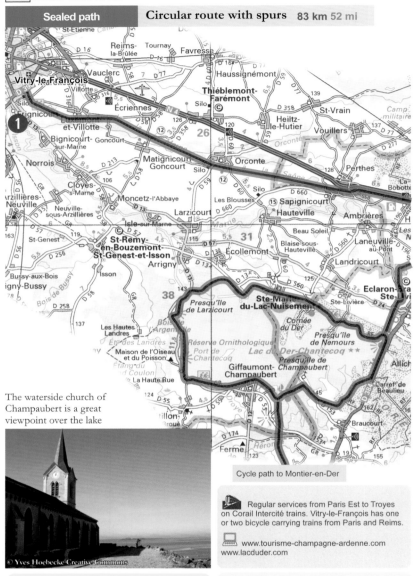

The waterside church of Champaubert is a great viewpoint over the lake

© Yves Hoebecke Creative Commons

Cycle path to Montier-en-Der

Regular services from Paris Est to Troyes on Corail Intercité trains. Vitry-le-François has one or two bicycle carrying trains from Paris and Reims.

www.tourisme-champagne-ardenne.com
www.lacduder.com

🚲 The enormous Lac du Der has a high quality 38 kilometre voie verte running round its perimeter. It is easy to get to by bike from Troyes (94 km), Vitry-le-François (21 km) and Saint-Dizier (12 km), the latter being linked to it by a high quality voie verte and Vitry by voie verte and a véloroute. The lakeside path often runs along embankments and has seats, picnic areas and observation points.

The lake is a considerable leisure facility with six beaches and much in the way of watersports and holiday activities. It's on major bird migration routes and the arrival of thousands of cranes in the autumn is a breathtaking sight.

There are little resorts on the south side of the lake at Giffaumont-Champaubert (electric bike hire here) and at Ste-Marie-du-Lac-Nuisement on the north. St-Dizier and Vitry-le-François are the nearest sizeable towns.

71 Champagne to Burgundy Canal

Sealed canal path   Vitry-le-François → Langres   **150 km** 93 mi

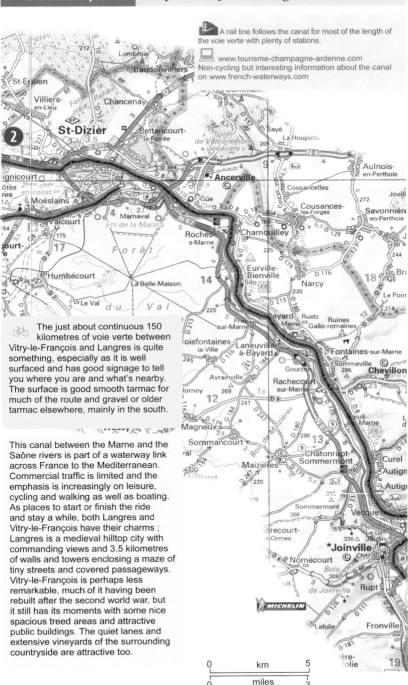

A rail line follows the canal for most of the length of the voie verte with plenty of stations.

www.tourisme-champagne-ardenne.com
Non-cycling but interesting information about the canal on www.french-waterways.com

The just about continuous 150 kilometres of voie verte between Vitry-le-François and Langres is quite something, especially as it is well surfaced and has good signage to tell you where you are and what's nearby. The surface is good smooth tarmac for much of the route and gravel or older tarmac elsewhere, mainly in the south.

This canal between the Marne and the Saône rivers is part of a waterway link across France to the Mediterranean. Commercial traffic is limited and the emphasis is increasingly on leisure, cycling and walking as well as boating. As places to start or finish the ride and stay a while, both Langres and Vitry-le-François have their charms ; Langres is a medieval hilltop city with commanding views and 3.5 kilometres of walls and towers enclosing a maze of tiny streets and covered passageways. Vitry-le-François is perhaps less remarkable, much of it having been rebuilt after the second world war, but it still has its moments with some nice spacious treed areas and attractive public buildings. The quiet lanes and extensive vineyards of the surrounding countryside are attractive too.

| 0 | km | 5 |
| 0 | miles | 3 |

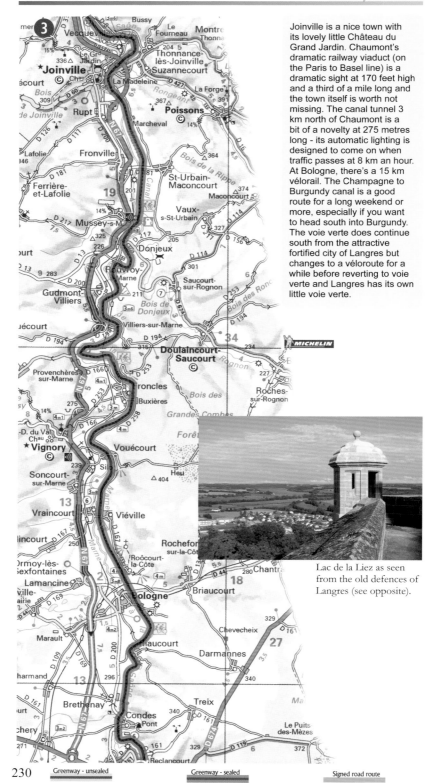

Joinville is a nice town with its lovely little Château du Grand Jardin. Chaumont's dramatic railway viaduct (on the Paris to Basel line) is a dramatic sight at 170 feet high and a third of a mile long and the town itself is worth not missing. The canal tunnel 3 km north of Chaumont is a bit of a novelty at 275 metres long - its automatic lighting is designed to come on when traffic passes at 8 km an hour. At Bologne, there's a 15 km vélorail. The Champagne to Burgundy canal is a good route for a long weekend or more, especially if you want to head south into Burgundy. The voie verte does continue south from the attractive fortified city of Langres but changes to a véloroute for a while before reverting to voie verte and Langres has its own little voie verte.

Lac de la Liez as seen from the old defences of Langres (see opposite).

Greenway - unsealed   Greenway - sealed   Signed road route

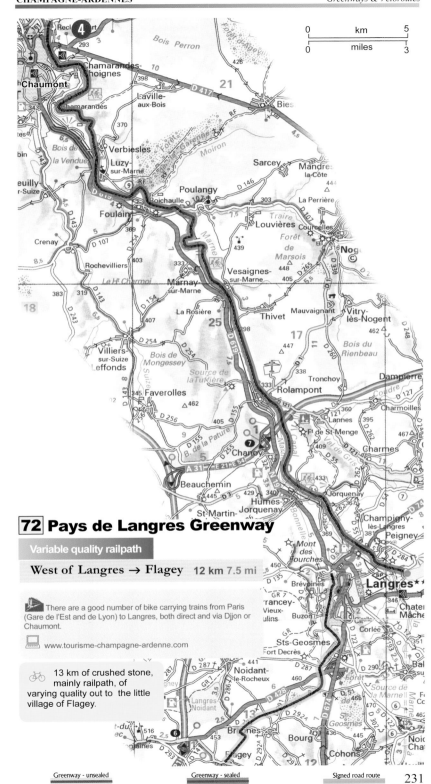

72 Pays de Langres Greenway

Variable quality railpath

West of Langres → Flagey   12 km 7.5 mi

There are a good number of bike carrying trains from Paris (Gare de l'Est and de Lyon) to Langres, both direct and via Djjon or Chaumont.

www.tourisme-champagne-ardenne.com

13 km of crushed stone, mainly railpath, of varying quality out to the little village of Flagey.

Greenway - unsealed   Greenway - sealed   Signed road route

Other Routes

73 Routes around Reims

Unsealed & unsealed railpath & towpath	Around Reims 53 km 33 mi

 Reims has good bicycle carrying rail links with Paris and Strasbourg.

Reims is a fine city and whilst the streets may not be flowing with Champagne, there are plenty of cellars to investigate and some fine cuisine to go with the wine. The city's most evident jewels lie probably in its glorious ecclesiastical architecture.

The 12 kilometre Coulée Verte which crosses Reims is a towpath route through a green corridor along the River Vesle and the canal, although much of it seems to be industrial. The central section is well treed with grassy areas. The path is well surfaced, tarmac with a parallel unsealed path for horses, and pretty much continuous. There are plenty of seats, picnic areas etc. but little helpful signage and not many access points. It's often very busy with walkers and joggers.

If the path were to be extended northwards, it could link to the 12 kilometres of towpath between Courcy and Berry-au-Bac which have been restored not that long ago, although the towpath between the two voies vertes is in practice cycleable. A similar situation exists to the south so there's knocking on for 40 kilometres of waterside riding in total.

Perhaps a little more scenic is the short (6 kilometres) but high quality path between the abbaye de Vauclair and the Center Parcs resort by the Lac de l'Ailette about 30 kilometres north west of Reims just over the border in Picardy. This is a newly built path through forest and by the lakeside with much of interest if you like flora and fauna, birds especially. Also over in Picardy about 20 kilometres from Reims is the 8 kilometre Evergnicourt to Guignicourt railpath but this is more of a commuter route between villages.

© Clelie Mascaret Creative Commons

Some of the Champagne company headquarters in Reims are eleaborate indeed. Here is the home of Pommery, found to the south-east of the town centre.

74 Châlons-en-Champagne

Canal towpath	Recy → Moncetz-Longevas 12 km 7.5 mi

 Plenty of bicycle carrying trains from Paris and Reims.

🖥 www.tourisme-champagne-ardenne.com

Halfway between Vitry-le-François and Reims, Châlons-en-Champagne has an excellent new length of voie verte alongside the canal. This will no doubt one day link up with the Champagne to Burgundy canal route at Vitry when it's part of the full Paris - Strasbourg cycle route. For the present, it's a treat for the locals and visitors to the town, offering a route into the heart of Châlons, notably Les Jards consisting of the Grand Jard, a French style formal garden, the Jard Anglais on the banks of the canal and the Petit Jard, a landscaped garden with arboretum. Cycle hire at the tourist office in Châlons, including children's bikes and electric ones.

Northern Burgundy & Franche-Comté

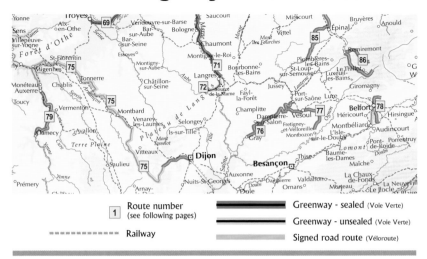

1 Route number (see following pages)	▬▬▬▬ Greenway - sealed (Voie Verte)
	▬▬▬▬ Greenway - unsealed (Voie Verte)
▬ ▬ ▬ ▬ Railway	▬▬▬▬ Signed road route (Véloroute)

If you are a fan of canals and cycling then you will love Burgundy.
This guide only covers the far north but you still get to enjoy two of France's
finest canal rides along the Burgundy and Nivernais canals (covered in the
touring route *Northern Burgundy*), part of the 800km long Tour of Burgundy
by Bike (around two-thirds finished at the time of writing). By contrast
northern Franche-Comté has little in the way of official cycle infrastructure,
though there are some fine routes further south.

Culture, Food & History

For much of its history the Dukes of Burgundy remained more powerful and controlled more
European territory than many kings. It is still one of the wealthiest areas of France today, though its
territorial ambitions have long disappeared. Many traces remain, for example in the incredible Ducal
palace at Dijon or the lovely abbeys of Fontenay and Ancy, all visited on the Northern Burgundy
touring route.
The area also has its own cooking description; à la bourguignonne means cooked in wine sauce
using one of the areas rich reds. Snails are a particular speciality, usually stewed in white Chablis
wine with various vegetables and finally stuffed with garlic butter.

Organised Holidays

Freewheel holidays offer cycling breaks along the Burgundy Canal and Yonne valley.
www.freewheelholidays.co.uk

Access to Burgundy

Paris Gare de Lyon to Dijon is only 1 hour 40 mins by TGV with reserved and payable bike space.

i **More Info**
www.burgundy-by-bike.com
has detailed online maps of
the main official signed routes
and a plethora of supporting
info.

Dijon is both cycle-friendly and beautiful

75 Burgundy Canal

Unsealed & sealed towpath

Migennes → Dijon
237 km 147 mi

Regular trains to Dijon from Paris Gare de Lyon (1hr45). For local journeys around the Burgundy Canal Laroche Migennes is the local hub along with Dijon, with lines south to Corbigny and Avallon and beyond.
www.burgundy-by-bike.com

Well-signed and good quality towpath for most of the length of the Burgundy Canal but north of Montbard the path is of interim standard only.

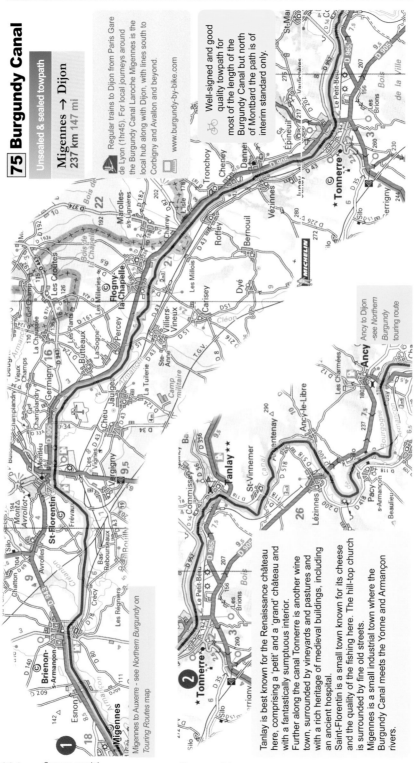

Migennes to Auxerre - see *Northern Burgundy* on *Touring Routes* map

Tanlay is best known for the Renaissance château here, comprising a 'petit' and a 'grand' château and with a fantastically sumptuous interior.
Further along the canal Tonnerre is another wine town, surrounded by vineyards and pastures and with a rich heritage of medieval buildings, including an ancient hospital.
Saint-Florentin is a small town known for its cheese and the quality of the fishing here. The hill-top church is surrounded by fine old streets.
Migennes is a small industrial town where the Burgundy Canal meets the Yonne and Armançon rivers.

Greenway - unsealed   Greenway - sealed   Signed road route

76 Saône voies vertes

Mainly sealed river towpath & railpath

Port-sur-Saône → Gray
67 km   41.5 mi

Direct bike carrying trains from Paris Gare de l'Est to Vesoul taking 3 hours 20 mins

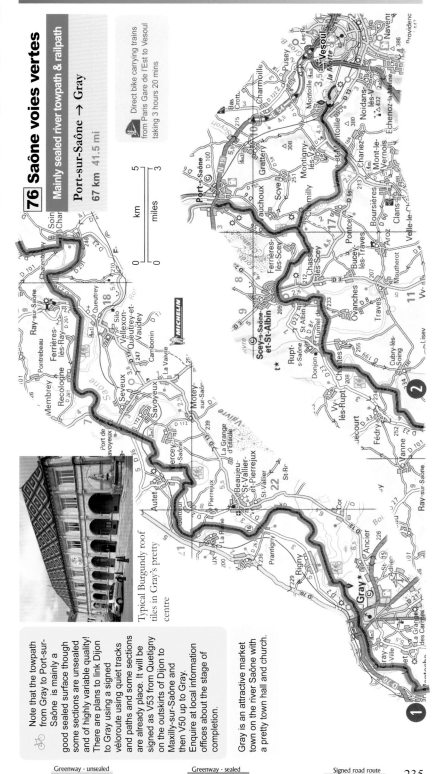

Typical Burgundy roof tiles in Gray's pretty centre

Note that the towpath from Gray to Port-sur-Saône is mainly a good sealed surface though some sections are unsealed and of highly variable quality! There are plans to link Dijon to Gray using a signed véloroute using quiet tracks and paths and some sections are already place. It will be signed as V53 from Quetigny on the outskirts of Dijon to Maxilly-sur-Saône and then V50 up to Gray. Enquire at local information offices about the stage of completion.

Gray is an attractive market town on the river Saône with a pretty town hall and church.

Greenway - unsealed   Greenway - sealed   Signed road route

77 Le Chemin Vert

Sealed path Vesoul → Fontenois-lès-Montbozon   **22 km** 13.5 mi

Direct bike carrying trains from Paris Gare de l'Est to Vesoul taking 3 hours 20 mins

Some of the tarmac is showing signs of wear but generally a pleasure to ride on.

One of the first old railways to become converted for cycling and walking, in the 80s. There are plans to continue the route south towards Besançon and EuroVelo 6.
Vesoul has an old centre of light stone dominated by a castle and the attractive church of St-Georges. Dampierre-sur-Linotte boasts several foodshops, a cafe and a restaurant.

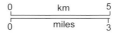

0	km	5
0	miles	3

Vesoul's attractive centre

78 Voies vertes around Belfort

Unsealed towpath	Essert → Montbéliard	24 km 15 mi
Sealed path	Belfort → near Roppe	18 km 11 mi
Sealed path	Belfort → Malsaucy (François Mitterand)	22 km 13.5 mi

Regular direct services from Paris to Belfort, including TGV services from Gare de Lyon and intercity services from Gare de l'Est. Note the TGV station at Belfort is around 12km from the centre.

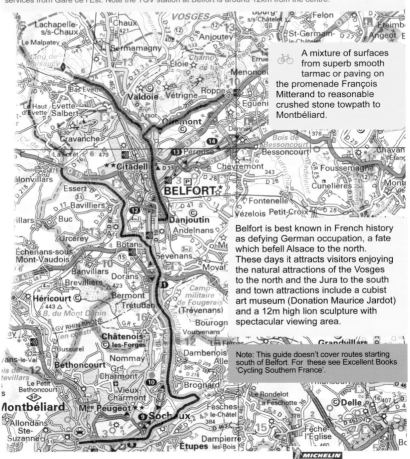

A mixture of surfaces from superb smooth tarmac or paving on the promenade François Mitterand to reasonable crushed stone towpath to Montbéliard.

Belfort is best known in French history as defying German occupation, a fate which befell Alsace to the north. These days it attracts visitors enjoying the natural attractions of the Vosges to the north and the Jura to the south and town attractions include a cubist art museum (Donation Maurice Jardot) and a 12m high lion sculpture with spectacular viewing area.

Note: This guide doesn't cover routes starting south of Belfort. For these see Excellent Books 'Cycling Southern France'.

Other Routes

79 Nivernais canal towpath and Yonne valley

Sealed towpath	Auxerre → Clamecy	61.5 km 38 mi

Covered in the *Northern Burgundy* touring route.

Lorraine

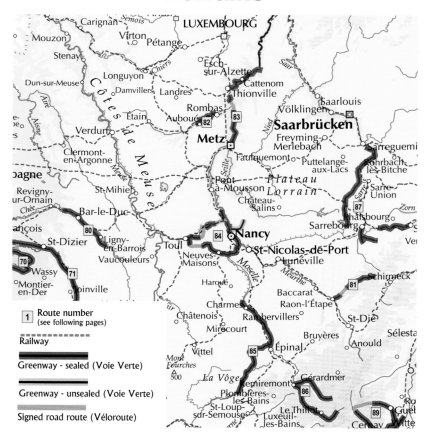

Legend:

1 Route number
(see following pages)

▬▬▬ Railway

▬▬▬ Greenway - sealed (Voie Verte)

▬▬▬ Greenway - unsealed (Voie Verte)

▬▬▬ Signed road route (Véloroute)

80 Ornain valley voie verte

Sealed Towpath   Fains-les-Sources → St-Amand-sur-Ornain   **29 km** 18 mi

Bicycle-carrying TGVs from Paris Est to Bar-le-Duc take about an hour and a half to two hours. There are direct bicycle-carrying trains from Nancy and some from Reims.

lorraine.voie.verte.free.fr

Another section of the developing major route along the canal de la Marne au Rhin which has been upgraded to voie verte runs for 29 km between Fains-les-Sources and Saint-Amand-sur-Ornain via Bar-Le-Duc and Ligny-en-Barrois. It follows a nice green valley on a gravel path (uncomfortable on a racing bike). See above website for detailed mapping.

Passes within striking distance of the Château de Marbeaumont at Bar-Le-Duc which merits a detour. Attractive villages along the way include Longeville-en-Barrois and Tannois. Naix-aux-Forges is the site of an ancient Gallo-Roman town.

Lorraine's cycle routes are a fine mixture; the most opportunities arise along the river valley of the Moselle, but there are also highly unusual opportunities for easy cycling in the heart of the mountainous and often breathtakingly beautiful southern Vosges, with two greenways starting at Remiremont. Overall, the intention for the region is a north - south cycle route incorporating the Moselle valley and the canal des Vosges and an east-west route based on the canal de la Marne au Rhin with Nancy and the Moselle Loop as the hub. The canal de la Sarre offers a long distance ride and it is intended that the Meuse valley also should.

Culture, Food & History

Less prominent culturally and historically than neighbouring Alsace, Lorraine is better known for the heavy industry of its north and its farm belt further south. However, it has one undoubted star. Nancy's city square, Place Stanislas, is one of the finest 18th century squares in the world. In the 20th century Nancy was a major centre in the Art Noveau movement. Lorraine has less Germanic influence than eastern neighbour Alsace, but Lorraine Franconian (a Germanic based language) is still spoken by a few. Parts of Lorraine were German from 1870 when France lost the Franco-Prussian War but were restored to France after the First World War. It was occupied again from 1940 - 44. Lorraine's most famous gastronomic contribution to French cuisine is the eponymous quiche. It's wines are less renowned, the best known probably being Côtes de Meuse and Côtes de Moselle, although the grey wine of Toul has a following also.

Organised Holidays

For a longer tour of the Moselle cycle path through France, Luxembourg and Germany from Metz to Koblenz, see www.mosel-radweg.de/en

Access to Lorraine

Great TGV train connections from Paris Est station mean both Metz and Nancy are only around 1.5 hours from the capital. The TGV service has reserved and payable bike space.

i More Info

There's lots of good info on **lorraine.voie.verte.free.fr** including details of how to get the excellent "Voies Vertes et Véloroutes de Lorraine" map (published 2010 though).

81 Plaine valley véloroute

Sealed paths and minor roads	Raon l'Étape → Raon-lès-Leau	28 km 17.5 mi

 Bicycle-carrying local services from Nancy to Raon l'Étape take about 1 hour

 www.ot-raon.fr for map leaflet of ths route

Running between Raon l'Étape (known as the Gateway to the Vosges) and tiny Raon-lès-Leau the cycle route running along the vallée de la Plaine is a mix of tarmac and concrete voie verte (17km) and signed route on quiet roads (11km). Smooth path with good facilities and signage.

This véloroute sometimes follows the line of a former railway, sometimes runs alongside the pretty river Plaine and passes the recently formed lac de la Plaine where there are swimming and other watersports. It connects the various villages such as picturesque Bionville and Vexaincourt of this lovely Vosges valley in the heart of forested mountains.

Voies vertes around Metz and the northern Moselle

82 Orne Valley path

Sealed Railpath	Rombas → Moineville 23 km 14 mi

Bicycle-carrying TGVs from Paris Est to Metz take about an hour and a half.

lorraine.voie.verte.free.fr

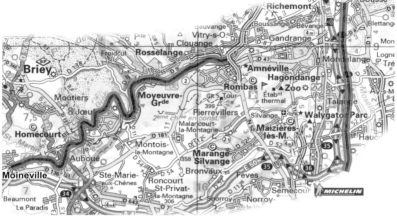

In a valley hit by steel making factory and mining closures this excellent white concrete voie verte follows the river in a surprisingly green and rural landscape. It has few interruptions, roads mainly going above it and has paths on both banks between Joeuf and Homécourt. It starts near Rombas, an ex steel town halfway between Metz and Thionville and runs out west to the small town of Moineville where there is a leisure park with everything from crazy golf to zip wires.

The iver Moselle runs through the heart of Metz

Greenway - unsealed   Greenway - sealed   Signed road route

83 Moselle river

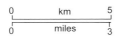

0 —————— km —————— 5

0 —————— miles —————— 3

The path along the Moselle from south of Metz north to Apach, only a kilometre from the borders of Germany and Luxembourg, offers some 60 kilometres of mainly voie verte which, if you forget to stop, will take you to Koblenz. Recent improvements mean the few remaining road sections are being put onto voie verte. Much of the route as it stands is good, smooth tarmac and the whole route makes for easy cycling. There's even a 10 kilometre section north of Thionville with path on both banks.

Urban areas are more prevalent in the south and the northern sections of the Moselle river route pass through some very picturesque vineyard areas. The train line along the valley means return journeys by train or cutting out bits you don't want to do are possible.

Metz has a good network of cycle lanes and cyclists are allowed to ride in pedestrian areas and parks and gardens. There is a good range of voies vertes in the surrounding area, although the nearest any of these come to the city is the 4 kilometres between the city centre and the Moselle path - existing links are not good but a proper cycle route should be in place shortly. There is a nice little railpath voie verte from Lessy near Metz out to Amanvillers (8 kilometres) but in places it's more for mountain bikes. Cycle hire and secure parking are available at the station in Metz and the rue d'Estrées and there is plenty of other cycle parking around the city. The capital of Lorraine is a lively and attractive place with many small waterways threading through it as well as the Moselle and Seille rivers between which it is built. There are nice public gardens and the museums and art galleries range from the collections of the long-established Cour d'Or museums to the exhibitions at the brand new Centre Pompidou-Metz. The golden-stoned cathedral is a major Gothic achievement, renowned especially for its very high nave and its stained glass.

Greenway - unsealed   Greenway - sealed   Signed road route   241

84 Voie vertes around Nancy
The Moselle Loop

| Waterside paths & roads | Nancy → Toul 72 km 45 mi |

Bicycle-carrying TGVs from Paris Est to Nancy in well under two hours. Several local stations on the Moselle Loop.

www.nancy-tourisme.fr for cycling maps of the centre of Nancy and the wider area. There's a little map leaflet on www.bassinpompey.fr covering most of the voie verte de la Mauchère and all of the voie verte de la vallée de l'Amezule. lorraine.voie.verte.free.fr

The longest traffic-free stretch of the Boucle de la Moselle runs from Custines, near Pompey, in the north, through Nancy and curls around south of the city to Sexey-aux-Forges. It runs alongside the river Meurthe into Nancy and then follows canals to Sexey-aux-Forges. The path is just about continuous but where there are junctions they require care. The quality of the surface is variable, there is little signage to speak of and the route across Nancy is not always straightforward. However, it's a very green and pleasant route even where it passes through industrial areas and despite any difficulties it's a good way to get across the city.

Other traffic-free sections of the loop which are in place run from Toul to Gondreville and Aingeray to near Liverdun. In practice, with connections on quiet minor roads, these combine to offer a signed 72 kilometre round trip. Ideal for a long day out with great waterside views.

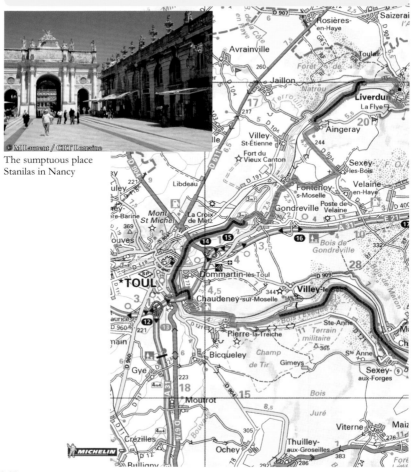

© M Laurent / CRT Lorraine

The sumptuous place
Stanilas in Nancy

Greenway - unsealed   Greenway - sealed   Signed road route

The Voie Verte de la Mauchère

Unsealed railpath   Custines → Jeandelaincourt **12 km** 7.5 mi

Voie Verte de la vallée de l'Amezule

Tarmac railpath   Lay-Saint-Christophe → Forêt d'Amance **20 km** 12.5 mi

Nancy is a city geared up to cycling with a network of cycle lanes, an automated bike hire system and good, downloadable cycle lane maps. For the visitor there are downloadable audio guides to the city and over the summer, a programme of guided tours by bike. The Maison du Vélo on rue Charles III offers repair and cleaning facilities amongst other things. The city's voies vertes comprise some 70 or 80 kilometres of high quality, mainly tarmac paths, much of them waterside and many of them connected up to form a good chunk of an evolving loop around the area.

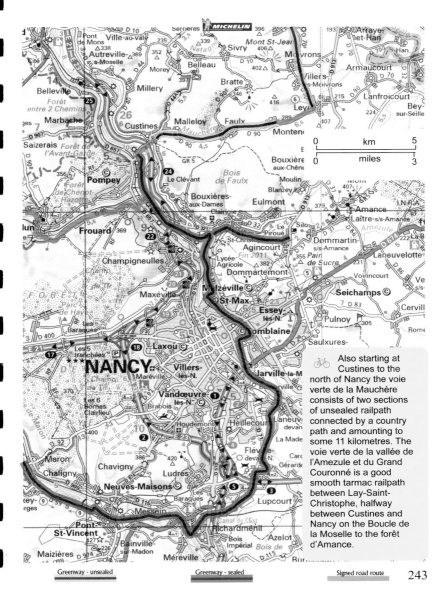

Also starting at Custines to the north of Nancy the voie verte de la Mauchère consists of two sections of unsealed railpath connected by a country path and amounting to some 11 kilometres. The voie verte de la vallée de l'Amezule et du Grand Couronné is a good smooth tarmac railpath between Lay-Saint-Christophe, halfway between Custines and Nancy on the Boucle de la Moselle to the forêt d'Amance.

Greenway - unsealed   Greenway - sealed   Signed road route   243

85 Vosges canal

| Sealed towpath | Socourt → Chamousey 36 km 22.5 mi |
| Sealed towpath | Girancourt → Fontenoy 32 km 20 mi |

It's about an hour by train from Nancy to Épinal but Charmes, Vincey, Châtel-Noméxy, Igney and Thaon-les-Vosges are also on the line. TGV service direct from Paris to Épinal.

lorraine.voie.verte.free.fr

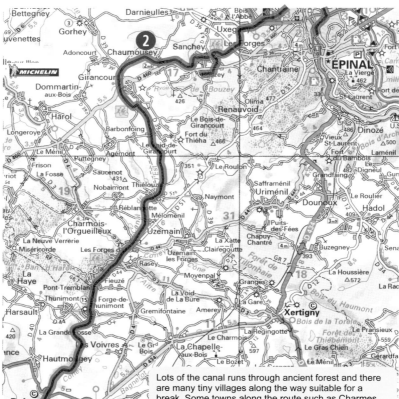

Lots of the canal runs through ancient forest and there are many tiny villages along the way suitable for a break. Some towns along the route such as Charmes and Thaon-les-Vosges are pleasant but not high points, although the art deco 'Rotonde' arts centre in Thaon-les-Vosges, built in the shape of a cross of Lorraine, is an interesting feature. Épinal on the Moselle, reached on a canal spur, makes a good place to stay, being a good way along the route and furnished with a range of attractions. It's also got nice parks and gardens and some good riverside bike paths. Just north of here, Golbey is the home of Moustache electric bikes, a new company producing several hundred city and trekking electric bikes a month. Little Fontenoy-le-Château comes complete with cobbled streets, some shops and some castle ruins, not to mention a museum of embroidery and metallurgy, both once important activities in the town. The large Lac de Bouzey near Chamousey has camping and a holiday park with beaches and swimming. The Vosges generally is a very attractive area and this ride of over 70 kilometres under the western side of the range is no exception.

Greenway - unsealed   Greenway - sealed   Signed road route

The Canal des Vosges offers a pretty much unbroken run on tarmac or other well surfaced towpath between Socourt in the north and Bouzey, near Chaumousey, in the south. There's then a short interruption on road to Girancourt, although this may by now be towpath voie verte also, and further tarmac path south to Fontenoy-le-Château near the border with Franche-Comté. One of the advantages of canal towpaths is that they tend to iron out the bumps in the landscape that roads do not and this one does it in style, passing through hills and valleys in the south particularly. In the north it parallels the River Moselle.

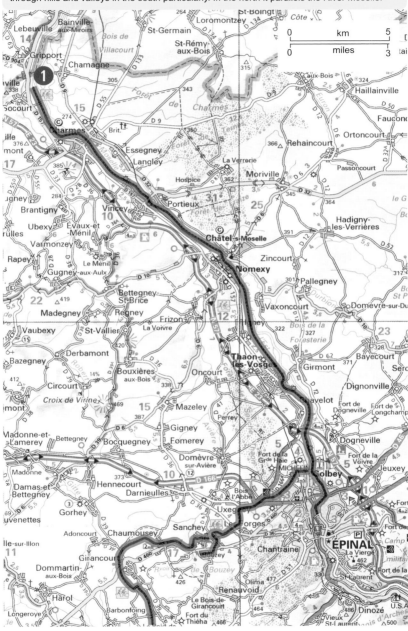

Greenway - unsealed   Greenway - sealed   Signed road route

86 The Vosges mountains

| Sealed railpath | Remiremont → Cornimont 23 km 14 mi |
| Sealed railpath | Remiremont → Bussang 30 km 18.5 mi |

Remiremont is an hour and a half by train from Nancy. TGV service direct from Paris to Remiremont.

www.lavoieverte.com Superb website giving map leaflet and loads of supporting info including services in all the towns and villages along the ride. Updated but briefer version at association.ballast.free.fr lorraine.voie.verte.free.fr

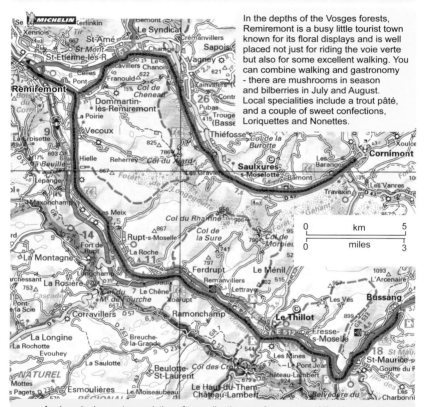

In the depths of the Vosges forests, Remiremont is a busy little tourist town known for its floral displays and is well placed not just for riding the voie verte but also for some excellent walking. You can combine walking and gastronomy - there are mushrooms in season and bilberries in July and August. Local specialities include a trout pâté, and a couple of sweet confections, Loriquettes and Nonettes.

A prize winning route consisting of two railpath spurs from south of Remiremont, a small town on the Moselle near its confluence with the Moselotte. The voie verte out of the town leads to a junction 3 kilometres away from where one spur follows the Moselle valley and the other that of the Moselotte, a road link between them to form a loop being possible. Entirely in tarmac and with reasonable signage and distance markers (sometimes it helps to use the pedestrian signage)

Like canals, railpaths tend to iron out the bumps in the landscape, but if you want to link the two spurs by road (between Cornimont at the end of the northern spur and either Ramonchamp or Le Thillot on the Moselle one), then bumps there will be. Gradients on both voie verte spurs are gentle at first becoming a little steeper in the later stages. Whilst Cornimont is the terminus of the northern voie verte, there is a signed véloroute up into the hills to La Bresse, a well known ski resort. In fact, the voie verte is used in the winter as a cross-country skiing path.

These routes run through some lovely Vosges landscapes, particularly the section along the Moselotte valley, although the Moselle section does have some stunning views, particularly on the return. Road intersections are more numerous on the Moselle spur which goes through more villages.

Greenway - unsealed   Greenway - sealed   Signed road route

© M Laurent / CRT Lorraine

Epinal (above) is an attractive base from which to explore the Vosges Canal (previous pages) whilst the old railway paths on this ride (below), branching out from Remiremont, are wide, very high quality and ideal for all users.

© M Laurent / CRT Lorraine

© Association Ballast

87 North of the Vosges mountains

Sarre Valley voie verte

| Sealed towpath | Saarbrucken → Gondrexange 74 km 46 mi |

For the Sarre Valley route, there are stations at Sarreguemines, Sarralbe and Sarre-Union. The cross-border tramway from Sarreguemines to Sarrebrucken carries bicycles. Direct bicycle-carrying trains from Nancy and Strasbourg to Sarrebourg. TGV service direct from Paris to Saarbrucken.

www.cc-sarrebourg.fr has maps of the cycle paths in and around Sarrebourg

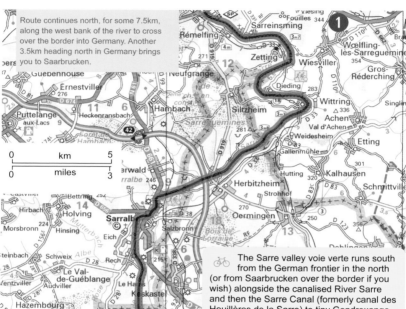

Route continues north, for some 7.5km, along the west bank of the river to cross over the border into Germany. Another 3.5km heading north in Germany brings you to Saarbrucken.

The Sarre valley voie verte runs south from the German frontier in the north (or from Saarbrucken over the border if you wish) alongside the canalised River Sarre and then the Sarre Canal (formerly canal des Houillères de la Sarre) to tiny Gondrexange about 10 kilometres west of Sarrebourg. Much of it is good, smooth tarmac and the path doesn't have many road crossings. Do watch out though; canal and towpath can sometimes be quite close together.

The countryside in the north is fairly unremarkable but becomes prettier the further south you go. Sarreguemines on the border was the head of the navigable River Sarre at one time and a fair commercial centre. Now it sees more leisure craft and has a small marina. It is also a bit of a voies vertes crossroads, short railpaths running out to Hambach and Grundviller to the west and Bliesbruck to the east. (It isn't actually a crossroads - the path to Bliesbruck starts in the suburbs). The southern end of the path is at Gondrexange, a large lake about 10 kilometres from Sarrebourg.

Greenway - unsealed   Greenway - sealed   Signed road route

Sarrebourg greenways

| Sealed railpath | **Sarrebourg area network** 22 km 14 mi |

Sarrebourg is creating a network of voies vertes to link the towns and villages in the area and connect to neighbouring areas. Currently consisting of three paths, Lorquin - Abreschviller (11km), Hesse - Troisfontaines (7km) and Hesse - Sarrebourg (4km), these are smooth, high quality paths often running through picturesque countryside with some nice views up into the mountains and forests. The canal de la Marne au Rhin runs south of Sarrebourg and its towpath will form part of a major cycle route between Paris and Prague, although in Lorraine little has been upgraded to voie verte as yet.

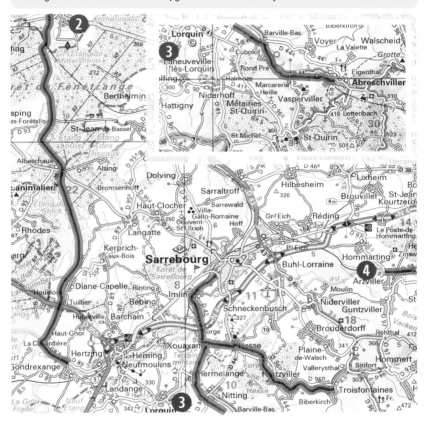

Lock-keepers voie verte

| Sealed towpath | **Arzviller → St-Louis** 10 km 6 mi |

The Lock-keepers' voie verte is a fairly recently created section of voie verte on the canal de la Marne au Rhin with a good smooth surface and a lot of canal type interest in the form of flower-bedecked cottages, 17 locks and an impressive boat-lift to bypass them. It runs from Arzviller to St-Louis where you can carry on along the canal towpath on the voie verte de la Zorn into Alsace and on to Strasbourg.

Greenway - unsealed   Greenway - sealed   Signed road route   249

Alsace

Undoubtedly one of the most cycle friendly regions of France. Strasbourg has one of the country's best developed city networks of cycle lanes - often the acid test of how serious a local government is about promoting cycling.

Having said that most official traffic-free routes suitable for easygoing leisure cycling lie in the east and north of the region; south and west lie the Vosges, which are hugely attractive but generally quite daunting for the cyclist. Our touring route gives you a taste though, with an easy route option up the Fecht Valley. Smooth rolling tarmac is the norm here too - great for cycling in all conditions.

There are also good cycling links across the German and Swiss borders if you want cycle routes with a multinational flavour.

Culture, Food & History

Alsace is very much its own little world, with a distinctive local language, the German dialect Elsässisch, distinctive and extremely colourful local architecture usually overflowing with geraniums and a history that has reflected its role as a pawn in the wargames of France and Germany. The art and architecture of Strasbourg and Colmar are of international renown.

This certainly makes for a fascinating contrast with mainstream French culture as does the Alsatian take on food and drink; again the Germanic influence is strong, with plenty of smoked meat and stews, the popular baeckoffe containing pork, mutton, beef and potatoes. The area has its own confectionery with tartes alsaciennes, featuring a variety of the local fruit, and some very distinctive white wines.

Organised Holidays

Amongst others : www.frenchcyclingholidays.com   http://hookedoncycling.co.uk
www.cycling-for-softies.co.uk   www.discoverfrance.com   www.utracks.com   www.headwater.com
www.inntravel.co.uk

Access to Alsace

Great TGV train connections from Paris Est station to Strasbourg making it a trip of only 2 hours 20 mins or so. The TGV service has reserved and payable bike space.

i More Info

www.tourisme67.com has a good selection of cycle routes in northern Bas-Rhin including some of the ones in this book. There are maps with brief notes in French, German and English.
pistes-cyclables-alsace.chez-alice.fr has brief notes and photographs of various routes throughout the region
www.bas-rhin.fr has a good map of cycle routes in Bas-Rhin
www.haute-alsacetourisme.com has good info on Haut-Rhin

88 Around Basel
Hardt forest voie verte

| Sealed track | Kembs-Loechlé → Munchhouse | 29 km 18 mi |

Huningue Canal

| Unsealed towpath | Huningue → Niffer | 17 km 10.5 mi |

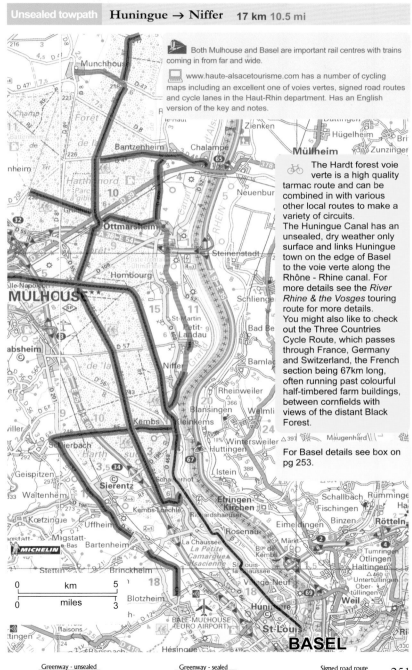

Both Mulhouse and Basel are important rail centres with trains coming in from far and wide.

www.haute-alsacetourisme.com has a number of cycling maps including an excellent one of voies vertes, signed road routes and cycle lanes in the Haut-Rhin department. Has an English version of the key and notes.

The Hardt forest voie verte is a high quality tarmac route and can be combined in with various other local routes to make a variety of circuits.
The Huningue Canal has an unsealed, dry weather only surface and links Huningue town on the edge of Basel to the voie verte along the Rhône - Rhine canal. For more details see the *River Rhine & the Vosges* touring route for more details.
You might also like to check out the Three Countries Cycle Route, which passes through France, Germany and Switzerland, the French section being 67km long, often running past colourful half-timbered farm buildings, between cornfields with views of the distant Black Forest.

For Basel details see box on pg 253.

| Greenway - unsealed | Greenway - sealed | Signed road route |

251

The voies vertes in the countryside around Basel and Mulhouse tend to be shortish routes on good sealed surfaces following pretty wooded valleys, other than the Hardt Forest path. They can mostly be linked to other routes to form good loop rides making this like the rest of Alsace a great area for easy leisure riding.

Both Mulhouse and Basel are bicycle very friendly. Mulhouse has a system allowing cyclists to override red lights in some places and plenty of two way cycle lanes on one way streets. They have four cycle parking areas under video surveillance and free bike usage for motorists who park in certain places, not to mention an automated bike hire system. Both cities allow bikes on their trams outside of peak hours. Basel has an underground bike park at the station with a choice of free parking or paid for parking with security along with bike hire, repair, toilets, lockers and coffee.

Thann lies at more than 1,000ft above sea level and is dominated by the 250ft spire of its minster. The town houses cellars that keep its famous wines. Adding to the venerable atmosphere are old town houses and a ruined castle, Engelsburg, above the town.

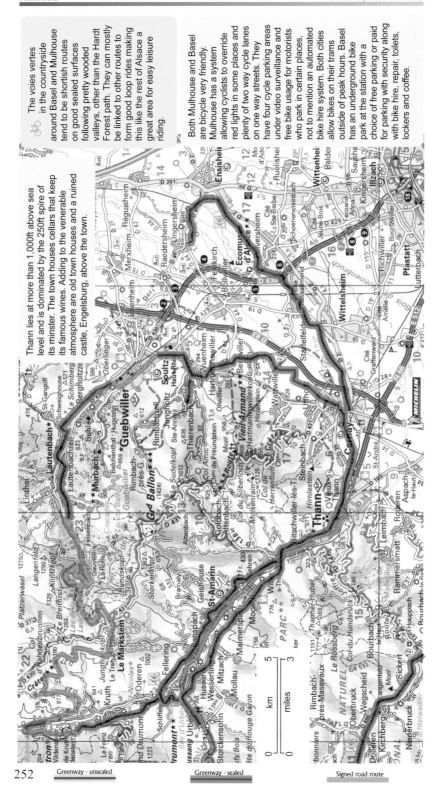

Greenway - unsealed   Greenway - sealed   Signed road route

Both cities are well worth some time. Mulhouse may not be as elegant as Basel but it has a selection of museums it would be difficult to match - the Cité du Train is the biggest railway museum in Europe but for those with a technical interest there are also the Schlumpf automobile museum, the EDF electricity museum and a textile museum. There are also museums of fine arts and history. Not that Basel is short on museums. The Kunstmuseum has an impressive collection of 19th and 20th century art and there are over twenty other museums in and around the city. Basel's old town is a delight, and the modern city has loads of absolutely top drawer buildings by the biggest names in architecture. Having said that, one of the nicest things you can do on a hot day in Basel is take a dip in the Rhine - blue signs indicate where it is safe to swim, orange where it isn't. Basel is the start of the *River Rhine & the Vosges* touring route.

Thann nestles in the spectacular Vosges mountains

89 Valleys west of Mulhouse

Thur valley voie verte

| Sealed paths & minor roads | Circuit from Ungersheim | 79 km 49 mi |

Doller valley voie verte

| Railpath | Burnhapt → Sewen | 20 km 12.5 mi |

Regular bike-carrying services from Mulhouse to Cernay.

www.haute-alsacetourisme.com has a number of cycling maps including an excellent one of voies vertes, signed road routes and cycle lanes in the Haut-Rhin department. Has an English version of the key and notes.

Greenway - unsealed   Greenway - sealed   Signed road route

90 East of Colmar

Rhône to Rhine Canal

| Sealed towpath | Artzenheim → Strasbourg   54 km 33.5 mi |

Colmar Canal

| Sealed towpath | East of Colmar → Artzenheim   14 km 9 mi |

Colmar is on the line between Mulhouse and Strasbourg but with trains also to Molsheim and a spur to Metzeral up in the hills.

www.ot-colmar.fr for a map of cycle routes around the town.

The route passes through not particularly remarkable villages and countryside. Colmar, however, is particularly remarkable. The entire town centre seems to be half-timbered buildings, ornate, carved balconies with flowers tumbling from them over narrow streets and canals but also of course a deluge of visitors. Alsace has many faces but Colmar along with nearby villages such as Eguisheim and Riquewihr are probably the best known one. It's a place where you may sometimes hear people speaking Elsässisch and indeed, some street name signs are bilingual.

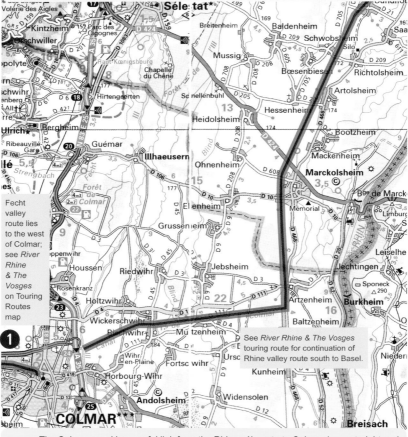

Fecht valley route lies to the west of Colmar; see *River Rhine & The Vosges* on Touring Routes map

See *River Rhine & The Vosges* touring route for continuation of Rhine valley route south to Basel.

The Colmar canal is a useful link from the Rhine véloroute to Colmar, long, straight and well-surfaced.

Greenway - unsealed   Greenway - sealed   Signed road route

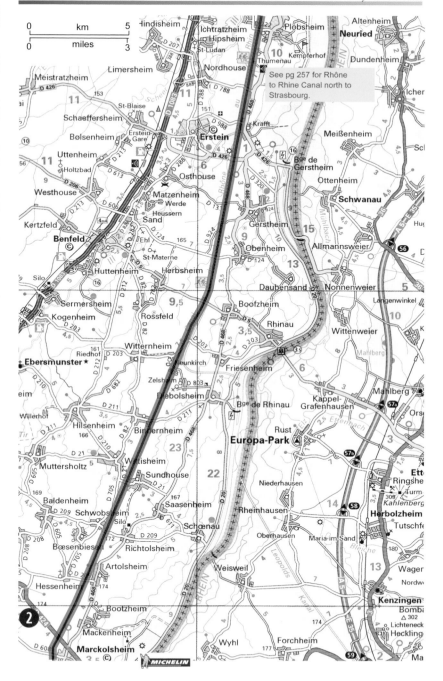

See pg 257 for Rhône
to Rhine Canal north to
Strasbourg.

91 Strasbourg voies vertes

Bruche Canal

| Sealed towpath | Strasbourg → Molsheim | 21 km 13 mi |

Molsheim to Wasselonne and Romanswiller voie verte

| Sealed railpath | Molsheim → Wasselonne | 17 km 10.5 mi |

Marne to Rhine canal

| Sealed towpath | Strasbourg → Lutzelbourg | 57 km 35.5 mi |

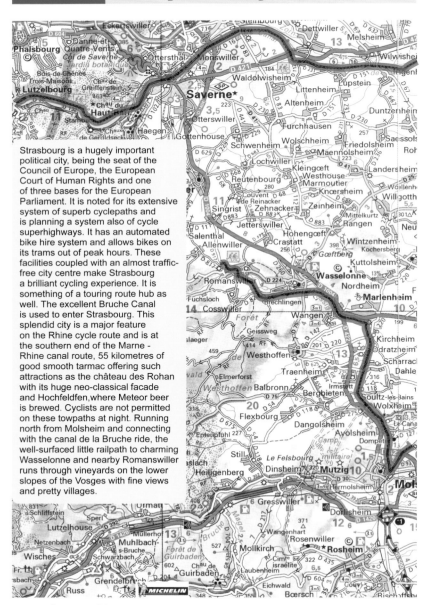

Strasbourg is a hugely important political city, being the seat of the Council of Europe, the European Court of Human Rights and one of three bases for the European Parliament. It is noted for its extensive system of superb cyclepaths and is planning a system also of cycle superhighways. It has an automated bike hire system and allows bikes on its trams out of peak hours. These facilities coupled with an almost traffic-free city centre make Strasbourg a brilliant cycling experience. It is something of a touring route hub as well. The excellent Bruche Canal is used to enter Strasbourg. This splendid city is a major feature on the Rhine cycle route and is at the southern end of the Marne - Rhine canal route, 55 kilometres of good smooth tarmac offering such attractions as the château des Rohan with its huge neo-classical facade and Hochfeldfen,where Meteor beer is brewed. Cyclists are not permitted on these towpaths at night. Running north from Molsheim and connecting with the canal de la Bruche ride, the well-surfaced little railpath to charming Wasselonne and nearby Romanswiller runs through vineyards on the lower slopes of the Vosges with fine views and pretty villages.

Greenway - unselaed   Greenway - sealed   Signed road route

Rail lines from/to Strasbourg for all these routes.

www.otstrasbourg.fr has maps and supporting notes (some in English) for the city and surrounding areas including the Canal de la Bruche ride, the Marne-Rhine canal and the Rhine cycle route north to Lauterbourg and south to Marckolsheim.

🚲 Generally high-quality well-surfaced tarmac routes.

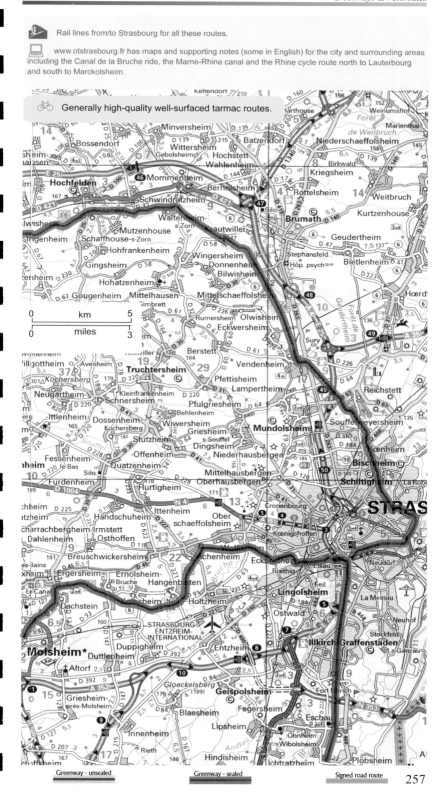

Greenway - unsealed   Greenway - sealed   Signed road route

92 Northern Bas-Rhin
Franco-German véloroute

Cyclepath	Wissembourg → Lauterbourg	24 km 15 mi

Rhine véloroute

Towpaths, cyclepath & quiet roads	Huningue → Lauterbourg	134 km 83 mi

Stations at Basel, Strasbourg and Lauterbourg with others in striking distance of the Rhine cycle route, particularly north of Strasbourg where the line is much closer to the route and there are many stations.

www.rhinecycleroute.eu www.tourisme67.com

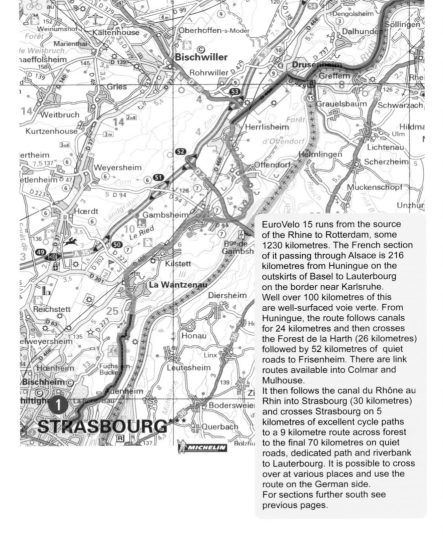

EuroVelo 15 runs from the source of the Rhine to Rotterdam, some 1230 kilometres. The French section of it passing through Alsace is 216 kilometres from Huningue on the outskirts of Basel to Lauterbourg on the border near Karlsruhe.
Well over 100 kilometres of this are well-surfaced voie verte. From Huningue, the route follows canals for 24 kilometres and then crosses the Forest de la Harth (26 kilometres) followed by 52 kilometres of quiet roads to Frisenheim. There are link routes available into Colmar and Mulhouse.
It then follows the canal du Rhône au Rhin into Strasbourg (30 kilometres) and crosses Strasbourg on 5 kilometres of excellent cycle paths to a 9 kilometre route across forest to the final 70 kilometres on quiet roads, dedicated path and riverbank to Lauterbourg. It is possible to cross over at various places and use the route on the German side.
For sections further south see previous pages.

Greenway - unsealed   Greenway - sealed   Signed road route

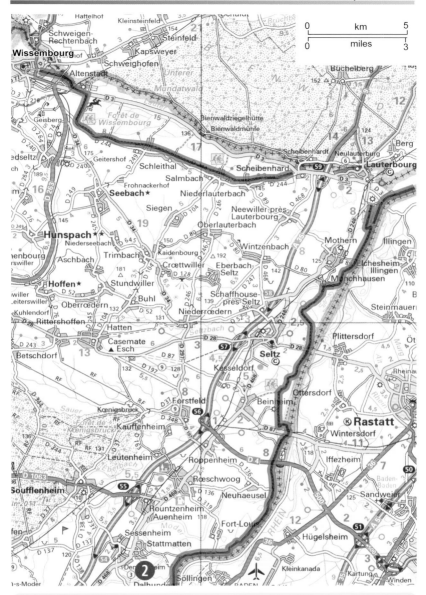

🚲 The Franco-German véloroute through fields and small villages between
    Wissembourg and Lauterbourg is the French section of a longer cycle route starting
and finishing in Germany and following the River Lauter. Although it's a véloroute in name, the
bulk of it is very much like voie verte. It's well-signed, well surfaced and not too challenging
and a route on the German side of the border between Scheibenhard and Wissembourg
makes a 46 kilometre circular ride possible. The route links in to the Rhine véloroute.

Greenway - unsealed   Greenway - sealed   Signed road route   259

Although much fought over with large parts of it destroyed in WWII (and many previous wars), Haguenau has retained some fine buildings including the former hospital and the current town hall. Also keep an eye out for the Synagogue, the Théâtre municipal and the Halle au houblon (hop hall). Perhaps most attractive though, are Haguenau's fountains. The medieval Saint-Georges fountain, the 18th-century Bee fountain (Fontaine aux abeilles) and the Dolphin fountain (Fontaine aux dauphins) in particular stand out. Haguenau forest to the north of the city is one the largest continuous forests in France.

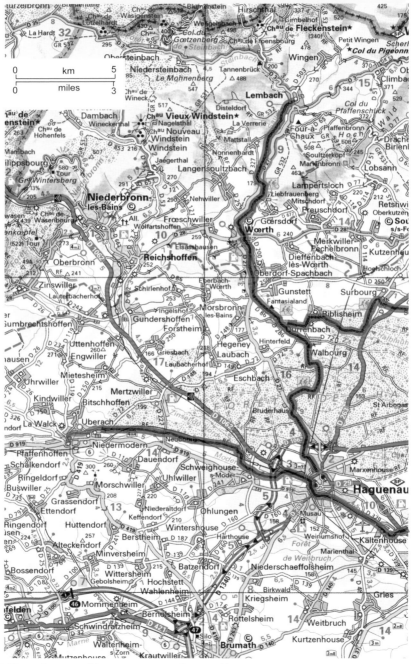

     Greenway - unsealed   Greenway - sealed   Signed road route

93 Around Haguenau

Lembach - Durrenbach véloroute

| Sealed Railpath | Lembach → Durrenbach | **13 km** 8 mi |

Pfaffenhoffen - Drusenheim véloroute

| Roads & paths | Pfaffenhoffen → Drusenheim | **32 km** 20 mi |

Haguenau - Betschdorf loop

| Sealed paths | Haguenau and back | **34 km** 21 mi |

Stations at Walbourg near Durrenbach, Haguenau and Drusenheim make these rides easily accessible from Strasbourg.

www.rhinecycleroute.eu www.tourisme67.com

The little railpath between pretty Lembach and Durrenbach is also well signed and well surfaced, linking the vallée de la Sauer and the forêt de Haguenau.

The véloroute between Pfaffenhoffen and Drusenheim via Haguenau is flat and well signed and uses cycle paths and quiet roads through woods and fields between the towns. Cross the Rhine on the ferry at Drusenheim and the route goes on via Bühl to Baden-Baden.

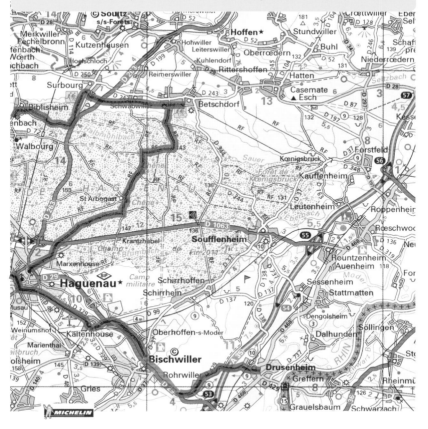

Greenway - unsealed   Greenway - sealed   Signed road route

FRENCH BIKING GLOSSARY

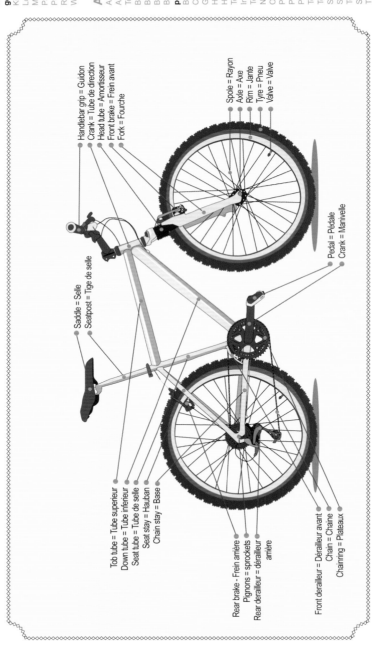

Handlebar grip = **Guidon**
Crank = **Tube de direction**
Head tube = **Amortisseur**
Front brake = **Frein avant**
Fork = **Fourche**

Spole = **Rayon**
Axle = **Axe**
Rim = **Jante**
Tyre = **Pneu**
Valve = **Valve**

Saddle = **Selle**
Seatpost = **Tige de selle**

Pedal = **Pédale**
Crank = **Manivelle**

Tob tube = **Tube superieur**
Down tube = **Tube inférieur**
Seat tube = **Tube de selle**
Seat stay = **Hauban**
Chain stay = **Base**

Rear brake - **Frein arrière**
Pignons = **sprockets**
Rear derailleur = **dérailleur arrière**

Front derailleur = **Dérailleur avant**
Chain = **Chaîne**
Chainring = **Plateaux**

FRENCH BIKING GLOSSARY

There are two route descriptions that you'll come across above all others. Here are the official definitions:

Voie Verte = Greenway

A track developed specifically for and reserved for non-motorised traffic. It is intended for pedestrians, cyclists, rollerbladers and the disabled (and in come cases horseriders). It must be accessible to the greatest number in the easiest possible manner. A voie verte can be urban or rural and may use, inter alia, disused railways, towpaths, forest roads, coastal paths and parkland.

Véloroute = Bike route

A medium or long distance route for commuting or touring, being linear, continuous, uniformly signed and safe. A Véloroute should be pleasant to cycle, avoiding excessive gradients as much as possible and will use the quietest roads and tracks available.

In addition AF3V, the French national association for voies vertes and véloroutes, used their own criteria to select routes suitable for inclusion in their guide and on their website:

Voie vertes should be longer than 12km (or 9km if part of a larger national route) continue without interruptions, be 2m or more wide, be officially open to cyclists and be comfortable to cycle on a hybrid type bike (VTC).

Véloroutes should be longer than 80km (or 25km if they are part of a longer national route), signed, use quiet roads and have some existing documentation in French.

Types of bike

Electric bike
Un vélo électrique
Hybrid bike
Un vélo de tout chemin (VTC)
Mountain bike
Un vélo de tout terrain (VTT)
Racing bike
Un vélo de course
Tandem
Un vélo tandem
Trailer
Une remorque

Directions & descriptions

Alley
La ruelle
At the church...
A l'église
Crossroads
Le carrefour
Cycle lane
La bande cyclable
Cycle path or track
La piste cyclable
Developed specifically for cycles
Aménagé
Facilities
Aménagements
Fork / split
La bifurcation
Go up / down the hill
Montez / descendez la colline
Minor road
Petite route
Path
Le sentier
Road
La Route
Roundabout
Le rond-point
Segregated from motor traffic
En site propre

Sign or information panel
Panneau
Signage / signed
Fléchage / jalonné / balisé
Straight ahead until
Continuez tout droit jusqu'à..
Surface
Revêtement
Surfaced smoothly (often sealed)
Enrobé lisse
Surfaced with gravel
Gravillonné
Surfaced with tarmac
Goudronné / asphalté
Towpath
Halage / Le chemin de halage
Track
La piste
At the traffic lights
Au feux
Turn left
Tournez à gauche
Turn right
Tournez à droite

Road instructions

Compulsory
Obligatoire
Except deliveries
Sauf livraisons
Except residents
Sauf riverains
Give way
Cédez le passage
Lorries entering/leaving
Sortie de camions
No entry (though not necessarily for bikes)
Sens interdit
One way (though not necessarily for bikes)
Sens unique

You do not have priority (with motor traffic)
Vous n'avez pas la priorité
Restriction / advice still applies
Rappel
Road closed (although not usually to cyclists - enquire locally)
Route barrée
Shared route
Route partagé
Uneven surface
Chausée déformée

Tourist information

Brochure
Une brochure
Leaflet
Une fiche
Tourist office
Office du tourisme / syndicat d'initiative

At the accommodation

Accommodation
Hébergement
Bed and breakfast
Chambre d'hôte
Bike parking
Un parking pour les vélos / parc de stationnement
Have you a space inside your hotel for our bikes?
Avez vous un coin dans l'intérieur de votre hôtel pour nos vélos
Campsite
Un camping
Garage
Un garage
Hotel
Un hôtel
We will arrive at.....
Nous arriverons a.....

INDEX

Major settlements (including all route start /finish points) in main text

265

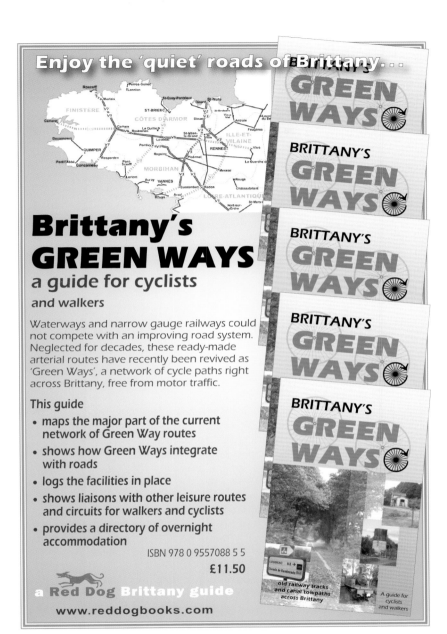

Morpheus